# Content

# FOREWORD

In 1851, William C. Nell stated, "There are those who will ask, why make a parade of the military services of Colored Americans?" He then criticized the "combination of circumstances (which) have veiled from the public eye a narration of those military services (of Coloreds) which are generally conceded as a passport to honorable and lasting notice of Americans." Patriots of color, all too familiar with the failure of America's commitment to the pledge of allegiance, have consistently contributed to the ideals expressed in the pledge. From the Revolutionary War to current military expeditions, African Americans have ignored the hypocrisy of the present and pursued the dream of the American Promise.

The Congressional Militia Act implemented on May 8, 1792 prohibited the enlistment of African Americans into the Organized Militia. However, African Americans did serve in Louisiana and several other states during the War of 1812, and in 1842 participated as infantrymen during the Dorr Rebellion in Rhode Island. Ironically, a company was formed in Providence in 1857 but the events at Harpers Ferry in Virginia two years later influenced state officials to disband the organization. The necessity for passage of a revised Militia Law on July 17, 1862 which entended military and naval enlistment to African Americans and the subsequent establishment of the United States Colored Troops, and the formation of African American militia organizations in states that included California, Louisiana and Massachusetts. Cognizant of the military contributions rendered by African Americans as combat and service support personnel, postwar northern state officials were encouraged to extend militia service to African Americans, and the majority of the southern state adjutant generals under the provisions of the Reconstruction Acts reluctantly admitted African Americans into their State Militia or National Guard.

The Maryland Adjutant General accepted the three African American companies into the State Militia, Baltimore Monumental City Guard in 1882, the Baltimore Rifles in 1884, and the Cumberland Allegheny County Guards in 1884 as Unattached which were formed into a provisional battalion during field maneuvers. Fiscal difficulties experienced after the deployment of guardsmen during the labor strike of 1894, the General Assembly authorized the adjutant general to disband, at his discretion, companies that had lost their strength and efficiency. In January 1895, the Baltimore Rifles and Cumberland Allegheny County Guards were disbanded and the Baltimore Monumental City Guard were reorganized into the First Separate Company on April 1, 1896. Rarely did the adjutant general request the services of this organization to perform domestic service and during the war with Spain the organization was only used for service at the Pimlico Race Track in Baltimore. After the federal activation of the National Guard and the implementation of the National Defense Act in 1916, men in the First Separate Company were assigned to Company I, 372nd Infantry Regiment, 93rd Infantry Division that was composed primarily of African American personnel. Commended for their excellent military service, the organization was reorganized after World War I as an auxiliary engineer company and further reorganized as the First Separate Company. This designation was revised in 1940 after the mobilization of National Guard organizations with the company reassigned to the 372nd Infantry Regiment as the Service Company. Post war realignment and reorganization influenced the National Guard Bureau and the Maryland Adjutant General to expand the organization into the 231st Transportation Truck Battalion.

African American personnel in the Maryland National Guard were not integrated into other units and throughout their service they were assigned as attached personnel. Segregation in the National Guard prevented expansion and the highest rank obtained within the organization was that of captain. All of the personnel were relegated to service within the company until formation of the battalion that permitted experienced personnel to service in higher grades with the 231st Battalion. The experiences personnel who in Korea, the termination of segregation within Maryland National Guard and the subsequent formation of the 229th Transportation and Supply Battalion is the significance of manuscript.

Brigadier General George M. Brooks, a graduate of Morgan State College, speaking before black war veterans, in 1989, stated, "So many have absolutely no idea of the role black soldiers played in the development of the United States. Here in Maryland, not many know the history behind Negro Mountain in Western Maryland." BG Brooks, after retiring from the Maryland National Guard, lectured and inspired many to pursue and revise the history books to reflect a balanced view of American history.

Louis S. Diggs received the "torch" from BG Brooks and herein tells the story of the All African American Maryland National Guard unit from Baltimore that was activated and served during the Spanish American War, World War I, World War II, and the Korean War. The focus of his manuscript is the 231st Transportation Truck Battalion, the only Maryland National Guard unit ordered to active duty during the Korean War. Mr Diggs renders a brief history of the founding and acceptance of this unit, originally called the Monumental Guard, and gives the reader a bird's-eye view of the trials and tribulations of being a black patriot in a white man's military.

Segregation was the official policy of the military, although convenience and military necessity, from time to time, had resulted in blacks and whites serving together. However, in 1947, under pressure from Paul Robeson, A. Philip Randolph, President of the Brotherhood of Sleeping Car Porters and Grant Reynolds, formerly a Republican City Councilman from Harlem who had formed the Committee Against Jim Crow in Military, a change was on the way. Randolph, in his testimony before the Armed Services Committee, advised that it was difficult for African-Americans "to shoulder a gun to fight for democracy abroad unless they get democracy at home." Up to this point, the most profound objection to segregation and inequality had come from black service members who had adopted the "double V" (victory abroad and victory at home) as a means of portraying their dissatisfaction with racism. Coupled with the courageous efforts of Congresswoman Helen G. Douglas of California, who placed in the Congressional Records a documented history of the contributions of African-Americans to the victory in World War II, the stage was set for further action.

President Harry S. Truman stepped front and center with his Committee on

Civil Rights which issued its report, To Secure These Rights which condemned segregation in general and specifically criticized segregation in the armed forces. The next year, on July 26, 1948, President Truman issued Executive Order 9981, establishing the President's Committee on Equality of Treatment and Opportunity in the Armed Services, and appointed Charles Fahy as Chairman. Additionally, Truman signed Executive Order 9980 creating a Fair Employment Board to eliminate racial discrimination in federal employment.

In recounting this extraordinary event, Brigadier General James L. Collins, Jr., Chief of Military History, stated, *"The integration of the armed forces was a momentous event in our military and national history; it represented a milestone in the development of the armed forces and the fulfillment of the democratic ideal."* He further stated, *"The experiences in World War II and the postwar pressures generated by the civil rights movement compelled all the services...to reexamine their traditional practices of segregation."*

This was not the case at the time. Truman was castigated and rebuked by the military establishment, under the Chairman of the Joint Chiefs of Staff, Omar Bradley, who resisted Executive Order 9981 presenting his view that the military was not the vehicle to implement social change. The newly created Air Force complied immediately to the President's directives. The army, navy, marine corps and coast guard practically ignored or subverted the President's directive which was crystal clear given his July 27, 1948 call for civil rights legislation. During the Fiftieth Anniversary Commemoration of Executive Order 9981, Lt. General Julius Becton, Jr., appeared on the Jim Lehrer NewsHour (July 31, 1998) and related his experiences with compliance to the Executive Order. Becton was a young black lieutenant at Aberdeen Proving Grounds (1948) in Maryland. The commander called his officers together and responded to the order by stating that as long as he was commander, there would be two officers' clubs, two NCO clubs, two swimming pools, etc. This attitude was prevalent throughout the military establishment and those commanders who supported the order were caught in a difficult situation since the hierarchy of the military was reluctant to pursue compliance. Becton, like most African-American military personnel, was accustomed to second class treatment. In a November 26, 2000 news article, written by Steve Vogel of the Washington Post News Service, Becton describes the disparity in treatment afforded prisoners of war and blacks. The story coincides with commentary from black soldiers regarding the humane treatment of German prisoners of war while black soldiers were treated as sub-humans. To this day, black soldiers feel humiliated by the experience.

James McEachin, author, actor, humanitarian and decorated Korean War Veteran, at the African American Month Convocation at Morgan State University, in February 2003, emphatically suggested that had war not broken out in Korea, the military would not have integrated for an extended period of time. Mr. McEachin who reenlisted to serve in Korea was wounded and nearly lost his life. History verifies Mr. McEachin's assertions. The Executive Order was not fully complied with until Secretary of Defense Robert S. McNamara expanded the military's responsibility to include the elimination of off-base discrimination detrimental to the military effectiveness of Black soldiers on July 26, 1963 - exactly 15 years after the original order.

From Truman's Executive Order through the early period of conflict in Korea, the United States Army and other branches of the military, excluding the United States Air Force, did not heed the order. Inefficiency and the urgency of war on the Korean Peninsula forced compliance to the Executive Order. The reduction in force, following World War II, had resulted in a military unprepared for war. The North Koreans crossed the 38th Parallel and captured Seoul with little or no resistence. After the United National Security Council passed a resolution condemning the attach and requesting assistance from member nations. Truman ordered military support for South Korea and President Sygman Rhee. Initial losses were great and with limited manpower, it became too cumbersome to assign personnel according to race. Thus, the military was swept up in the currents of history and forced to desegregate.

Today, segregation and institutional discrimination has been, by and large, obliterated; however, individual prejudice remains a primary target of a vigilant military.

Louis Diggs began his military career in 1950 with the Maryland National Guard and served in the Korean War; he retired from the Regular Army in 1970 which covered the most dramatic social change ever to occur within the United States and its military. His service spanned two wars and several major conflicts - the Berlin Crisis, the Cuban Missile Crisis and more. He witnessed first hand the military struggle against institutional racism. Correspondingly, he witnessed the military reaction to desegregation in civilian society. His insight is invaluable to the understanding of black patriotism.

Before writing this chronicle of African-Americans in the Maryland National Guard, Diggs published books and articles detailing the histories of blacks in Baltimore County to include the Oblate Sisters of Providence, the first African-American Order of Nuns. While these may be important documentaries of black survival, his dissertation detailing the saga of the Monumental Guard is paramount to the understanding of American history and the determination of his community to move beyond the reality of America and pursue the dream.

*"I pledge allegiance.....to the Republic for which it stands. One*
*nation under God. Indivisible with liberty and justice for all."*

Charles Johnson, PhD
Professor of History, Morgan State University

Clarence "Tiger" Davis
Delegate, Maryland General Assembly

# Acknowledgements

I must first thank God for providing me with the strength, knowledge and wisdom to complete this book that I have had a burning desire to write for many years. I must also give thanks to my wife, Shirley Washington Diggs for all of her encouragement, patience, and support to complete this book, as well as our four sons, Louis Diggs, Jr., Blair Diggs, Terrance Diggs and Fredric Diggs. With all this strength behind me, there was no way that I could not have completed this task.

I must thank the one man who made a difference in my young adult life, who showed me what a real man was about during the Korean War. That man is retired First Sergeant Lloyd R. Scott, Sr., my platoon sergeant. From the time I joined the 726th Transportation Truck Company in 1950 until I reenlisted in the Regular Army and left the 726th in Korea in 1951, Sergeant Scott left an indelible spot in my life, and he has played a significant role in seeing that one of the members of the old Maryland National Guard unit take the time to put the history of the unit in book form. He has been my greatest motivator.

I cannot forget the motivation General George Brooks provided me before his death. When I first approached him about my desires to document the history of the 231st Transportation Truck Battalion, I clearly remember him saying that numerous people had put our history in book form, but to have a person who served with the unit document our history will result in a book written from the heart.

I must also thank my friend, retired Master Sergeant Nathaniel Pope, the current historian of the Veterans of the 231st Transportation Truck Battalion. Sergeant Pope, though he did not join the 231st until the unit returned from duty in Korea, has expressed much love for the unit, and has a tremendous desire to see the history of the unit documented in book form. I cannot thank him enough for all of the material, documentation, photographs, and other memorabilia that he has provided me over the past year or so, which takes up a great part of this book. I dare say that the many photographs in this book came from his personal collection. He really has helped to bring the organizations alive in this book.

Many thanks also to Lt. Colonel Wayne Johnson, Jr., the Battalion Commander of the 229th Support Battalion, and his staff for recognizing the contributions of the 231st Transportation Truck Battalion and its history and heritage by the truly wonderful dedication ceremony held at the Lt. Colonel Melvin H. Cade Armory on December 14, 2002. I am sure that none of the many people in attendance will ever forget that marvelous activity.

# Dedication

I am dedicating this book on the history of the 231st Transportation Truck Battalion to two members of that battalion - The Late Retired Brigadier General George M. Brooks and a sergeant in the 726th Transportation Truck Company who took many young, inexperienced men, newly assigned to the company, new to military life, and especially new to life in Korea during the war. That strong, very concerned leader of men is Retired First Sergeant Lloyd R. Scott, Sr.

When I became acquainted with Sergeant Scott, it did not take me long to realize that here is a leader with strong leadership abilities, who had the ability to make younger soldiers want to bring the best out in ourselves. He was not the kind of leader that would punish or push you to the end to get the best out of you, but the kind of man who reached inside of you to bring the best out. It was not long before all of us were marching so good, 'til none of the other two companies could compete with us.' Sergeant Scott molded each of us throughout our training in summer camp in 1950 and later in 1950 when we were activated and sent to Camp Edwards, Massachusetts to learn to become soldiers in the active army. I have never seen Sergeant Scott berate any of the men in the company, or make any of us seem small. When we erred on the rifle range, or had difficult in catching on to the skills of driving those hugh 6X6 trucks, Sergeant Scott had a truly unique way of making it clear that we must put more of ourselves into the learning process, and it worked.

I contribute the leadership skills that I learned from Sergeant Scott to the many wonderful assignments I received during my twenty year career in the Regular Army, including my best assignment when I served as the Sergeant Major of the ROTC Detachment at Morgan State College where only the most qualified non-commissioned officers leaders could serve. That was back in 1957.

The other person who I dedicate this book to is the one leader in the 231st Transportation Truck Battalion who rose from the rank of Private in 1943 to become the first African American Brigadier General in the Maryland National Guard in 1979 when he was promoted to that high grade by the then Governor Harry R. Hughes.

I recall encountering General George Brooks as a young soldier in the Guard, and though I never worked for him directly, I found him to be a soldiers' soldier. He understood the enlisted men, and had a unique skill to always get the best out of everyone who came into contact with him.

General Brooks was commissioned a second lieutenant in the 231st Transportation Truck Battalion in 1946. He served with the unit in Korea during the war, and was one of those dedicated African American officers of the 231st who petitioned the Governor of Maryland to permit the unit to allow any one to join the unit without regards to race, creed or color. He refused to rejoin the unit after the war until they were permitted to integrate. It was a long, hard battle, but thanks to officers like

General Brooks, integration of the National Guard became a reality.

My personal relationship with General Brooks came about several years ago. I have for years had a burning desire to write a book about the history of the 231st Transportation Truck Battalion. When I met General Brooks, he strongly urged me to bring my dreams into reality; His encouragement was one of my greatest motivators. He shared much information about the unit with me, but I was so deeply involved in researching and publishing books on the histories of many of the forgotten African American communities in Baltimore County, and was not able to give much time to writing about the 231st. Unfortunately in 2001, General Brooks passed away, and I was at a lost on gathering additional information about the unit; however, his lovely wife, Mrs. Amelia Brooks, and his son, Dudley Brooks, made information that the General had collected, available to me.

The late Brigadier General George M. Brooks, the first African American in the Maryland National Guard to be promoted to the rank of general. He served with Headquarters and Headquarters Company, 231st Transportation Truck Battalion in Korea during the Korean War.

Retired First Sergeant Lloyd R. Scott, Sr. He served with the 726th Transporation Truck Company in Korea during the Korean War

# Introduction

It is my intention to enlighten the wider community of the military contributions made by African American men in the metropolitian area of Baltimore, Maryland, to include quite possibly African American men from other counties in Maryland, beginning around 1879, some 16 years following the Civil War.  I assume that some of these men might possibly have served in one of the several African American regiments that were formed in Maryland during the Civil War.  The men that I am referring to were some seventy African Americans in the 1870s who wanted strongly to be recognized by the Maryland National Guard.  These men had practiced for quite a while so that they would be able to make a more than acceptable presentation whenever they would be judged militarily. The unit was quite unique because it was made up of all African American men, from the lowest private to the highest ranking officer.  They knew that the Maryland National Guard consisted of Major General Hubbard, the Adjutant General of Maryland and members of his staff would be extremely hard to convince that their unit was more than qualified to become part of the Maryland National Guard, and the chances for their acceptance was extremely limited, but they refused to give up on their trying.  The commanding officer of the unit had approached the Maryland National Guard and their political representatives in Annapolis, without much success.

In 1879, after all of the practice, they finally got their opportunity.  The Adjutant General of Maryland finally decided to observe this group of African Americans to see what they would bring to the National Guard.  The Adjutant General, with his staff, got to review this group of African Americans as they went through all of the military routines.  The unit must have been truly outstanding because the Adjutant General decided that they should become a part of the National Guard.  Rather than incorporate this unit of all African Americans into the Maryland National Guard, it was decided that they would be accepted as a "Separate Company" of the National Guard.  Prior to this acceptance, the men called themselves "The Monumental City Guards," a name that stuck with the unit for many years.

In 1898, the First Separate Company was ordered to active duty to support  the Spanish American War.  The unit was not sent to Cuba, rather they were ordered to remain in the United States performing duty stateside during the entire length of the war.  This is not to say that the unit was not prepared for war, it is just that they were not given the opportunity.  The Maryland National Guard was activated at the same time, and they did participate in the Spanish American War; however, the First Separate Company was relegated to only pitching tents in Pimilico.  In 1902, the Maryland National Guard was again activated to combat Pancho Villa who was terrorizing the inhabitants along the Texas border, but the First Separate Company was not activated.

World War I was a completely different story for the First Separate Company, because they were ordered to active duty in 1917 as Company I of the 372nd Infantry Regiment in the provisional 93rd Division, and sent to France to fight not with an American unit,but with the French 63rd Division in Sector "Argonne West," where it saw front line duty. Later the unit was transferred to the 157th French Division, the famous "Red Hand Division" where it saw duty at "Hill 304," one of the most stubbon sectors to give way. The unit was cited twice for conspicuous bravery; many men received the Distinguished Service Cross, and several cited by the American Command. Several men from the unit were individually decorated with the French Croix de Guerre.

In 1940, the unit was redesignated as Service Company, 372nd Infantry Regiment, and on March 10, 1941, the unit was inducted into Federal Service again. During World War II the unit performed guard duty at strategic points along the Eastern Seaboard of the United States, and on May 3, 1945, the unit left for duty in the Hawaiin Islands and received credit for participation in the Asiatic-Pacific Campaign. In 1946 the unit was inactivated and reorganized as Headquarters and Headquarters Detachment, 231st Transportation Truck Battalion in April 1947 under the direction of the Maryland National Guard.

In August 1950, the 231st Transportation Truck Battalion and all three of it's truck companies, the 147th, 165th and 726th Transportation Truck Companies were ordered to active duty to support the Korean War effort. The make-up of the unit had not changed since its inception in 1879, that is, it consisted of all African Americans, from the lowest enlisted man to the battalion commander. The battalion had just returned from its annual summer encampment in Camp Pickett, Virginia. The Headquarters and Headquarters Company, 231st Transportation Truck Battalion with the 147th and 726th Transportation Truck Companies left Baltimore shortly after being inducted into federal service, with the 165th Transportation Truck Company leaving Baltimore a little later. The Battalion Headquarters with the 147th and 726th Transportation Truck Company departed for training in Camp Edwards, Massachusetts, while the 165th Transportation Truck Company eventually departing for duty at Fort Story, Virginia. Before 1950 came to an end, the 726th Transportation Truck Company landed in Pusan, Korea on December 31, 1950, and became the first United States National Guard unit to step foot in Korea to support the Korean War, while the Headquarters and Headquarters Company, 231st Transportation Truck Battalion set foot on Korea soil on January 1, 1951. The two units remained in Korea until the mid-1950s, but they never served together. The 231st picked up numerous truck companies, while the 726th served primarily under the 70th Transportation Truck Battalion. Both units performed their duties well in Korea, and received numerous unit distinctions. Both units became integrated in 1951 when segregation of Army units became a reality.

The 147th Transportation Truck Company, though it trained with the 231st Transportation Truck Battalion and the 726th Transportation Truck Company in Camp Edwards, Massachusetts, did not follow the Battalion and the 726th to Korea, instead, they were deployed to do duty in Germany, with the 165th Transportation Truck Company remaining in Virginia, doing their share for the Korean War effort.

As the men from these units returned to Baltimore, Maryland, it was the desire of many of the men to return to their old National Guard unit; however, the colors of the 231st Transportation Truck Battalion was still in Korea. General Reckord, the Adjutant General of Maryland wanted the 231st to be returned to National Guard status in the same segregated format as it was before the Korean War. The officers of the 231st refused to return to the old segregated ways, and they began a petition against having the 231st go back to their old segregated ways. General Reckord refused to have the unit integrated, and for some time there was a standoff between the Adjutant General and the officers of the 231st. Determined to have the old segregated 231st Transportation Truck Battalion, General Reckord promoted Jesse Peaker, a member of the 231st, to the rank of Captain and put him in charge of reactivating the Battalion in the same organizational structure as it was before being ordered to active duty for the Korean War, and Captain Peaker did just that; however, because of the pressures caused by the petitioning officers of the 231st, they were eventually permitted to become an integrated organization, beginning initially as the 229th Transport and Supply Battalion, and over the years have been reorganized into numerous other organizations, but always as an integrated organization.

This book actually ends it account and history of the old "Monumental City Guards" and "The First Separate Company" in the late1950s when the unit ceased to become a distinctive African American organization with African Americans officers and African American enlisted men; however, several pages have been devoted to sharing some information and photographs from the units that succeeded the 231st Transportation Truck Battalion when it became an integrated organization.

Before closing this introduction, I would like the readers to know that the Monumental City Guard was not the only African American Militia company from the Baltimore area at the time they were organized in 1879. I was able to visit a web site that carried information on articles in the Washington, DC "Grit" and the Washington, DC "Bee.," which indicated that there were two other African American militia units operating, or which both were accepted into the Maryland National Guard. The Monumental City Guard was organized in 1879 and admitted into the Maryland National Guard in 1882. In a response that I received from the owner of the web site, Roger D. Cunningham, he notes that two years after the Monumental City Guard was accepted into the Maryland National Guard, the Baltimore Rifles and the Baltimore City Guard were also admitted. In reviewing the "Grit" and the "Bee," it is obvious that both the Baltimore Rifles and Baltimore City Guard were African American military units like the Monumental City Guard. There were several articles of these units having active social lives, visiting with each other for competitive drills, holiday parades and banquets. According to Roger D. Cunningham, the Baltimore Rifles were disbanded in 1895, followed by an unknown date that the Baltimore City Guard were disbanded. It was around 1896 when the Monumental City Guard was renamed the First Separate Company. Mr. Cunningham also sent me a copy of the September 23, 1899 "Bee" which indicated that the War Department had announced the organization of two Black Regiments, the 48th and 49th USVI to serve in the Phillipine War, led by White officers, with the African American press pushing for a third regiment composed of Black Officers. C.A. Fleetwood from Maryland was recommended for Colonel, but the War Department was not interested in the proposal.

# Chapter 1

**(Contributions of African Americans from Maryland from the Revolutionary War to the Civil War)**

It would truly be unfair to our African American ancestors who so bravely served our great country throughout the history of our country to say that the African American men of Maryland started a few years prior to the Spanish-American War of 1898. True, the African American men from Maryland began as an entire, separate unit, made up of African American officers and enlisted men on February 20, 1879, and began their military history in the Maryland National Guard as a "The First Separate Company" from 1882 until the late 1950s, with a long war history of serving during the Spanish-American War, World War I, World War II, and lastly, the Korean War.

This book will highlight the history of the Monumental City Guards, the First Separate Company from its very beginning, and it's various reorganization, but it will give an accountability of the unit during the Korean War, which afterwards marked the end of the unit as a "separate," segregated company. The stories of the then Headquarters and Headquarters Company, 231st Transportation Truck Battalion, the 147th Transportation Truck Company, 165th Transportation Truck Company, and the 726th Transportation Truck Company, all which started as the First Separate Company, through interviews, photographs and various memorabilia, etc.

First, the readers of this book should be made aware that African American soldiers fought in every war of our country, and in every battle has acquitted himself with credit and honor. Maryland African American soldiers have contributed their share in the past to the fame and fortune of American life and accomplishments, and while the records of their early efforts are not so clear and concise, these are sufficiently bright to point the way and indicate the extent of that service.[1]

During the Revolutionary War, Koger notes that "Maryland, at first, as did other colonies, made no effort to use Negroes in the Revolutionary War. As time went on and the stress and strain of that struggle began telling upon the manpower, not only did Maryland suffer Negro troopers, but made bids for them. The fact that there may be little to say as to the numbers engaged, may be accounted for in that there were no separate units for colored. The Whites and Colored were assigned without regard to color. A system of 'substitution' was used wherein a person drafted might have another answer the call for him. With a promise of freedom for service and with the assurance of having sufficient food and clothing, one needs no stretch of the imagination to know that among the hundreds of substitutes on the Maryland roster, that a large number of these were former slaves and free Blacks, paid well to perform this service. In George Washington's immediate command were 60 Maryland Negroes."[2]

Legislation passed by the General Assembly indicate the gradual change of face in admitting Negroes to the Army:

An Act for Procuring more troops passed in March, 1778 says, among other things: "..........nor any servant whatever until emancipated and set at liberty."

The Act of October(sic), 1780 provided, "That any able bodied slave between 16 and 40 years of age, who voluntarily enters the service and is passed...........may be accepted as a recruit."

The following year (May, 1781) the Assembly provided, "..........and all freedmen although Blacks and mulattoes........ shall be taken in to the militia and be subject to the draft as above."

The same year provisions were made for the enrollment(sic) of 700 Colored militia. As victory approached this plan was abandoned.[3]

That the Negro was used for the heavy work as labor for the Army and Navy may be assured.[4]

Koger also notes that during The War of 1812, most of the war was fought by our Navy, and over one-sixth of the Navy of that day was comprised of Negro sailors. It may be certain that the skill and experience of the Maryland Negro, acquired along the Chesapeake Bay, was used in that conflict. As with all wars of our country, it may be assured that Negro labor was employed in the handling of supplies and transportation. It may be recalled that when Baltimore was being threatened by invasion, the City Council issued a call upon its citizens to erect works of defense and her citizen soldiers to man them in that conflict. Negroes in great abundance answered that call. It has been variously estimated that at least three hundred Negroes served along with others in the defense of the city.[5]

On August 7, 1814, the City Council of Defense issued the following:

"WHEREAS, the Commanding Officer has requested aid of the citizens in the erection of works of defense of the City etc................the free people of color will................assemble tomorrow, Sunday morning at 6 o'clock at Hampstead" "............that the owners of slaves are requested to send them to work on the days assigned in the several districts" In other ways too did the Maryland Negro pay penalties. Niles Register (Sept. and Oct. 1813) Vol VII, gives graphic accounts of numerous kidnapping and selling of Negroes into Canada and the British West Indies. Fully fifteen hundred Negroes along the Chesapeake paid this price.[6]

The Civil War saw thousands of African Americans from Maryland coming to the defense of their country. From the records within the archives of Maryland maybe found not only the complete account of the engagements, number of African American troops, etc., but a complete roster of the members thereof. There were six regiments with a total strength of 8,718 in the Army, and within the Navy were 657 enlisted men. The entire causalities were more than fifteen hundred. One regiment, the 7th U.S. Colored Volunteers, was at Appomattox, Virginia, when Lee surrendered to General Grant.

Under General U.S. Grant in his campaigns in Virginia, the siege of Petersburg, his siege and capture of Richmond and triumphant entry there; with General B. F. Butler's expedition in North Carolina and the glorious victories of that campaign; an excursion into South Carolina, Florida, New Orleans and Texas and garrison duty in some of these states after the War, the Maryland Volunteers gave good account of themselves and made glorious history.[7]

Following  are the names and organizing dates of the six U.S. Colored Troops from Maryland:

Fourth Regiment Infantry U.S. Colored Troops:  Organized in Baltimore, July-September, 1863.

Seventh Regiment Infantry U.S. Colored Troops:  Organized beginning September 1863 with men from Baltimore and Eastern Shore.

Ninth Regiment Infantry U.S. Colored Troops: Organized in November, 1863 with men from over the entire state.

Nineteenth Regiment Infantry U.S. Colored Troops: Organized in Benedict in December, 1863 with men from Southern Maryland and the Eastern Shore.

Thirtieth Regiment Infantry U.S. Colored Troops: Organized in February and March, 1864, principally with men from the Eastern Shore.

Thirty-Ninth Regiment Infantry U.S. Colored Troops:  Date organized in Baltimore, unknown date, with men from all over the State.[8]

Sgt Rufus Pinckney from Baltimore.
Winner of French Croix de Guerre
(Bronze Star); Purple Heart.
Displayed contempt for danger.
(Photo from the book, "The Maryland
Negro in Our Wars.")

Sgt William Butler, Salisbury,
Maryland's greatest hero.  French Croix
de Guerre, US Distinguished Service
Medal.
(Photo from the book, "The Maryland
Negro In Our Wars.")

1st Lt Walter T. Webb.
(Photo from the book, "The
Maryland Negro in Our Wars.")

Sgt Alexander Malone.
(Photo from the book, "The
Maryland NegroIn Our Wars.")

# Chapter 2

(The Monumental City Guard)

Captain William K. Spencer

February 20, 1879 saw the first independent military company of all African Americans in Baltimore formed by Captain Thomas H. Lewis who had high hopes of becoming a part of the National Guard. After many trials and disappointments, this dream was realized on February 20, 1882 when the outfit was formally recognized as a part of the Maryland National Guard with the status of a "separate company.[9] Prior to that, it was known as "The Monumental City Guard."[10]

Captain Thomas H. Lewis had a difficult time in his attempts to have the State of Maryland acknowledge his independent company of African American men. The following, reproduced from the publication, "Freestate Guardian, 1991," provides information on just what it took for such acceptance:

"It was on a cold day, some 16 years after the Civil War that a company of men waited to be inspected. As a freezing wind blew, the soldiers shivered in formation. Their blue uniforms were immaculate. Brass had been polished and re-polished. Their Civil War era muskets almost glowed, while the leather crossbelts of their haversacks and cartridge boxes smelled of the "blackballing" the men had religiously applied during the preceeding days.

Captain Thomas H. Lewis, the commander, stood in front of his men, worried and impatient. The 70 men of the company, too, realized that this was no ordinary inspection. Success today would be a victory not only for the company, but for many others as well. Unlike every other military organizations in Maryland, this one, including its officers, consisted entirely of African-Americans. If the men did well, they would become an official part of the Maryland National Guard, its first and only African American unit. The inspector would be none other than the Adjutant General of Maryland, Major General Hubbard. Major General Hubbard had his doubts about the success of this project. Many of Maryland's guardsmen had fought for the South during the Civil War; in fact, many had been slave owners. It was Captain Lewis who finally convinced him to at least give this unit a chance.

The unit called itself "The Monumental City Guard," that was formed on February 20, 1879. At first the unit was little more than a military club. It had no official status. The men, some of them former slaves, and many of them veterans of the Union Army's all-Black regiments, collected equipment and weapons and learned to drill in the hopes of one day becoming guardsmen in their home state of Maryland.

Captain Lewis worked hard to gain acceptance for his men by the state. He made many trips to Annapolis, lobbying on behalf of the unit. Finally, after two years, the Adjutant General said he would give this unit a chance. Now that day was at hand. When Major General Hubbard and his staff arrived, Lewis called the Monumental City Guard to attention. As the Adjutant General approached, the unit presented arms and Captain Lewis reported. The inspection then began.

At first the soldiers performed the manual exercises, the "School of the Soldier" as it was known then, including stationary drill and individual loading and firing of their muskets. The men then progressed until they were demonstrating company battle drill, going from column into line, firing by platoon and ending with bayonet charge.

Except for an occasional comment among themselves, the general and his staff gave no indication of how they felt. After the inspection, Captain Lewis went to talk to General Hubbard. To Lewis' delight, General Hubbard told him he was extremely impressed with the company. He would go back to Annapolis and talk to the governor. On February 20, 1882, the Monumental City Guard was officially accepted as part of the Maryland National Guard. Since units at that time were not racually mixed, and this was one of a kind, it would have the status of a separate company, unattached to any regiment.

The command of the African American unit was passed to Captain Lloyd Young who remained as the commander only for a short period of time when command was passed on to Captain William R. Spencer who reorganized the unit into a field unit in

1883.  Under the leadership of Captain Spencer, the company developed into a more proficient group.  The drills were standardized in accordance with army regulations and the seriouness of the men and the high standards set by the unit attracted men of high caliber.[11]

In 1883, the First Separate Company participated in the observation of the landing of "Lord Baltimore" in the city harbor.  The company was the only Black outfit in the parade.  It was also during this year when Captain William R. Spencer took command of the First Separate Company.  Drills became more serious and the work as well as the caliber of men attracted to the company became even higher.[12]

Retired Master Sergeant Nathaniel Pope, the historian of the Veterans of the 231st Transportation Truck Battalion, provided the author with a roster of the original Monumental City Guards dated March 15, 1882, that he discovered in the archives of the LTC Melvin H. Cade Armory.  This roster lists Captain William K. Spencer as the commanding officer, and not Captain Thomas H. Lewis.  This roster is dated less than one month after the unit was formally accepted in the Maryland National Guard.  Research has not uncovered why the change of command took place in such a short period of time; however, the following is a listing of the members of the Monumental City Guard that were mustered into the Maryland State Militia:

Captain William K. Spencer
First Lieutenant Peter Wilson
Second Lieutenant Jesse L. Dandridge
First Sergeant James H. Moore
Second Sergeant Charles H. Brooks
Third Sergeant Benjamin R. Douglass
Fourth Sergeant William Walker
Fifth Sergeant John Mitchell
First Corporal John Ray
Second Corporal Henry B. Evans
Third Corporal George W. Scott
Fourth Corporal Emory R. Jackson
Fifth Corporal Stith Purahan
Sixth Corporal Henry Brown
Seventh Corporal Joseph W. Wilson
Eighth Corporal Matthew W. Morton
The following Privates:
    Moses Askins
    George Ash
    Louis Burke
    George W. Brown
    Samuel Brown
    Benjamin Bishop
    John W. Bishop
    Benjamin Burley
    Thomas Blackwell

Louis T. Coleman
Handy Coleman
James Cottman
Joseph H. Collins
Basil Cowdy
Stephen Dickerson
William G. Darry
Louis Davis
George Dexter
James Evans
Bush Evans
James M. Fredericks
George Goodwin
B. A. Gatewood
Theodore Gasaway
Clementine Gasaway
John Hurst
Sidney Johnson
Daniel Johnson
Robert Johnson
Charles Johnson
Samuel Johnson
Davy Jones
William H. Jones
Charles H. Jones
Lorenzo S. Jones
William Jardon
Alfred Kelly
James La Prade
Alfred Mackey
Hezekiah Mapp
Frank Mason
Charles Mosby
Nathaniel Nevitt
Washington Owens
Nicholas A. Pike
James P. Paul
P. H. Quarles
William Rawson
William Robinson
Thomas Stevens
Joseph Sheaf
John N. Smith
John S. Savoy
Joseph Turner
Roderick Twine
Charles Twine

| | |
|---|---|
| Arthur Thomas | Abraham Williams |
| John S. Thomas | Joseph Wright, Jr. |
| James White | Henry Watts |
| William Wells | Thomas H. Young |

The officers of the Monumental City Guard faced a difficult problem in those days. The two top officers after the units being in existence for a while, Captain Spencer, and a First Lieutenant Henry Ryan, Jr, were both senior officers in their grade in the Maryland Guard. Since Captain Spencer was an African American, he could serve only in this one unit. There were no other African American units in Maryland. He could not even move up to a staff job because the unit was not part of a larger regiment. Since there was no major's slot for him, he could never be promoted. First Lieutenant Ryan, also an African American, could not be promoted until Captain Spencer left. They both would spend several decades locked into their ranks.

Two officers from the all African American
First Separate Company, MD National Guard
(Photo provided by ret MSG Nathaniel Pope)

First Separate Company in the early 1900s
(Photo provided by Mrs. George M. Brooks)

Members of the First Separate Company
from MD's National Guard when assigned to
Camp McClellan, Alabama in 1917.
(Photo provided by ret MSG Nathaniel Pope)

The First Separate Company from Maryland's
National when the unit was serving in France
during World War I. 1917 photograph.
(Photo provided by ret MSG Nathaniel Pope)

# Chapter 3

## (Spanish American War)

In 1896, the unit was officially redesignated as the First Separate Company, although everyone continued calling it the Monumental City Guards. At the outbreak of the Spanish American War, the First Separate Company was ordered to active duty, and was the first to pitch tents in Pimilico and while it was never sent to participate in the Spanish American War, it actually was in the Federal Service until the close of that conflict.[13]

Charles Johnson, Jr., noted that during the Spanish American War of 1898, the company experienced several humbling incidents when the military forces of the United States was called to active duty. Maryland's National Guard was activated and the First Separate Company was the first to pitch its tents at Pimlico, where the Regiment was being mobilized. However, the First Separate Company did not accompany the Regiment to Cuba. It remained in Baltimore during the entire crisis. Perhaps its failure to move with the regiment was due to the fact that it was not on the "recognized" list of of the National Guard. A fuller recognition was not bestowed upon the organization until 1902. Maryland's National Guard was activated again on July 5, 1916 to help combat and effect the capture of Pancho Villa who was terrorizing the inhabitants along the Texas border. Again, the First Separate Company was not activated.[14]

# Chapter 4

## (World War I)

At the outbreak of World War I, the First Separate Company had about sixty-five men and three officers. On June 25, 1917 and on August 3, 1917, sixty-seven men from the First Separate Company were rushed to Pittsburgh, PA for interior guard duty; later, about sixty-five recruits joined these men and on October 30, 1917, the company was transferred to Camp McClellan, Alabama, and on January 1, 1918, it was send to Camp Stuart in Newport News, Virginia. It was here that the First Separate Company was organized into Company I, 372nd Infantry in the provisional 93rd Division. It sailed for overseas duty on March 30th, on the USS Susquehanna, arriving in St. Nazaire, France on April 13th and assigned to service with the French 63rd Division on May 26th, and took up sector "Argonne West" where it saw front line duty. The company was transferred to the 157th French Division, the famous "Red Hand" Division on July 2nd and saw service at "Hill 304," one of the most stubborn sectors to give way. The company saw front line services throughout the war, and was twice cited for conspicuous bravery; fifteen men received the Distinguished Service Cross, and two were cited by the American Command. Ten men from the company were individually decorated with the French Croix de Guerre. The company was demobilized on March 3, 1919 at Camp Sherman, Ohio, and on August 5, 1921, the First Separate Company was again organized as part of the Maryland National Guard with Captain William Crigler, Lieutenant Thomas Chatmon, and later, Lieutenant Leroy Clay.[15]

The history of the 229th S & T Battalion noted that after World War I when the unit was again redesignated as the First Separate Company, Infantry, it remained that way for seventeen years;[16] however, Koger notes that sometime after the ending of World War I, with the taking over of the regular militia by the Federal Government, a Guard for the State was deemed advisable. In that setup one battalion of two companies was allotted to members of the First Separate Company. The governor of Maryland appointed the then Major William Creigler with the responsibility of recommending the personnel of his official family. The unit was designated the Eleventh Battalion, Maryland State Guard, and was called for active duty. The officers included: Major William Crigler, commander; Major Maceo Williams, Captain Nelson Williams, Captain E. Walter Shervington, Captain Lewis A. Johnson, Medical Corps, Captain Henry Ryan, Captain William Brady, 1st Lieutenants John Holt and Alonzo Dorman; 2nd Lieutenants Herbert Moulton, Nichols, Virgil S. William and William J. Credit.[17] Unfortunately, Koger did not indicate the specific dates the 11th Battalion were an active or inactive unit, and how the unit related to the First Separate Company; however, it appears that the "Guard for the State" and the "Maryland National Guards" were separate and distinct units.

The Baltimore Afro-American Newspaper, December 31, 1974 - January 4, 1975, notes that the company was reorganized and federally recognized as Company A, 140th Auxillary Engineer Battalion, Maryland National Guard. One year later it was redesignated as the First Separate Company, Infantry. It remained as such for seventeen years.

Members of Company I, 372nd Infantry. They fought with the French Red Hand Division during World War I. 1917 photograph.
(Photo provided by ret MSG Nathaniel Pope)

Major William Creigler, Company Commander, Company I, 372nd Inf. He served in several capacities from 1921 to 1941.
(Photo provided by ret MSG Nathaniel Pope.)

General Warren D. Hodges, the Adjutant General of Maryland, presents award to CPL Parron, one of three men of the Monumental Guard left from WWI.
(Photo provided by ret MSG Nathaniel Pope)

A representative from the Embassy of the Republic of France presents the Croix de Guerre in honor of Co. I, 372nd Inf (Monumental City Guard) for service in WWI. Presented to Co C, 58th Supt Bn and the 243rd Engineer Co.
(Photo provided by ret MSG Nathaniel Pope,)

General Warren D. Hodges, the Adjutant General of Maryland, presnts an award to Lieutenant Colonel William Brady, one of only three members of the old Service Company remaining from World War I. (Photo provided by ret MSG Nathaniel Pope)

French officer and General Warren D. Hodges, the Adjutant General of Maryland, placing a battle streamer from service during World War I as the First Separate Company. Activity took place in 1981. (Photo provided by ret MSG Nathaniel Pope)

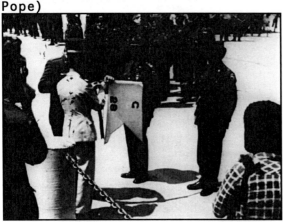

French Officer and General Hodges placing a battle streamer on the guidon of Company C for service during World War I. Captain Edward Ballard was the Company Commander. Activity took place in 1981. (Photo provided by ret MSG Nathaniel Pope)

Members of Company C, 58th Support Battalion in formation at awards ceremony of the Embassy of the Republic of France presenting the Croix de Guerre for service during World War I. 1981 activity. (Photo provided by ret MSG Nathaniel Pope)

French officer making presentation to SSGs Clinton Nichols and William Hutchinson at an awards ceremony for World War I activty. (Photo provided by ret MSG Nathaniel Pope)

Albert Dunton who served in the First Separate Company during World War I. One of his nephew, Robert Dunton, served with the 231st Transportation Truck Battalion. (Photo provided by Robert Dunton)

The original 4th Regiment Armory (old Richmond Market Armory) as it appeared in the early part of the 1900s.
(Photograph copied from the original drawing that currently hangs in the 5th Regment Armory)

Richmond Market Armory as it looks today. This is a rear view of the Armory. It was incorporated into the extension of the Maryland General Hospital on Howard Street many years ago. It was in the rear of the Armory on Linden Avenue where the 231st Transportation Truck Battalion soldiered.
(Photograph provided by Louis S. Diggs)

# Chapter 5

## (World War II)

In 1940, the company was redesignated as Service Company, 372nd Infantry Regiment; seven months later, on March 10, 1941, the unit was again inducted into Federal Service. During World War II, the company performed guard duty at strategic points along the Eastern Seaboard of the United States. On May 3, 1945, the 372nd Infantry Regiment left for overseas duty in the Hawaiian Islands and received credit for participation in the Asiatic-Pacific Campaign. On January 31, 1946, the unit was inactivated, and Service Company, 372nd Infantry Regiment was reorganized as Headquarters and Headquarters Detachment, 231st Transportation Corps Truck Battalion in April 1947 in Baltimore, Maryland under the direction of the Maryland National Guard. The battalion was located at the time in the old Richmond Market Armory on Howard Street and Linden Avenue in Baltimore. The battalion consisted of the Headquarters and Headquarters Detachment and three truck companies: The 147th Transportation Truck Company, the 165th Transportation Truck Company, and the 726th Transportation Truck Company. In 1950, the battalion was reorganized again as Headquarters and Headquarters Company, 231st Transportation Truck Battalion, with no changes to the three truck companies within the battalion.[18]

Several of the officers of Service Company, 372nd Infantry Regiment, former members of the First Separate Company of the Maryland National Guard when they were activated for duty during World War II. The second from the left is then Captain Vernon F. Greene. Others are: not known
(Photo provided by Larry Gibson)

At head of troops, on left side is then Captain Vernon F. Greene marching members of Service Company, 372nd Infantry Regiment from the 5th Regiment Armory in Baltimore, Maryland. They are the former members of the First Separate Company of the Maryland National Guard, and have been ordered to active duty during World War II.
(Photo provided by Larry Gibson)

Lieutenant Colonel Vernon F. Greene, who served in the First Separate Company, Service Company, 372nd Infantry Regiment during World War II, and commanded the 231st Transportation Truck Battalion during the Korean War.

World War II photograph of Retired Lieutenant Colonel Lorenzo (Bus) Felder, who served with the 165th Transportation Truck Company of the 231st Transportation Truck Battalion when they were activated for duty during the Korean War.
(Photo provided by Ret LTC Lorenzo (Bus) Felder)

Captain Leroy A. Clay, the Commanding Officer of ServiceCompany, 372nd Infantry when the First Separate Company was ordered to active duty during World War II.
(Photo from the book, The MD Negro in Our Wars)

# Chapter 6

## (Korean War)

In August 1950, the battalion was ordered to active duty to support The Korean War effort. This activation came just as the battalion and the three truck companies were returning from their annual summer camp at Camp Pickett in Virginia. Several recruiting teams were organized to recruit personnel for fill the numerous vacancies within all of the units. On the last day of August 1950 members of Headquarters and Headquarters Company, 231st Transportation Truck Battalion, 147th Transportation Truck Company, and the 726th Transportation Truck Company massed in formation in front of their military home, the Richmond Market Armory, and, led by SFC Lloyd R. Scott, Sr., and assisted by SGT George (Tony) Thomas, both members of the 726th Transportation Truck Company, were marched down Howard Street, passed the old Mount Royal Train Station, over the Howard Street bridge, made a left turn and marched up North Avenue to the freight train station on North Avenue at the foot of the bridge and boarded a train that took them to Camp Edwards in Falmouth, Massachusetts where the units went through intense training, both physically and with the old World War II GMC deuce-and-a-half trucks. The 165th Transportation Truck Company was the last to leave, but their destination was not Camp Edwards, but Fort Story, Virginia. According to the Freestate Guardian, date unknown, in an article written by Major John C. Andrews, HQ-STARC, the original active duty orders had kept none of the four units together, and earmarked them for Camp Edwards, Fort Story, Camp Lawton, Washington, and Fort Hauchua, Arizona.[19]

This all African American Transportation Truck Battalion was not the only African American military unit from the Baltimore area that was called to active duty to support the Korean War. One week after the 231st Transportation Truck Battalion was order to active duty, the 376th Engineer Construction Battalion became the first Army Reserve unit called to active duty to support the Korean War. The difference between these two African American units are (1) the 231st was a Maryland National Guard unit and the 376th was an Army Reserve unit. The 231st was made up totally of African Americans, enlisted and officers, while the 376th was made up of African American enlisted with all White officers.

The 231st Transportation Truck Battalion with its three truck companies were pretty well understrength. During summer encampment in June and July 1950, the officers were seemingly aware of the impending call to active duty, so the training at Camp Pickett, Virginia was more intense than usual; however, there were numerous military veterans in all of the units. The Baltimore Afro-American newspaper that was published sometime in July or August 1950 noted some of these veterans, such as:

The Battalion Commander, Lt. Colonel Vernon F. Greene, served as adjutant of the 372nd Infantry Regiment during World War II.

Captain James H. Gilliam, 165th Transportation Truck Company served with the 92nd Infantry Division in World War II and was honored with the Bronze Star for valor.

Captain Lester C. Hudgins, Headquarters and Headquarters Company, 231st Transportation Truck Battalion served with the 3101st Quartermaster Service Company during World War II and fought in New Caledonia and Europe.

1st Lieutenant George P. Dawson, Headquarters and Headquarters Company, 231st Transportation Truck Battalion served with the 401st Port Company during World War II and fought in Africa, Italy and the Philippines.

1st Lieutenant George M. Brooks, Headquarters and Headquarters Company, 231st Transportation Truck Battalion served with the 1323rd Engineer General Service Regiment during World War II and fought in France, Luxemburg, Belgium, Germany and the Philippines. (Note: 1st Lieutenant Brooks rose to the rank of Brigadier General in the Maryland National Guard).

2nd Lieutenant William A. (Box) Harris, 726th Transportation Truck Company served with the 3078th Ordnance Transportation Company during World War II and fought in the Rhineland and Central Europe. He was also in the Normandy invasion.

2nd Lieutenant Lorenzo (Bus) Felder, 165th Transportation Truck Company served in the US Marine Corps during World War II and fought in the Marshall and Gilbert Islands.

2nd Lieutenant Thomas Briscoe, 147th Transportation Truck Company also served during World War II.

2nd Lieutenant Emerson W. Brown, Jr., 726th Transportation Truck Company served in both theaters of operations during World War II.

Chief Warrant Officer Earl W. Jackson, 726th Transportation Truck Company served with the 372nd Infantry during World War II.

Chief Warrant Officer Wilbert F. Armstead, Headquarters and Headquarters Company, 231st Transportation Truck Battalion served with the 372nd Infantry during World War II. He joined the National Guard in 1930.

First Sergeant Albert J. Smith, 147th Transportation Truck Company served with the 372nd Infantry during World War II. He joined the National Guard in 1926.

Master Sergeant James H. Smith, Headquarters and Headquarters Company, 231st Transportation Truck Battalion served with the 362nd Infantry during World War II.  He joined the National Guard in 1929.[20]

In addition to the above officers, Warrant Officers and non-commissioned officer, it is a known fact that numerous Non-commissioned officers from all of the units served in the military during World War II, with some who had many years of National Guard experience  These World War II and well seasoned veterans were greatly needed in all of the units because the units were badly understrength and consisted of mostly very young men with no military experience.

By the end of November 1950, training ended for Headquarters and Headquarters Company, 231st Transportation Truck Battalion and the 726th Transportation Truck Company. On December 6, 1950, these two units entrained for a very long train ride to Seattle, Washington where they boarded an old converted liberty ship named "Sergeant Sylvester Antolak."  On December 31, 1950, the 726th Transportation Truck Company unloaded in the port of Pusan, Korea, and on the following day, New Year's Day, 1951 Headquarters and Headquarters Company, 231st Transportation Truck Battalion also unloaded in the port of Pusan, Korea.  When the 726th Transportation Truck Company stepped off the ship, they were the first U.S. National Guard unit to enter Korea in support of the war effort.

Shortly after arriving in Korea, the Headquarters and Headquarters Company, 231st Transportation Truck Battalion and the 726th Transportation Truck Company were separated.  The 231st was assigned to I Corps and had several truck companies assigned to it, while the 726th was assigned to the 70th Transportation Truck Battalion in X Corps, and they went their separate ways.

According to the same Freestate Guardian article, the two units saw a lot of each other during the maximum effort to shift the 3rd Infantry Division between Corps fronts.  This was a secret operation - runs in one direction were made under strict security and in the other with "lots of noise, lights, and radio chitchat" to mislead the enemy.  Both the 231st and 726th spent over four years on active duty. Most of the Maryland Guardsmen rotated home in 1952.  On February 21, 1955, the 231st and 726th returned to State status with eight Korean War campaign Streamers, two Meritorious Unit Citations, and a Korean Presidential Unit Citation.[21]

As far as records being kept by Headquarters and Headquarters Company, 231st Transportation Truck Battalion of their activities in Korea, there is much of their history that was maintained, and has been documented; however, there is no record of the activities in Korea of the 726th Transportation Truck Company.   The following history of Headquarters and Headquarters Company, 231st Transportation Truck Battalion during their tour in Korea was extracted from an unknown document provided the author by Retired Master Sergeant Nathaniel Pope, the Historian of the Veterans of the 231st Transportation Truck Battalion:

"The battalion debarked at Pusan, Korea on 4 January 1951 and encamped there until 16 January 1951 when they moved to Taejon, Korea. (Note: the 726th Transportation Truck Company actually debarked from the troop ship at Pusan, Korea on December 31, 1950 and the Headquarters and Headquarters Company, 231st Transportation Truck Battalion debarked on January 1, 1951. These two units separated as soon as they debarked).

On 26 January 1951, the battalion was split. The operation, maintenance and medical sections moved to Chonan in order to have better supervision over the assigned companies: the 42nd, 49th, 74th and 396th Transportation Truck Companies. The administration and supply sections remained at Taejon. The battalion was under control of Eighth United States Army and was supporting the I Corps United States Army. During this period Battalion Headquarters handled all matters of supply and administration giving the companies more time for operation and maintenance.

From Chonan, Korea, the Battalion Operations, Maintenance and Medical Section and assigned companies moved to Suwon, Korea on 20 February 1951 with the administrative section moving to Chonan, Korea. Operations consisted mainly of hauling Class I, III and V supplies to the 3rd and 25th Infantry Division Supply Points. The battalion trucks were aso used on several occasions as decoys to simulate movements of troop and supplies.

In April the Spring Offensive made it necessary to withdraw the Battalion Operations, Maintenance and Medical Section to Youngdong-Po, and the administrative section to Suwon. All during the fight in Seoul, the Battalion remained in Youngdong-Po hauling supplies and troops within range of small arms fire to aid in stopping the advance of the enemy.

In May 1951, the United Nations Summer Offensive began. The X Corps United States Army advanced so fast that the entire battalion was placed in support of the Corps and worked on a round the clock operation, hauling supplies from Suwon to Wonju. The 3rd Infantry Division was also moved from I Corps to X Corps in an effort to continue the advance.

On 7 June 1951, the 231st Transportation (Truck) Battalion (Forward) CP moved from Youngdong-Po to Uijongbu. Battalion (Rear) CP was moved to Uijongbu and joined the Battalion (Forward) CP.

On 29 October 1951, the Battalion found itself in the position of supporting two Corps, I Corps and IX Corps. The impending attacks of the enemy made it necessary to build up forward Supply Dumps. To accomplish this, the Battalion was to receive the 505th Transportation Company and the 665th Transportation Company, attached for operations only.

The 514th Transportation Company and the 42nd Transportation Company were committed on a round-the-clock operation in the support of IX Corps. IX Corps provided a Liaison Officer to the 231st Transportation Truck Battalion to coordinate operations.

The rotation of troops from Korea imposed many problems on the Battalion.  Replacements from the United States had to be trained to operate on Korea roads,  To alleviate the situation, the 351st Transportation Highway Group organized a Drivers Training School.  However, in the Specialist Field, the prospective rotatees had to train their own replacements before they could rotate.

On 28 November 1951, the 665th Transportation Truck Company was assigned to the Battalion, but continued to support IX Corps.  During the month of December 1951, units of the Battalion were engaged in the task of replacing the 1st Calvary Division with the newly arrived National Guard Division, the 45th Infantry Division.  This move called for a high degree of coordination and timing in order for it to be completely smoothly and swiftly.  This operation was accomplished by three major moves.

The 60th Transportation Truck Company was moved from the east coast of Korea to the Uijongbu area and was assigned to the 231st Transpoprtation Truck Battalion on 4 April 1952.  On 22 July, the 20th Transportation Truck Company moved from Yongdong-Po from the east coast, and was assigned to the 231st.

As of the end of December 1952, the Battalion had 9 truck companies attached:  The 20th, 42nd, 43rd, 49th, 60th, 73rd, 121st, 514th and 665th Transportation Truck Companies.

When the cease fire was announced on 27 July 1953, the Battalion began to stress other activities beside operations.  Some of these were extensive sports programs, educational programs, building programs, safety programs, fire prevention programs, and the Armed Forces Assistance to Korea Program.

Operations continued to be heavy.  It was the job of this Battalion to move troops from positions in the demilitarized zone to locations behind the zone.  In addition, the Battalion was employed in "Operation Little Switch," "Operation Big Switch," and "Operation Swap."  In Operation Little Switch, wounded and sick prisoners were exchanged.  In Operation Big Switch, the 43rd Transportation Truck Company with a platoon of the 49th Transportation Truck Company moved to Munsan-ni to haul Korean and Chinese prisoners from the lines.  The 121st Transportation Truck Company with one platoon of the 665th Transportation Truck Company moved to Munsan-ni to haul the American and other UN troops back from the lines.  In Operation Swap, all prisoners that did not wish to go back to their country were placed in enclosures guarded by Indian troops to await decisions as to their future.  All units taking part in Operation Big Switch were also involved in Operation Swap and Operation Little Switch.

On 20-21 January 1954, the Battalion took part in "Operation Reclaim."  The mission was to move Communist prisoners who refused repatriation from the Indian Camp in the Demilitarized Zone to Inchon for shipment to Formosa.

On 16 May 1954, on the first phase of the withdrawal of United States troops from Korea began.  The Battalion at this time committed two truck companies, the 121st and the 665th Transportation Truck Companies, to move the 40th Infantry Division.  These units moved to the 40th Infantry Division area and operated directly under the 40th Infantry Division Transportation Officer.  This operation ended on the 19th of June.

On 1 September 1954, the 43rd Transportation Company (Lt Truck) moved to the 25th Infantry Division area and operated directly under the 25th Infantry Division Transportation Officer.  This operation ended on 7 October 1954.

On 4 October 1954, the Battalion (Forward) CP, 49th, 107th, 514th and 665th Transportation Companies (Lt Truck) moved to II Corps to support a ROKA Corps redeployment.

Reorganized and redesignated 1 April 1954, as Headquarters and Headquarters Company, 231st Transportation Battalion (Truck).  On 21 February 1955 the unit was deactivated in Korea and on the following day, 22 February 1955 was reactivated Headquarters and Headquarters Company, 231st Transportation Battalion (Truck) with four (4) companies:  Headquarters and Headquarters Company, 147th Transportation Company, 165th Transportation Company and 726th Transportation Companyunder the Maryland National Guard."

There being no record of the activities of the 726th Transportation Truck Company during their years of service in Korea during the war, the reader should read the interviews of the former members of the 726th that were obtained.  Unfortunately, none of the officers of the 726th, nor the First Sergeant, are still alive.  Thanks to the remarkable remembrances of the then Sergeant First Class Lloyd R. Scott, much of the activities of the 726th during his tour of duty in Korea are detailed in his interview.  There are several other interviews of non-commissioned officers of the 726th are included, and should provide a pretty good overview of the history of the activities the 726th was involved in during the Korean War.

The 147th Transportation Truck Company departed Camp Edwards for service in Germany, while the 165th Transportation Truck Company saw most of its service in Fort Eustis, Virginia.

The experiences of many of the members of the Headquarters and Headquarters Company, 231st Transportation Truck Battalion 147th, 165th and 726th Transportation Truck Companies are told in this book via interviews, photographs and other memorabilia by these members.

## (Korean War Interviews)

## Interview - Ret Major James Anthony Porter, a member of Headquarters and Headquarters Company, 231st Transportation Truck Battalion who served in the Korean War

**Samuel A. Porter, Major, Retired**

My name is Samuel Anthony Porter. I was born on August 27, 1918 in Middle River, Baltimore County, Maryland. I attended public school in Baltimore City from the kindergarten to the fifth grade, then I spent one year in a Baltimore County school, then attended Douglass and Carver High Schools in Baltimore City. I graduated from Carver High School that was located on Lafayette Avenue and Carey Street in Baltimore City. After graduation I took various odd jobs, with most of the time being employed by the US Public Health Service at the old Wyman Park Hospital in the city.

During World War II, I was drafted into the military. I started my military service at Fort George G. Meade, Maryland, then transferred to Aberdeen Proving Grounds, then to Egland Army Air Base, from there to Tuskegee, Alabama, then to Officers Candidate School where I was commissioned a Second Lieutenant upon graduation. I was commissioned in the Infantry, but eventually transferred to Armor where I was then assigned to Fort Hood, Texas. I was assigned to the 758th Light Tank Battalion. I served in Italy during the war. At the conclusion of World War II I was transferred to the reserves as a First Lieutenant. That was in 1945. Not long after that, in 1946, I joined the 231st Transportation Truck Battalion of the Maryland National Guard, stationed at the old Richmond Market Armory in Baltimore.

During the early stage of my military service, I married Vanessa Russell on June 6, 1942. We have two daughters who are Vanessa Antonette Porter and Marcia Porter. I was later remarried to Dorothy Grooms. We have one daughter, who is Toni Edwena, and a step son named Kevin Porter.

I came out of the military in December of 1945 as a first lieutenant, and then went to work for several places like the American Stores Company on Pennsylvania Avenue, which was a good job, but didn't pay very much, and the US Postal Service where I worked as a Temporary employee during the Christmas holidays. I was fortunate enough to have been selected for a position as a clerk in the downtown post office where I worked twelve hours a day, six days a week. Later I was selected to work in the parcel post area which was great because my hours became more regular. Later on I was selected for numerous decent jobs in the postal service. I ended up as the Postmaster in White Marsh, Maryland where I remained until the 1970s when I retired.

In 1946, my good friend, Joe Locklear, got me interested in the Maryland National Guard. Joe was a member of the all African American National Guard unit that met at the old Richmond Market Armory. Colonel Brady was the commanding officer would only consider my appointment as a second lieutenant. I refused to accept a demotion. It was not until Colonel Vernon F. Greene took over as the commanding officer, when he offered me a position in the battalion as a first lieutenant. I accepted the assignment. I was in a reserve unit, but it was like a paper unit. I was the only officer assigned and there was only one sergeant assigned. I didn't care for that situation. In accepting the assignment in the 231st Transportation Truck Battalion, I ran into good friends like Donald Parker, James Gilliam, and others. I was assigned to the 165th Transportation Truck Company under James Gilliam. There were two other truck companies under the 231st, which were the 147th and 726th Transportation Truck Companies. Major Parker never took any crap off of anyone. These were typical situations during the time of a segregated army.

In August of 1950, when I was on vacation with my family, I received a telephone call from Colonel Vernon F. Greene informing me that the battalion was ordered to active duty to support the Korean War effort. I didn't like that at all. At that time I was assigned to Battalion Headquarters as Battalion Maintenance Officer.

I recall that when we were activated, the Headquarters and Headquarters Company, 231st Transportation Truck Battalion and the 147th and 726th Transportation Truck Companies were sent to Camp Edwards, Massachusetts in August of 1950. The 165th Transportation Truck Company remained back in Baltimore for a while, and then they were sent to Fort Eustis, Virginia. At Camp Edwards, we had quite a job training the young men in the battalion. I had much experience on just about all types of armament. One of the chief objectives during the training cycle was rifle marksmanship. My experience really came into play then as I was a marksman with the 6mm mortar, light machine gun, BAR, water cooled machine gun, 75, 50 and 37mm weapons, etc.. I will never forget once when we had the troops on the rifle range with Sergeant Vernell Parker when a general visited the range and asked me how things were going with the troops. As he watched the troops train, he indicated how pleased he was that things were going so well.

Before November 1950 came to an end, Headquarters and Headquarters Company, 231st and the 726th Transportation Truck Company were enroute to Korea. The 147th Transportation Truck Company was sent to Germany. By January 1, 1951, we landed at Pusan, Korea and was mustered into service immediately. I don't know why, but the 726th Transportation Truck Company was separated from us and went off into a different direction in the war. Our battalion picked up the 47th, 49th and 396th Transportation Truck Companies. We had never met any of the officers in these newly assigned units. Our duties were to support I Corps to supply them with the necessary transportation to transport Class IV items, ammunitions, and troops to the front lines. We also established what was called a road patrol which had various truck parts and fluids traveling the routes of vehicles in the battalion so as to keep the trucks rolling. It was my duty as the Maintenance Officer to ensure that a minimum of 500 trucks were rolling on the road twenty-four hours a day.

I remember an interesting thing happening when we first arrived in Korea. We were assigned to I Corps Headquarters when we were called to report to a Colonel Franklin who instructed us to send ten trucks to a certain point with drivers. When our drivers arrived at the destination point, there were numerous White drivers just sitting around shooting the breeze while our drivers were overworked trying to accomplish their mission. When we confronted Colonel Franklin about this situation, we were rebutted, and when Major Donald Parker approached Colonel Franklin about the problem, they had heated words, but Major Parker got his point about the situation, and believe me, that never happened again.

I remained in Korea for almost two years. In May 1952, I was able to rotate home. Duty was really rough, but I would like to say that the 231st Transportation Truck Battalion did its share of duty in Korea, and did it well. Some of the places that the 231st ended up during my tour of duty was Pusan, Inchon, Yong-dong-po, Ascom City, Ujion-bo, and Seoul. If I remember correctly, during my tour, the battalion was always assigned to I Corps. There was always a problem keeping spare truck parts on hand. I never will forget when once we were joined with some British officers, and we all got to be pretty good friends. There was Colonel Greene, Major Cade, Captain Dawson, Warrant Officer Holt, Captain Brooks, myself, and we were all drinking and having a great time. We mentioned that booze was hard to come by, and to our amazement, after the British officers left, Major Cade got a call from one of the British officer who said that there was a British ship in the Inchon harbor and there were numerous cases of whiskey on board for us. When we picked up all that liquor, we found that by dealing with enlisted men in the right kind of positions, that you could wheel and deal when you had liquor to trade. We put in a requisition for some ordnance parts to a certain supply point, and when the sergeant in charge found out we had all this liquor to trade, we got just about everything we needed, and I mean everything. The 2 1/2 ton truck that I took was loaded to the point where the springs were going to give out. Just to give one an idea of what that British liquor got for us, we had shoe packs, all kinds of parts, a dump truck, two ten ton wreckers, five extra 2 1/2 ton trucks, etc.

I personally hated my tour in Korea. The winters were simply cruel, the summers were too hot, and you could not get away from the Kimche odor that permeated throughout the country. When I returned to the United States, I did have a desire to return to my old unit in the Maryland National Guard, but many of the officers, myself included, had no desire to return to the old segregated 231st Transportation Truck Battalion. Thirteen African American Officers signed petitions to integrate our unit. General Rekord, the Maryland Adjutant General said that "there would be no integrated Maryland National Guard unit as long as I breath." Many organizations like the Urban League, NAACP, Pittsburgh Courier, every group that was for integration supported our effort. African American officers had no promotion opportunities in the National Guard outside of the 231st, and since all of the units were segregated, we were stuck in jobs with no upward movements. Eventually, the old 231st Transportation Truck Battalion was redesignated as the 229th

Transport Supply Battalion, and was in fact integrated. Around 1964, I was the S2 in the newly designated battalion, and I could only secure intelligence clearance for African American officers, so there was really not much change at all. When the unit went to Camp AP Hill in Virginia, the White band would come around to our area and would only play Dixie or Swanee River. Normally, when the band arrived in your troop area, you were supposed to come outside and show them your support. We said to heck with the band. One day, Colonel Felder said to me, "Send one of your men down to ration breakdown, I have something that your boys would like, watermelons and pork chops." Now, I was already turned off by his use of "your boys, " but when he said what it was, I remarked back to him, "Colonel, if you make it cantaloupes and lamb chops, I'll send troops down right away." He didn't like my response.

I stayed with the unit for quite awhile, serving primarily as an umpire during the training sessions. I remember once when I was sent to observe and rate the 229th Truck Company in Chrisfield, Maryland. They were being tested. They did so badly on the test that I recommended that the unit be disbanded. The company commander told me if he ever catch me on his side of the Bay Bridge, look out. He was a state trooper. Two years later, that same company was up in IGMR, Pennsylvania, and I was the only African American and was the only umpire. This time, the unit was excellent on their tests, and I rated them accordingly. I never will forget when later, a bunch of us flew down to the Eastern Shore for an inspection trip, and the members of the unit never forgot me, and broke ranks to greet me. The White Colonel that I was with was amazed by the action of the men towards me, and later said to me that he had never seen such a display of affections towards an African American officer when a superior White officer was with him. This was the greatest thing that had ever happened to me while I was a member of the Maryland National Guard.

The following interview was extracted from a book, title unknown, in which the then Captain Simon Porter was interviewed:

"Captain Simon Porter, Headquarters, 231st Transportation Truck Battalion: After we landed at Pusan we headed north, moving several times before settling in at Uijongbu, above Seoul. We were with I Corps at this time and had five truck companies attached to us for logistical support. Sometimes we had more, sometime less, but it was usually four or five companies. I was battalion maintenance officer and had a crew of about twenty or so mechanics; about half Americans and half Korean, to keep the trucks running. One afternoon I noticed a lot of activity in the hills to the north of us about 3,000 yards away, It looked like the hills were covered with ants, all moving. I told Colonel Green, the C.O., 'I think I see some gooks up in the hills.' He said, 'No, Tony, I don't think so. I was sure and replied 'The hell it isn't!'

An hour and a half or so later the word came from I Corps, 'Withdraw and quickly!' We had a number of vehicles on deadline waiting for parts, I didn't want to leave them for the Chinese or destroy them. We hooked up a bunch of cables and moved out. I don't recall how far back we went to how long it was before we went back to Uijongbu.

Porter, who had served in Italy during World War II, remained in the National Guard. He retired as a major with over thirty years service."

**A Tribute to Chief Warrant Officer Joseph B. Locklear Who Served With Headquarters and Headquarters Company, 231st Transportation Truck Battalion When They Were in Korea During The Korean War From His Daughters**

My sister, Josephine, and I: how close we were as children--sharing almost everything--a room, clothes, secrets, treats, friends, toys, and most importantly, our pride in and love for our Dad, CWO Joseph B. Locklear. Overlooking the humanly faults and weaknesses each one of us has, we found his many strengths to predominate his character.

Dad's greatest strength was his dedication to our nation and its military organizations. Practically all of our lives, Dad was an active member of a military organization--the Maryland State Guard, the Maryland National Guard, the US Marine Corps, the US (Regular) Army, the Army Reserves, and the Baltimore Chapter of the Montford Point Marines. When age eventually compelled him to retire from active membership in the Army Reserves, he adorned his automobiles, until his death in 1990, with ROA license plates--Reserve Officers Association.

Josephine and I beamed with pride when we saw Dad in his uniform, or saw him performing as a soldier alongside his military buddies. Our memories contain countless snapshots of Dad instilling in us a snippet of US History, or benefits of having military affiliation, or a hands-on opportunity to learn something new.

As little girls during World War II, Josephine and I often had grandstand-type views of the many, many parades that marched along Howard Street. Dad took us to the Richmond Armory where we had unobstructed views from the large second-story windows of the military units marching to, and sometimes from, deployment. From 1945-1946, when Dad was a US Marine stationed at Montford Point (Camp LeJeune, NC), my sister and our mother traveled by train to visit him for a week. The three of us stayed on post at the Hostess House and were treated to a tour of the camp and free movies every evening. As a National Guardsman, we also got the opportunity to visit Dad on Family Sundays at the various summer encampments. There, we were sometimes treated to memorable experiences such as a ride in a Jeep, a meal in a mess hall, and ping pong in the post's recreation hall. It was while traveling with our mother (Margaret) aboard the old Western Maryland Railroad to Camp Ritchie in the late '40s that Josephine and I met the son and daughter of CWO Thomas Owens. The two mothers, just as the four children, became acquainted and eventually, good friends. That friendship developed into a strong and lasting one; one that still exists today among the five of us remaining. During the time that the men of the 231st Transportation Truck Battalion were in Korea, a close bonding emerged among many of the wives and children. Many times, Josephine and I, along with the Owens children, were delegated to babysit the younger children of this informal "sisterhood of wives" when the ladies went out on their R & Rs.

We saw Dad continue to avail himself of opportunities to enrich his membership as a National Guardsman, and later, as an Army Reservist by attending many schools the Army offered. His collection of certificates for successful completion of those courses was numerous and the trek was not always easy; especially when, as time has a habit of doing, Dad found himself to be one of the older enrollees. Among the character traits of CWO Joseph B. Locklear that I will forever admire are dedication, perseverance, tenacity, and love-of-country.

Your girls are proud of you, Dad.

Respectfully submitted,
Lillian Locklear Alston (Daughter #2)

CWO Joseph B. Locklear, just before he retired from military service. He served with the 231st Trans Truck Bn for years, and was with the unit in Korea during the Korean War.
Photo provided by Josephine L. & Lillian L. Alston)

Margaret V. Lindsay Locklear, the wife of Retired Chief Warrant Officer Joseph B. Locklear who served with the 231st Trans Truck Battalioon in Korea during the war. (Photo provided by Josephine L. and Lillian L. Alston)

Left is Josephine Locklear Alston and her sister, Lillian Locklear Alston. They are the children of CWO Joseph B. Locklear who served with the 231st Trans Truck Battalion in Korea during the war.
1970s photograph
Photo provided by Josephine L. & Lillian L. Alston)

Center is Margaret V. Locklear with her two daughters, on the left is Josephine Locklear and Lillian Locklear. Photo taken at the Hostess House at Montfort Point where their husband/ father was stationed during World War II.
1945 photograph
Photo provided by Josephine L. & Lillian L. Alston)

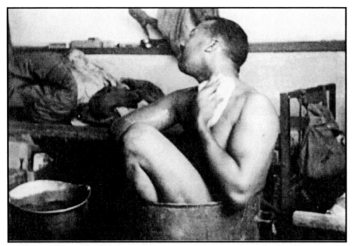

SFC Joseph B. Locklear taking a bath in Korea during the war. He was assigned to Hq & Hq Co, 231st Trans Truck Bn.
1951 photograph
Photo provided by Josephine L. & Lillian L. Alston

Joseph B. Locklear who was with the Hq & Hq Co, 231st Trans Truck Bn when they were in Korea during the war. He was wearing a Korean "A" Frame.
1951 photograph
Photo provided by Josephine L. & Lillian L. Alston

Willie Horne who was a member of Hq & Hq Co, 231st Trans Truck Bn in Korea. He eventually became a Chief Warrant Officer in the unit.
1951 photograph
(Photograph provided by Josephine L & Lillian L. Alston)

Captain Lester Hudgins who served with Hq & Hq Co, 231st Transportation Truck Battalion when they were in Korea during the war.
1951 photograph
(Photograph provided by Josephine L. & Lillian L. Alston

# Interview - Retired Master Sergeant Claude Henry Patterson, Jr., a member of Headquarters and Headquarters Company, 231st Transportation Truck Battalion who served in the Korean War

Claude H. Patterson, Jr., MSG, retired. He is pictured here as a Colonel in the Maryland State Guard

My name is Claude Henry Patterson, Jr. I was born on April 10, 1927 in Roland Park on Providence Street in a community called Hoes Height. My father was Claude Henry Patterson, Sr., and my mother's name was Ruth Harris Patterson. My mother was from Baltimore, Maryland, and my father was from Appomattox, Virginia.

My siblings are Patsy Patterson and Charles Patterson. I grew up in Roland Park. In 1934, my father purchased a home down on 42nd Street when they built some new houses there. This was right off of Evans Chapel Road, just a few blocks from Providence Street. I attended school down on Falls Road where the two new high schools are now located, right off of Coldspring Lane, only back then it was an old wooden building. I do recall the number of the school which was PS #158, and it was an elementary school for African American children who resided in the area. I completed school there, and was then sent to Booker T. Washington Junior High School, PS #130, and then to Douglass High School, PS #450. I graduated from Douglass in the 1940s. After graduating from high school, I went to work in the clothing industry, working first for Kay Burn Clothes out of New York. They had a store on Park Avenue, just off of Howard Street, on the second floor. The factory was out on Pulaski Street. I was a salesman. They later relocated on Baltimore Street in a building where the Sun Newspaper was located. From there I worked for North Carolina Mutual Life Insurance Company. I was a debit clerk, and from there I went into ordinary insurance. I stayed with them for years before I finally went to work for Baltimore City. I retired from Baltimore City as a health inspector, and as a housing inspector. When I retired, I was in charge of the Complaint Department. I did attend Morgan State College in 1946. I majored in academics, and I did graduate.

My first wife was Gladys Williams. Her father was the minister of First Baptist Church over on Caroline Street. We were married from 1946 to 1998. We had three children who are: Ricky, Robin and Jeffrey.

I first got involved with the Maryland National Guard from my cousin, Sam Wilson. He talked me into joining the Guard in 1941 when they started the Minute Men, and from there into the State Guard, and that's when the State Guard was doing all the guard work around Baltimore, like Glen L. Martin Bridge, and all the water reservoirs, and other facilities and structures. We were located in Prettyboy Dam when I first enlisted. I would say that back then we were part of the African American Maryland State Guard because at that time the First Separate Company had been called to active duty during World War II, and then they organized the Minute Men which were also located at Richmond Market Armory, and then they were moved to the State Guard. We remained with the State Guard until we were mustered into the National Guard in 1946. The Minute Men, stationed at the Richmond Market Armory, were all African Americans, however, they did have White Minute Men that were located at the 5th Regiment Armory. In the Minute Men we primarily had drills on Wednesday nights. We really did not do much other than drill and instructions. I did remain with the State Guard. In the State Guard, back then, I attained the rank of corporal. When I was mustered into the Maryland National Guard in 1946, I was assigned to Headquarters and Headquarters Company of the 231st Transportation Truck Battalion. I have always been assigned to Headquarters Company. I was in Headquarters Medics, serving as a surgical technician.

In 1946 we had drill on Wednesday nights, then we had drivers training on Sundays, and the best thing about it was that we had just as many people come out on Sundays for drivers training because you didn't get paid for the Sunday drill. We always had 100% attendance on Sundays. We took drivers training downstairs in the market of Richmond Market Armory. They kept so many trucks in the market and so many out in Pikesville. We used the trucks stored in the market to take the men out to Pikesville for training on Sundays. They had some large garages in Pikesville. There was all type of training that we had to undergo such as drivers training, NCO classes, medical classes, etc. During the summer time we went to camp. We went to Camp Meade, Maryland, AP Hill, Virginia, Camp Pickett, Virginia, Fort Bragg, North Carolina, Fort Eustis, Virginia, Camp Lee, Virginia, and Indiantown Gap, Pennsylvania. Summer camp was all training, and by being truck companies, we would transport the White troops into the field, and that type of thing. It was primarily our job to transport them back and forth.

When I first joined the Maryland National Guard, Colonel Brady was the commander for a very short time. It was not long after that when Colonel Vernon F. Green took command of the battalion. Colonel Brady was also the commander of the state guard. After Colonel Greene, it was Colonel Hudgins who took command, which was after the unit returned from duty in Korea. Sometime later, Colonel Cade took command of the unit. Colonel Hudgins was the company commander in Korea and Colonel Cade was the battalion staff training officer. Colonel Cade used to take us out in the night time in Korea to look for the North Koreans.

Before we were activated in 1950, the unit was in Camp Pickett, Virginia. We were always last in the parades, and when we marched before the grand stand, and we really did look sharp as we usually did, we were told that General Mark Clark was in the grand stand, and he turned around and said to General Reckord, "I would like to have those troops." Then, we had another week in camp. When we got back home that Saturday morning, and on that Sunday morning, my father had called me and said that we had been called up for active duty. It was in the Sunday newspaper. We all had to report the next morning to the unit in Richmond Market Armory, and began to pack up and prepare to go on active duty. We left the Richmond Market Armory to go to Camp Edwards in Massachusetts. That was around the middle of August in 1950. We remained in on post from August 1950 until December of 1950 when we left there for Seattle, Washington by train. From Seattle, we were put on a troop ship and off we went for duty in Korea. I never will forget the name of the boat that we were on. It was called the US Sylvester Antolock. That was a really rough ride over there. We landed in Korea later in the month of December 1950, but we had to stay on the boat for a while because we did not have overcoats. When we landed in Pusan, Korea and was sent up north almost immediately. I recall that the 726th Transportation Truck Company, that had always been a part of the 231st Transportation Truck Battalion, and was on the same boat with us, had been separated from the battalion when we arrived in Pusan. However, there were quite a few other truck companies that had been assigned to our unit. I recall that we had an Alabama unit attached to us, and several others. When our battalion was activated, we had three truck companies assigned, the 147th Transportation Truck Company, the 165th Transportation Truck Company, and the 726th Transportation Truck Company. The 147th was sent to Germany, the 165th was sent to Fort Eustis, Virginia, and the 726th stayed with the battalion until we actually arrived in Korea in December 1950.

During the Korean War, all of the support battalions had a medical unit assigned to it, and I was assigned to the medical unit of the 231st Truck Battalion. I served all during the Korean War as a surgical technician. We took care of sick call daily of all units attached to the battalion, and any type of medical problem that came up. I never will forget one morning, right after sick call, some Koreans rushed into the tent and said that some Koreans had been ambushed and shot about a mile from our area, and they wanted us to send some medics to the area to help. We did, and we speedily went to the area in our ambulance, and sure enough, to make a long story short, some guy was robbing Korean trucks, an American, but what happened this time, the Korean shot it out with him, and he was shot, lying in the rice patties. He was shot dead! Several of the Koreans were also killed.

I remember one night when Colonel Cade got us and we went up on the front line. We would take the trucks up, let the gates down hard to try to bring the Koreans out of the mountains. I don't recall that it ever worked. Another night when we went up on the front line, the guys, the Infantry men were in foxholes, and they told us to leave the area quickly because it was a pretty hot area, then one night we were in Chonan, or one of those towns we were told that we had to leave the area fast because the Koreans were coming over the hill sides quickly. Chinese, and sure enough, we left the area really fast, so fast that we had to leave some of our equipment. That was the Chinese's game to overrun the units and take their equipment. We had two incidents like that. I recall the next morning we could see them caught up the in the barbed wire, etc. It was a terrible sight.

When 1951 rolled around and integration became the way of life, our unit was no longer a segregated unit. We had a White unit from Georgia assigned to the battalion, and I really can't recall any problems when that happened. Those guys were really very nice to work with. The battalion itself was not integrated until we returned to America. I was one of the first ones to rotate from Korea because my enlistment was up before we even left for Korea, and I was on an extension of service, so when the extension of service was up, I was sent back home.

When I returned to Baltimore, I went to the Fifth Regiment Armory to rejoin the National Guard, but I was told that I could not join the guard because there were no Black units in the Maryland National Guard's 29th Division at that time, and we had to wait until the 231st was returned from duty in Korea, and that was what I had to do. The 231st did not return to Maryland for about two and a half years, so I lost time. It was when Jesse Peaker organized the new company. I joined the unit at that time. I was again assigned to Headquarters and Headquarters Company. It was not a battalion at that time. The unit was the Headquarters and Headquarters Company. General Reckord had made Jesse Peaker a Warrant Officer and then he was later promoted to Captain. At the time he organized the unit, he was a Master Sergeant. Actually, he was a Captain in the State Guard, but a Warrant Officer on the federal side. That was sometime around 1953. We did not return to the Richmond Market Armory, rather we were stationed at the Edmondson Avenue Armory. When we were first organized in 1953, meeting were held at the home of Jesse Peaker, then we got the armory on Edmondson Avenue, but we did go back to the Richmond Market Armory. When all of the units that made up the 231st Transportation Truck Battalion were reorganized, the Edmondson Avenue Armory was too small, so we returned to the Richmond Armory. From there we came into the new Armory.

Some of the officers that made up the newly reorganized 231st were young members of the unit were made officers. I recall Leonard Ford, Howard Duvall and myself were to be sent to Officer Candidate School, but by being on orders to go to Korea, we were not able to attend the school. Just before I was returning to the states from Korea, they wanted us to go to Japan to OCS, but after being in Korea for two years, I was ready to return home to my wife and two children, so all of us refused to sign up for OCS.

I remained with the 231st Transportation Truck Battalion. I had almost 40 years with the State and National Guard. I retired as a Master Sergeant. When integration started, they wanted some of us to go down to Annapolis, but no one wanted to go, so Sergeant Edward Watties, who eventually made Warrant Officer, and I were the first two to go to Annapolis to drill. We stayed down there for about six months and then the National Guard had a reorganization which brought the Quartermaster Battalion to Baltimore which caused half of the unit to leave the Guard because they did not agree to the transfer of the unit. After that, Warrant Officer Griffin from the Fifth Regiment Armory informed me of an opening in the S2 Section, which I did apply for, but received a letter indicating that someone else was selected. Unfortunately the person selected did not last long in the position, which opened the position for me. That was in the 58th Brigade. From there, DISCOM was started, and I was fortunate enough to transfer into that organization as a Master Sergeant.

After I was retired from the Maryland National Guard, the Maryland State Guard had been started up again. I recall that Tom Briscoe was a member of the unit already. By my being a Master Sergeant in the National Guard, I was able to start in the State Guard as a Warrant Officer. Company commanders were needed, so I was then commissioned a Captain and assigned to Cade Armory. From that assignment, I was continually promoted in the G4 Section. I was the Assistant G4 Officer for a while, and when the G4 Officer himself passed, I became the Acting G4 Officer, and eventually was promoted to Full Colonel in 2001.

The State Guard was different from the National Guard. They are the back-up for the National Guard. You are trained to take over the armories when the National Guard was activated, otherwise you are trained to assist the civilian personnel. There is still an active State Guard. I retired from the State Guard in July 2002. The military has been my life.

One of the things that I can really remember was my wife and her relationship to my military experiences. My wife never complained of the many times that military assignments took me from our home for those many years I belonged to the guard. I missed many holidays because of drilling schedules, etc. My wife retired as a Social Worker, and she dealt with senior citizens. General Feddert gave her a plaque at her retirement for her achievement of being a dedicated wife to a National Guardsman. That was one of the main pleasurable thing I remember about my many years serving in the National Guard.

I truly hope this book about the 231st Transportation Truck Battalion and their wonderful past is successful.

Sgt Claude Patterson, a member of Hq & Hq Co, 231st Trans Truck Bn when they were in Korea during the war.
1951 photograph
(Photograph provided by Josephine L. & Lillian L. Alston)

## Information provided by an individual who was assigned to the a truck company that was under the 231st Transportation Truck Battalion in Korea after the unit was integrated

I heard from an individual who was assigned to the 42nd Transportation Truck Company that was under the 231st Transportation Truck Battalion after the battalion was integrated and most of the original personnel had returned to the United States.

The person was John D. Warner who resides in St. Clair Shores, Michigan. He wrote to me sometime in January of 2002 after I had posted information on one of the Military web sites, seeking information from men who had served with either the 726th Transportation Truck Company or the Headquarters and Headquarters Company, 231st Transportatation Truck Battalion in Korea during the war. John D. Warner had arrived in Korea in late 1951, and though he was not assigned to either the 726th or the 231st, his unit was under the 231st, and he shared various documents and photographs with me about the 231st Transportation Truck Battalion between 1951 and 1952.

I will share the following letter that John D. Warner had written to me:

"Dear Louis,

I don't have too much info or pictures of people from the 231st. I have many pictures and remembrances of the 42nd Truck Company from September 1951 to September 1952. Much was accomplished mainly through the efforts of Captain David M. Nero. He was from the Oakland, California area I believe.

Collectively, we upgraded, built and established what was a showcase operation. We built permanent buildings for the orderly room, mess hall, post office, PX combined and a fine enlisted man's club. We put in permanent showers by damning a stream and piping in water from the mountains. We had a company laundry with sewing machines and indgenous labor for many of the chores. We paid them with the profits from beer sales from the club.

All tents were outfitted with wood floors. The club had eight booths, a nice bar with plenty of room. We had a piano purchased in Seoul and a bass fiddle. Dances were held periodically with girls brought in from Special Services in Seoul. Personnel were known to come in from miles around to experience our endeavors to make them feel at home.

We were the first company to receive fifty new GMC Hydromatic Trucks and related vehicles. What a difference it made in our operations. They were great and made the driving for the guys somewhat a pleasure. They also promoted the company as a showcase as many inspections were made by upper "Brass." We were visited by various generals on three occassions.

All this and much more was accomplished through Captain Nero. He picked the right people to do the work and we hired much local labor to get the carpentry done. We also paid them with profits from selling beer.

Captain Nero scrounged much fine lumber, paint, nails, varnish and beautiful plywood for our building projects. We had electricity from the time I arrived until I left. We had a generator when I arrived and I got two more by hook and crook. So we always had one in operation. We put up poles and wired the whole place.

The first night the club opened we sold 75 cases of beer and much spirits. The dance hall section of the club was used for movies. Through all this I was the company handyman, telephone repairman, electrician, part time dispatcher, and E.M. Club Manager (What a racket). I was very fortunate. I didn't get on more than six convoy runs during my whole tenure. The guys were always gone and at times it wasn't easy for them. I also kept a time sheet for the indigenous labor that was provided and paid for by the Army. We had a fine interpreter who was a great help. Also a barber who could speak pretty good english.

We got ice every day for our beverages from a school teacher in Ujiongbu. He in turn took all our company garbage and trash. We had three dogs, "Blackjack," "Butch," and "Daisy."

Well, that's probably enough rambling. I hope you can read this. I'm not much of a typist. I'm 74 years old now, retired from Michigan Bell Telephone. Been partially incapacitated for over three years, Life has been good though. No complaints.

Good Luck and All the Best to You and Yours,

John

Note: John was nice enough to send me a copy of a Special Orders published by Headquarters, 2131st Transportation Truck Battalion when they were in Korea dated 16 September 1962, plus a picture from his hometown local newspaper that showed a chapel called "The Trucker's Cathederal" built by the 231st Transportation Truck Battalion which was located in Uijongbu, and several pictures of buildings of his company area and of the 231st Transportation Truck Battalion which are shown with the photographs.

Louis S. Diggs
Author

**Persons assigned to the Headquarters and Headquarters Company, 231st Transportation Truck Battalion in November 1950. Official copy of unit roster cannot be located. These names came from the unit photograph taken at Camp Edwards, Massachusetts in November 1950**

LT. COL. Vernon F. Greene
MAJOR C. Parker
CAPTAIN Melvin Cade
CAPTAIN L. Hudgins
CAPTAIN S. Porter
1ST LT George Brooks
CWO W. Armstead
CWO John Holt
1ST SGT J. Smith
MSGT Jesse Peaker
MSGT C. Hicks
MSGT C. Hurd
MSGT R. Gardner
SFC A. Henderson
SGT C. Edmonds
SGT G. Spears
SGT J. Livingston
SFC Joseph Locklear
SGT J. Hill
SGT V. Clarke
SGT L. Ford
SGT E. Wilkerson
SFC T. Randall
SGT H. Spencer
PVT W. Horne
CPL J. Lopes
PFC G. Johnson
CPL H. Rawls
PVT W. Stewart
PVT M. Guerrier
PVT R. Goslee
PFC R. Dawson
CPL J. Donelson
PVT V. Yates
PFC G. Voss
PVT F. Youngblood
PVT G. Battle
CPL J. Hall
CPL W. Potter
PVT W. Floyd
PVT W. Boswell

PFC J. Reaves
CPL W. Bland
PFC W. Ferebee
PFC R. Murdock
PVT T. Costlee
PVT C. Nero
PVT F. Russell
CPL P. Baytop, Esq.
CPL Claude Patterson
PVT T. Wilson
PFC H. Watley
PVT W. Green
PFC A. Salsbury
CPL J. Greer
PVT J. Broaddus
CPL G. Gross
PFC A. Williams
PFC H. Brown
CPL C. King
CPL W. Stevens
PFC H. Duvall, Esq.
PFC A. Griffin
PFC J. Spruell
PFC E. Bland
CPL J. Evans
PVT W. Graves
CPL W. Byrd
PFC H. Bates
PFC B. Thomas
PVT T. Wilson
PFC H. Watley
PVT W. Green
PFC A. Salsbury
CPL J. Greer
PVT J. Broaddus
CPL G. Gross
PFC A. Williams
PFC H. Brown
CPL C. King
CPL W. Stevens

PFC H. Duvall
PFC A. Griffin
PFC J. Spruell
PFC E. Bland
CPL J. Evans
PVT W, Byrd
PFC H. Bates
PFC B. Thomas

# Photographs provided by members of Headquarters and Headquarters Company, 231st Transportation Truck Battalion

Unit photograph of Headquarters and Headquarters Company, 231st Transportation Truck Battalion when the unit was stationed at Camp Edwards, Massachusetts before it was sent to Korea in late 1950.

"The Club" of a unit under HQ, 231st Transportation Truck Bn when they were in Korea during the Korean War. (Photo provided by John D. Warner, who was in a unit under the 231st in Korea)

Inside "The Club" of a unit under HQ, 231st Transportation Truck Battalion when they were in Korea during the Korean War. (Photo provided by John D. Warner, who was in a unit under the 231st in Korea)

Part of the compound of the 231st Transportation Truck Battalion when it was in Korea during the war. (Photo provided by John D. Warner. who was in a unit under the 231st in Korea)

The Chapel of the 231st Transportation Truck Battalion when it was in Korea during the war. (Photo provided by John D. Warner, who was assigned to a unit under the 231st in Korea)

First Sergeant of, Hq & Hq Co, 231st
Trans Truck Battalion in Korea.
1951 photograph
(Photo provided by Willie Horne)

CPL Willie Horne, member of Hq & Hq Co,
231st Trans Truck Battalion in Taegue, Korea.
December 1951 photograph
(Photo provided by Willie Horne)

Ambulance unit from the 231st Transportation Truck Bn in Korea during the war.
(Photo from a book written about the 231st
in Korea. Title of book and Authos is not
known)

Market place in Teajon, Korea. Photo taken by Corporal Willie Horne, member of Hq & Hq
Co, 231st Trans Truck Battalion in Korea.
1951 photograph
(Photo provided by Willie Horne)

Captain Lester Hudgins, Hq & Hq Co, 231st Trans Truck Bn in Seoul, Korea in 1951. (Photo provided by Willie Horne)

SGT James Hill, Operations Section of Hq & Hq Co, 231st Trans Truck Bn in Youngdongpo, Korea in 1951. Name of other soldier is not known. (Photo provided by Willie Horne)

Captain George Brooks, Operations Officer, Hq & Hq Co, 231st Trans Truck Bn in Pusan Korea in 1951. (Photo provided by Willie Horne)

L to r: CPL Sprulls, SGT Brown, SGT Wilkerson, PFC Gozalee, PFC Willie Brown and other unknown members of Hq & Hq Co, 231st Trans Truck Bn in Korea in 1951 (Photo provided by Willie Horne)

CPL Willie Horne, Hq & Hq Co, 231st Trans Truck Bn in Youngdongpo, Korea in 1951. (Photo provided by Willie Horne)

**Interview of Captain Bedford Bentley (Deceased), Commanding Officer, 726th Transportation Truck Company (Maryland) who served in the Korean War, contained in the book titled "A Very Long Weekend"**

Captain Bedford T. Bentley, Commanding
Officer, 726th Transportation Truck Company in
Korea

"We loaded everything we had on flat cars and went up to Camp Edwards, Massachusetts. The trip from Baltimore took about two days. We had signed up some new men before we left but were still a long way from out full complement. At Edwards we filled up to full strength fairly fast. Most of the new men were Regular Army or recalled Reservists and didn't need basic training. We did, of course, have to give basic to the recruits. We gave them a combination of basic and truck driving training and it worked out quite well. A commander always wants more time for training, but I thought we were in pretty good shape when we shipped out."

Bentley, who had served in World War II with the famed "Red Ball Express" transferred to the Army Reserve upon his return from Korea. He retired as a major in 1972.

The following is the second interview of Captain Bentley also contained in the book titled "A Very Long Weekend":

"We moved up to Taegu and went to work. We were assigned to a truck battalion but I can't recall which one (Author's Note: That battalion was the 70th Transportation Truck Battalion). Every morning I'd tell battalion how many trucks I had available then they'd give me the day's mission. Generally the three platoons would go out on separate assignments, we rarely worked together as a company. As a rule the trucks would be back in by nightfall although occasionally they would be gone twenty-four hours or longer.

North of Taegu the roads were in terrible condition, really more like one lane trails. The engineers worked on them constantly. That, along with the cold weather, lack of spare parts, and the fact that most of the trucks were World War II leftovers caused twenty, to as much as fifty percent of the trucks, to be on deadline at any given time.

At this time the front was fluid and we moved around quite a bit. All in all it was quite an experience."

In the front row, center, is Lt. Bedford T. Bentley when he served in Europe during World War II. He was the Commanding Officer of the 726th Trans Truck Company in Korea. 1940s photograph
(Photo provided by Bedford T. Bentley, Jr.)

Lt. Bedford T. Bentley in Europe during World War II where he was assigned to a "Red Ball Express" Trans Truck Company. 1945 photo
(Photo provided by Bedford T. Bentley, Jr)

Lt. Bedford T. Bentley, center, with his wife, Barbara Fletcher Bentley, on his left. Name of lady on right is not known. Photo was taken in the Club Sudan Cabret Restaurant in Harlem, NY in the 1940s.
(Photo provided by Bedford T. Bentley, Jr.)

Captain Bedford T. Bentley with his family. L to r are daughters Benita and Burly, and son, Blaine. His wife, Barbara, is in rear. Date of photo is not known.
(Photo provided by Bedford T. Bentley, Jr.)

L to r: James Newby, SGT Vernon Marshall, Capt Bedford T. Bentley, Winzer Anderson, Carlissa Hardy, Cpl Haste, Unk., Unk., amd Paul Milburn, members of the 726th Trans Trk Co in Korea in 1951.
(Proto provided by Ret 1SG Lloyd R. Scott, Sr)

Major Bedford T. Bentley at the Sheridan Reserve Center in Baltimore. He did not return to the Maryland National Guard after returning from Korea. 1970s photograph.
(Photo provided by Bedford T. Bentley, Jr)

**Interviews of First Lieutenant Joseph Bracy (Deceased), Executive Officer, 726th Transportation Truck Company in the Korean War, were contained in several books or publications. One of the books is titled "A Very Long Weekend," The title of the other book is not known.**

Left to right: SGT Charles Gilmore, 1st Lt. Joseph Bracy, and
Sergeant Sam Wilson, of the 726th Trans Truck Company in
Korea. 1951 photograph.
(Photo provided by ret 1SG Lloyd Scott, Sr.)

"December 31, 1950, New Year's Eve, a night for celebrating and parties; a time to reflect on the year past and a time to look ahead to the new year. As they huddled and tried to keep warm in their tents on the outskirts of Pusan, the men of the 726th Transportation Truck Company (Maryland) were not partying on celebrating. They were thinking of the past five months and what the future might bring. One hundred and thirty-four days after mobilization the first Army National Guard unit had arrived in Korea.

After we unloaded we went into an encampment area where there a lot of troops. I recall that the first night staying in a squad tent with some a artillery officers. They were saying, 'Why did you embark from those ships? We came this way expecting to get on them.' They said we would not be able to go forward, that it was impossible. The Chinese had overrun their outfit and they had lost all their equipment and taken many casualties. Their whole attitude was one of defeatism. General Ridgeway soon changed that. This was the situation we walked into.

Bracy, who had received a battlefield commission in World War II, resumed his career with the Social Security Administration, becoming assistant bureau director for administration. He also remained in the Guard, retiring after 26 years service as a major.

Four more National Guard truck units came ashore the next day, January 1, 1951. Two of them, the 167th (Pennsylvania) and 231st (Maryland) Truck Battalion Headquarters Companies, had been detachment size when mobilized but were soon expanded to company strength. Their mission was to provide administrative and logistical support to truck companies assigned to them.

These units might be Guard or Regular Army outfits and number anywhere from four to as many as ten companies. The two headquarters companies operated under Corps control; the 167th went to IX Corps, while the 231st joined I Corps.

By January 8, the men of the 726th had been joined by five more National Guard truck companies. The 107th and 252nd (Alabama), the 715th (District of Columbia) and the 121st and 131st (Pennsylvania).

The 726th TTC that landed on New Year's Eve hailed from Baltimore, as did the 231st Headquarters Company. Commanded by Captain Bedford Bentley, the 726th trained at Camp Edwards, Massachusetts, before heading for Korea. There was nothing unusal about these two outfits except for one thing. Both units were manned 100 percent by African Americans".

First Lieutenant Joseph Bracy, Executive Officer, 726th Transportation Truck Company (Maryland):

"We finally got unloaded and began drawing equipment. We had to mount the .50 caliber machine guns and we weren't that familiar with their operation, but we got them on the mounts and then tested them. We went up to Taegue and then on our first mission, moving elements of the 1st Cav at night.

I hadn't become familiar with the division's code names yet; I went with the lead platoon and I saw this road sign that said 'Danger Forward.' I thought, Oh God, are they trying to tell us something!' Later I learned this was the code name of the 24th Infantry Division's forward command post (CP). Those first week things were pretty disorganized."

As Bracy, and the other National Guard truckers headed north, one outfit, the 121st TTC went south. Assigned the mission of truck support at the POW compounds on the island of Koje, the Pennsylvania unit spent its entire Korean tour in this capacity. The POW's now numbering over 40,000, had been held in the Inchon area as late as mid December. When it became apparent that the Communists would soon recapture Inchon, they were moved to Pusan, and then to Koje, a small island off the southern Korean coast."

This final interview of First Lieutenant Joseph Bracy, occurred when he was the Commanding Officer, 715th Transportation Truck Company (District of Columbia):

"One thing I experienced over there, I saw the Army integrated while I was in Korea. I was commanding the 715th Transportation Truck Company out of Washington, DC, when it happened. I'd left the 726th TTC and taken over the 715th around the first of February 1952, when their C.O. rotated home.

I had been with the unit about a month when the integration began. There was no advance notice or fanfare. If you needed x number of truck drivers or maintenance personnel you sent a request in and they send you qualified replacement. I saw my unit go from 100 percent black to 60 percent white, 40 percent black inside of four months.

In many of the units they did it overnight, You went to bed 100 percent black or white and the next day people transferred in and out, and that night your unit might be only 70 percent black or white. For some reason my outfit was integrated gradually as new people were needed. I think this was probably a better way to do it; over a few months' time.

I got a new first sergeant and a new mess sergeant, both Regular Army and both white. They were very good people, tremendously efficient. Not many people realize how vital a good mess sergeant is to a unit.

We had not one racial difficulty. The only problem I had was when the MPs were ticketing the truck drivers. The MPs were very tough on speeding; with the poor roads and the possibility of accidents this was understandable. At times the white fellows said the MPs were picking on the black drivers and wanted to protect them, and I had to calm them down. When I left in May 1952, I was the only black officer in the company. We had no problems at all."

# Interview - Retired First Sergeant Lloyd Robert Scott, Sr., a member of 726th Transportation Truck Company, who served with the 726th in the Korean War.

Left to right:  SFC Bradford, SFC Lloyd R. Scott Sr, and First Sergeant Albert Brooks, members of the 726th Transportation Truck Company in Korea.  1951 photograph
(Photo provided by Ret 1SGT Lloyd R. Scott, Sr.)

My name is Lloyd Robert Scott, Sr.  I was born a Junior, but I have a son named after me that I named Junior, so I changed by name to Senior.  I was born on October 7, 1926 in Baltimore, Maryland, on Pierce Street.  In 1950 I was assigned to the 726th Transportation Truck Company, 231st Transportation Truck Battalion of the Maryland National Guard.  My parents were Robert Lloyd Scott and my mother was Gladys Keyes.  I was reared by my grandmother, Elizabeth Parren, who was from Calvert County, Maryland.  I have no siblings.

My wife is Effie Williams Scott.  Her brother, Donald Williams, was also in the Guard with me.  He was assigned to the 165th Transportation Truck Company that went to Fort Eustis, Virginia. We got married on November 3, 1950, just before I left to go to Korea while I was still stationed in Camp Edwards, Massachusetts.  We have fifteen children:  Natalie Jones, Ronald, Lloyd, Jr., Anthony, Diane, Patricia, Melvin, Michael, Valerie, Geraldine, Richard, Saundra, Rochelle, James, Sandra, the youngest.

Growing up in Baltimore, when I was residing on Boyd Street in South Baltimore, I started school on Lemon and Freemond Avenues, from there I went to Booker T. Washington Junior High School, and then on to the old Douglass High School.  I did not graduate, instead, I quit school in the 1940s to work to help my grandmother.  I did lots of odd jobs, including scrubbing steps, but I liked driving trucks.  I remember one job that I really enjoyed was working for Martha T. Washington Canning Company down on Liberty Street and Clay Street.  I was a bus boy, dishwasher, whatever jobs I could get.  I finally got a job at Glenn L. Martin Company where I worked for eight years.  I had to leave there because I did not have a car, and it was really difficult getting back and forth from work.  In 1947 I worked for the Merchant Marines, and I enjoyed that because I had opportunities to see different parts of the world, like England and Scotland.  Around 1947 a good friend, Frank Palmer, introduced me to the Black unit in the Maryland National Guard. Back then the units were soldiering over a market on Howard Street, called Richmond Market Armory. There is a hospital there now. I joined the 726th Transportation Truck Company in 1948, which is where I remained until we were called to active duty in August of 1950. I remember First Sergeant Albert Brooks who was the first sergeant at that time.

The 726th Transportation Truck Company was known for its strong marching abilities, and was one big happy family. In 1950 I had worked my way up to platoon sergeant, then acting field first sergeant. I recall Sgt Sam Wilson was the field first sergeant when I was the platoon sergeant. It was from Sam Wilson where I learned my marching abilities and how to drive a 2 1/2 ton 6X6 truck. I'll never forget him. I recall when all of the truck companies would go to camp with the 29th Infantry Division. Being all Black units, we were always on the end of everything, but we were always the best at camp. No one could beat us when it came to marching. We always looked forward to summer camp so that we could show off our marching abilities. Even when we were enroute to Camp Edwards, Massachusetts and we had to load on to a train down at the depot on North Avenue near Mount Royal Avenue, our units marched from the old Richmond Market Armory, past the Fifth Regiment Armory, past the Mount Royal Railroad Station, down Howard Street, over the Howard Street bridge, up North Avenue into the train depot at the end of the North Avenue bridge. Man! we did some serious marching back then.

When we were alerted for active duty, we had just returned from summer camp in Virginia where we marched for General Mark Clark. I say it today, that we looked so good marching for General Mark Clark that "we marched ourselves to Korea." We were just that good, and we heard that the General really liked to see us march. I recall that all of the units that made up the 231st Transportation Truck Battalion was under strength. The Headquarters and Headquarters Company of the Battalion, the 147th Transportation Truck Company, the 165th Transportation Truck Company, and the 726th Transportation Truck Company. I remember that several recruiting teams had to be made up to scout throughout Maryland for young men to join the units. I was assigned to one of those recruiting teams. I was working with Lt.William (Box) Harris, Lt. Coscoe Williams, Sgt Baughn, Sgt Carter, Sgt Gilmore, and myself. Our team took off for Eastern Shore, Maryland where we visited factories, and other places where young Black men worked. We stayed on Eastern Shore for three or four weeks, and were quite successful in gathering numerous men for our company.

In early or mid-August, all of the units took off for Camp Edwards, Massachusetts. We took the rest of our training in Camp Edwards. All we knew is that we were training to go overseas. We were learning how to retrieve trucks bogged down in mud, driving in severe winter weather, etc. We loaded up on a train in early December 1950 and headed for Seattle, Washington where we were loaded on a boat, and by the end of December, our unit, with the Headquarters and Headquarters Company of the 231st Truck Battalion, landed in Pusan, Korea.

One of the things we had to get used to right from the bat was the odor that permeated all over Pusan; it was like crabs that had been eaten and the uneaten parts were wrapped in paper and left out in the sun for days; it was an odor that you could not get away from, but I have to admit that you eventually got used to it. By the time we got to Taegue, the 726th Truck Company broke off from the 231st Truck Battalion. The battalion remained in the rear, and our truck company was really broken up into platoons. We were assigned to different Infantry units. We did not see each other for a long time. Our two platoons, by operating separately caused some problems with the mechanics from the base company trying to locate us to keep up the maintenance on the trucks, and we were spread out all over Korea. As we tried to get used to driving our trucks in Korea, it just got harder as time went by. In the mornings when we finally got the trucks started in the severe cold weather, the roads were like round top roads, and it was just like a sheet of ice. The trucks would sit still and slide off the road. By the middle of the day when the sun would come out and things finally warmed up, we had the horrible experience of the odor from the human excretion that the farmers used in their farming. God! not only was the odor terrible, but as you walked around, you'd get the mud and stink in your boots and you'd smell up everything. One experience I will never forget when we arrived in Pusan was in the chow line. They had a big open sided tent, and right across the road was a prison camp, and all along the fence line were open trenches for the North Korean prisoners, and they would wait until we went to chow when they would decide to use their facilities. It was always so bad that we always had to lower the sides of the tents if we wanted to stomach eating breakfast.

Some of the White troops that we ran into treated us like we were equal, which we knew better. Things were moving so fast that there really wasn't a lot of time for prejudice to play a real role in life. We all had to watch our backs at all times, and the Whites knew it as well as the Blacks. The 726th was supporting the 24th Infantry Division and the 1st Calvary Division. We would move material and troops up to a certain point near the front lines, and the service companies of the divisions would take over. I always felt uneasy while driving over Korea into unknown territory. People would come out of the hills just to look at you because many had never seen Black Americans, and we were always at a disadvantage because we were not able to distinguish between a North Korean and a South Korean. When the Chinese inter-vened, it was not difficult to tell a Korean from a Chinese. Believe me, when the Chinese did get involved in the war, then things really got tough on everyone.

During big pushes both back and forward as the front line moved, we all had to move out at a moments notice. The only thing familiar to us was the routes we traveled, either the Red Diamond or the Green Diamond. If you were on a Red Dia-mond run then you knew you would end up somewhere near the front lines, and danger was always there. If you were on a Green Diamond run, then you were usually in a safe zone behind the lines moving troops or material, they were commercial access routes. Danger was always around the corner because the roads would be sabotaged, or a kid would be waving at you with one hand, and as soon as you got close, then he would throw a grenade at your truck. Our unit had never experienced such action by children, but we were warned by units throughout Korea to be on the lookout for such tactics, especially when traveling through towns and villages where people were not so friendly.

The officers that made up the 726th Truck Company while we were in Korea included: Captain Bedford T. Bentley, the company commander, Lt. Joseph Bracy, a platoon leader, Lt. William (Box) Harris, a platoon leader, Lt. Emerson Brown, a platoon leader, and Warrant Officer Jackson, the Motor Pool Officer. Most of the time, our unit was under the Tenth Corps in Korea.

When our unit was not making truck runs, life in our area was like being in a bivouac, or training area. We had time to take care of our personal needs, clothing needs, supplies, and we spent some times on those needs because our troops would be on driving missions for weeks at a time, and there was no time to take care of yourself, so everyone really used the free time we had in our bivouac area. We didn't have much social time because we were always camped out in the fields, quite a distance from towns and villages. When we went on R&R (Rest and Recuperation) to Japan, Okinawa, or other places. I never had the time to take R&R.

The average person in the 726th Transportation Truck Company remained in Korea was for just about a year. Most of us left in 1951, and we left our colors in Korea. By the time I left in 1951, there were not many of the original members of the unit from the National Guard days still with the unit. I recall when I rotated back to the Zone of Interior, I left with lst Sgt Albert Brooks, Callissa Hardy, and another young man rotated with me. I recall Frank Palmer remained in the military, Louis Diggs, and a couple other guys opted to reenlist in the Regular Army.

The worst experience I encountered in Korea was having a mission and driving over those really rough roads at a speed that you couldn't handle. You were forced to drive at a very slow speed, and at night, it was even worst because you couldn't see the pot holes and drop offs from the roads that caused much damage to our trucks. The situation was really terrible when we would have to drive through unfamiliar territory in the extreme darkness of might not knowing who or what you would encounter. It was nightmarish most of the time on those trips, and we would have to spend week after week driving under those conditions. Guns were always going off in the distance; those were the heavy artillery, and when the guns stopped firing, then fear hit our hearts because of the rumors that would be flying around that Charlie (Chinese) broke through the lines and was on his way towards the rear. Man! that was scary because you didn't know what to expect. When we would take off in convoys, we had to drive using the night time lights (little slits in the headlights - we called them "Cat Eyes") that almost made you drive blinded. I mean the nights in Korea were absolutely pitch black! I recall when we had stopped at the base of a mountain and we thought we would turn around and head back deeper into the rear echelon, but the Lieutenant from the infantry unit that we were transporting said to stay fast, that they were going to dig in around us; that this was the only way out. We knew what the deal was then, so they dug in and eventually moved up towards the front and dropped napalm on the mountain. Man! That scared the crap out of all of us. The lieutenant never did come back, and the guys that did, jumped on our trucks, and we got the hell out of there real fast. We had .50 caliber guns mounted on our trucks, but all the drivers could carry was small carbines. The only uplifting thing while serving in the Korean War was receiving our mail from home. It seemed as though your letters took forever getting to you, but when you finally got a letter from home, all of the activities during the war just took a back seat.

When I finally left Korea in 1951, I went to Osaka, Japan where we waited for a flight to the United States. It was a crazy flight because I was looking to have some kind of parachute on, but not so as it turned out. It was great just getting to Japan because then we got some real food for a change, none of the "C" and "K" Rations out of cans that we had gotten used to for the last year. After getting a change of uniforms, and having to give up most of the souvenirs that we collected, we boarded a nice flight to Camp Kilmer, New Jersey. We didn't stay there long, just long enough to be processed through, and in a day or so, we were on the way home. We were discharged from active duty in New Jersey.

When I returned from Korea, the only jobs available to African American men were porters, janitors, cooks, drivers, etc. I had a family to take care of, so I took a job in the Reads Drug Store out on Belair Road as a porter. I had other little odd jobs, but I eventually got a job in the 5th Regiment Armory in publications. I distributed literature to various units, and eventually, I applied for a position at the Cade Armory as a technician, plus I was still in the National Guard. I eventually made First Sergeant, and I stayed in this capacity until I eventually retired from the National Guard and the State. I retired in 1986.

I never will forget when Warrant Officer Jesse Peaker, who always went to bat for our unit. We had lost the Richmond Market Armory when it was converted to be part of the hospital. Our unit ended up in an old firehouse on Edmondson Avenue at Bentalou Street. When we were reactivated after all of the units under the 231st Transportation Truck Battalion were converted back to Maryland State National Guard control. It started with the 147th Truck Company, which was the mother company of the 231st. Our unit was changed to the 229th Transportation Battalion, and our units were changed to Company A, B, C, etc. We even had an all White company that was stationed in Annapolis in the battalion. It later became the Supply and Transport Battalion. In 1968 our battalion was disbanded, and we then came under an Engineer unit in the 28th Division in Pennsylvania. By then we were in the Cade Armory. Initially it was called Northwest Armory. It was the officers of the old 231st caused it to be changed to Winchester Armory, and eventually it became Cade Armory. Our goal now is to have Cade Armory designated as a historical site, and we are currently on the road doing just that.

# Interview - Claude Donald Urquhart, Jr., a member of 726th Transportation Truck Company, who served in the Korean War.

Claude Donald Urquhart, Jr.

My name is Claude Donald Urquhart, Jr., I was born on January 6, 1928 in Baltimore, Maryland. I currently reside at 5006-102 Hollington Drive, Owings Mills, Maryland 21117.

My mother was Gertrude Green Urquhart, and my father was Claude Donald Urquhart. Both are deceased. I have no siblings.

I attended elementary school in Trenton, New Jersey; I attended PS #130, Booker T. Washington Junior High School in Baltimore, and PS #450, Douglass High School, also in Baltimore where I graduated from. I attended what was then Morgan State College. While at Morgan State College, I joined the Enlisted Reserve Corps (ERC) and completed the ROTC Basic course. When the Korean Conflict started in 1950, I was notified by the Enlisted Reserve Corps that I was called to active duty in July, 1950. Since I was not assigned to a specific unit while in the reserves, I was aware that the 231st Transportation Truck Battalion of the Maryland National Guard was being activated, so in July, 1950, I enlisted in the Maryland National Guard and was assigned to the 726th Transportation Truck Company of the 231st Transportation Truck Battalion. The entire battalion, with all three of its assigned truck companies were ordered to active military service in August, 1950.

After we were activated, we were notified that we would be going to Camp Edwards in Massachusetts for training. I was happy to be going North because I was afraid that we would be sent to a southern camp. While at Camp Edwards, I made the best of the situation, and enjoyed myself whenever possible.

Being called to active duty for the Korean Conflict, our guard unit was given refresher training, and it did not take a genius to realize that we were going to be sent to Korea; it was just a matter of time when we left. In November, 1950, the 726th Transportation Truck Company, with the 231st Transportation Truck Battalion boarded a train, and was bound for duty in Korea.

We arrived in Pusan, Korea in January, 1951, and disembarked the night of our arrival. We were directed to squad tents where we spent that night. It was cold and we had no cots to sleep on, so we scrounged around for some cardboard. In the morning, we were assembled, the companies were given vehicles and assigned to various units. My company, the 726th Transportation Truck Company, was assigned to the 1st Calvary Division. There were two major routes in South Korea, Green and Red. The Green routes were used to bring supplies from the port to supply depots, and the Red routes took the supplies to the front lines. Our company used both routes and hauled all types of supplies and personnel. The roads were dirt and barely wide enough for two trucks to pass each other. Only officers and sergeants were allowed to take out a ten, or more, truck convoy, however, things got hectic and some corporals were assigned as convoy leaders. There were times when I took a convoy out and didn't return to my compound for a week or more. Sometimes the compound would have been relocated and I would have trouble finding it. Our trucks ran twenty-four hours a day, seven days a week. No sooner then we returned to the compound, the trucks were refueled, given a quick check, and sent out with a different driver. I was a convoy leader for about seven months before being promoted to Sergeant First Class. With that promotion, I was made Company Supply Sergeant. I worked in that capacity for the remainder of my tour in Korea.

In March, 1952, I contacted hepatitis, and was sent to a hospital in Koyota, Japan where I remained in the hospital until the end of April, 1952. I was then sent to Camp Drake in Japan, to await my return to the United States.

I rotated to the United States in June, 1952 and was assigned to Fort George G. Meade, Maryland. On June 4, 1952 I was released from active duty. At that point, I returned to my studies at Morgan State College, married Constance L. Urquhart and had my family, my daughter, Gabrielle A. Urquhart. I got a position with the Division of Parole and Probation, State of Maryland, where I remained employed until retirement in 1986.

Claude Urquhart when he was serving in the
Korean War in 1951.
He was assigned to the 726th Trans Truck Co.
(Photo provded by Claude Urquhart)

# Interview - Ret SFC Louis S. Diggs, a member of 726th Transportation Truck Company, who served in the Korean War, and made a 20+ year career in the Regular Army

On the right is Louis S. Diggs, with his older brother, the late George A. Diggs, Jr. George was a member of the 24th Infantry Regimenton the front lines in Korea, when he spent Christmas of 1951 with his brother, Louis who was in the rear.
(Photo provided by Ret SFC Louis S. Diggs)

My name is Louis S. Diggs. I was born on April 13, 1932 on Dewey Avenue in Baltimore, Maryland, in a small African American community called "Hoe's Heights," located not far from Falls Road and Coldspring Lane in East Baltimore.

My mother was Agrada Francis Deaver Diggs and my father was George Augustus Diggs. My mother was born in Baltimore, Maryland and my father was born in Piney Grove in Boring, Maryland. Both are deceased.

I had four siblings: George Augustus Diggs, Jr., who is deceased; Janice Celestia Diggs Langley, who is deceased; Lawrence Prentiss Diggs, who is deceased, and Nettie Agrada Diggs Holley. All of my siblings were born and reared in Baltimore City.

My schooling began at PS #104 on Carey Street, PS#108 on School Street, a school down on Gilmor Street, near Lafayette Avenue, PS#130, Booker T. Washington Junior High School, and another Junior High School on Francis Street, and finally PS #450, Douglass High School where I quit in 1950. Later in life (1975), I was able to complete my high school through the GED program. In 1976 I earned an Associate Degree at Catonsville Community College; in 1979 I earned a Bachelor of Arts Degree from the University of Baltimore (Cum Laude), and in 1982 I earned a Master of Public Administration Degree also at the University of Baltimore. I did post graduate studies at George Washington University in Washington, DC.

On June 20, 1950, I joined the 726th Transportation Truck Company of the Maryland National Guard. At that time they were located in what was the Richmond Market Armory on Biddle Street in Baltimore, Maryland, just in the shadows of the hugh 5th Regiment Armory where we as African Americans were not permitted to soldier in. When I first learned that five days after I joined the 726th, that a war had

64

broken out in Korea, I really was not overly concerned because being only eighteen years of age, and not hearing any one in the unit talk about Korea, I didn't see any reason to be concerned. First of all, I had a strong desire to join the Regular Army because I was having a very hard time in school. There was a Baltimore City Police Officer by the name of Sergeant Violet Hill Whyte who was after me like white on rice. I was a very mischievous boy, not really bad, just mischievous with a great dislike for school. I played hooky from school a lot and as a result, I must have failed three or four times at Booker T. Washington Junior High School. When I would hook school, my favorite place was Druid Hill Park where several of us would go to and play around the water's edge where you could rent boats. I would lie on the grass and day dream all day long. Well, Sergeant Whyte knew this was a favorite place for the kids to play hooky, so you always had to be on your alert. Sergeant Whyte had no intentions to helping you stay in school, only to make sure that you stayed in school. I was often threatened by her to be sent to the Juvenile Prison for Black Boys in Cheltenham. I knew several boys who were sent there and came out harden criminals. I knew if I stayed in Baltimore that I would eventually end up in Cheltenham. So, after graduating from Junior High School, I went to Douglass High School, where my problems became exacerbated. I sort of liked high school, and I particularly loved typing, so I took up typing in school where I ended up as the only boy in a class of about fifty girls. I took so much ribbing from the boys, including fighting. Just about every day I had to fight just to prove that I was all boy. I just gave up and decided to quit school. I think I passed to the tenth grade in June of 1950 when I decided not to return to school. Besides, I was eighteen years old, so school was not mandatory.

I was actually afraid to enlist in the Regular Army, so I decided to try the National Guard, and perhaps by September of 1950, I'd be somewhat used to military life and could then join the Regular Army. When I enlisted in the Guard, it was only a couple of weeks when we were off to summer camp in Camp Pickett, Virginia. That was when we all learned that the entire 231st Transportation Truck Battalion was to be federalized in support of the Korean War. We returned to Baltimore either late July or early August of 1950 when we were all informed of being called to active duty. I really thought about getting out because actually, I was still in high school, but my lifelong friend, Sidney (Chico) Dorsey who was my neighbor in the 1500 block of Stricker Street, decided that we would use this opportunity and make a break from Baltimore. So, off to war we both went.

Our unit was initially ordered to Camp Edwards in Falmouth, Massachusetts on August 19, 1950. All of the units made preparation to depart from the Richmond Market Armory, and it was then that the reality of the situation stepped into my life. We were all issued new summer uniforms and began the long Battalion march up Howard Street, over the bridge leading to North Avenue, did a left turn on North Avenue and marched up the second part of the bridge for about four blocks when we got to what appeared to be some type of loading dock for trucks at the railroad yard right at North Avenue and Mount Royal Avenue. I loved to march, and felt good about finally getting away from Sergeant Violet Hill Whyte and Baltimore, when I spied my mother and my little sister, Nettie (Peggy). Now that was when the reality of my situation set in. I began to panic, what could I do away from my mother. I only left Baltimore one time before. All of the mothers and wives were lined up as we marched into the train yards, and you could tell that everyone began to be unnerved. They did allow everyone a few minutes with their loved ones before we had to board the train. Man! I think everyone cried all the way to Massachusetts.

The unit did not stay at Camp Edwards very long. We had just returned from Summer Camp, so much of the basic training was not required. Most of the time was spent on learning how to drive the 2 1/2 ton 6 X 6 trucks, that really, not many of us learned. Our next shock came just a few months after arriving at Camp Edwards. In November, we were alerted for overseas duty. The Battalion was then split. Actually, the 165th Transportation Truck Company did not join us in Camp Edwards. They eventually went directly to Fort Eustis, Virginia. The Headquarters and Headquarters Company, 231st Transportation Truck Battalion and my unit, the 726th Transportation Truck Company were ordered for duty in Korea. The 147th Transportation Truck Company was ordered to Germany.

By late November of 1950 we had boarded a troop train and took this extremely long train ride across the country to the state of Washington. Actually, I thought we would never get out of Texas. I recall when we got to somewhere in Nevada, I think it was Las Vegas, when several of us eased into town to buy booze and snacks, and I found out that segregation was in full effect. Most places wouldn't even sell us items. Finally, I think we found a place with a side or back counter when we got what we wanted. We didn't stay very long. Perhaps it was by mid-December of 1950 when we finally loaded onto a converted liberty ship named Sgt. Sylvester Antolak. That was truly the most raggediest ship in the navy, but by the end of December of 1950, we were finally able to disembark in Pusan, Korea. I understand from reading several earlier books that our unit and the 231st were the first United States National Guard unit to step foot in Korea to support the war.

It was quite an experience itself serving in Korea. I will never forget the odor that permeated the entire country; it was an odor that I cannot explain. It took a long time to get used to that odor. My job in the 726th was to serve as the Company Clerk and a truck driver. Most of my time was spent in the orderly room with First Sergeant Albert Brooks, but there was such great need for truck drivers that I also spent many hours driving a 2 1/2 ton 6 X 6 truck hauling everything from manpower to napalm bombs all over Korea. When we first arrived, some of us many great mistakes in handling these really big trucks. It was so bitter cold that you had to be very careful never to touch the metal of the truck with your open hand. It would actually freeze onto the truck and you would lose much of your skin. Even the roads were always frozen, even though they were dirt roads. Many times we would drive off in convoys at night and many of us would slide off the road, but when the sun came up in the morning, it would melt the ice. I recall hauling other African Americans from the 24th Infantry Regiment of the 25th Infantry Division, back from the front lines and would see the pain and misery in their faces. It made me glad that I was not assigned to combat. I think the most dangerous things we would haul would be napalm bombs from the boats in Inchon to the big air base in Seoul. I recall having to help 8th Army headquarters evacuate Seoul in the winter of 1951, crossing the Han River when the bridge was blown up and we had to drive on the ice. Now, that was a scary situation. Sergeant First Class Lloyd Scott was our platoon leader, and we were with him most of the times we went our on various missions. He was a great leader, and he realized that many of us were still boys, or young men without a lot of experience, so he looked over us like a father. He truly made men out of most of us. I always respected him, and wanted to emulate him as a leader.

I remained with the 726th until July of 1951 when I was transferred to Battalion Headquarters. Our unit was already separated from the 231st Battalion and we were under a White Battalion called the 70th Transportation Truck Battalion. It was during this time when I saw the great opportunity to make the military a career. I was assigned as a Personnel Administrative Clerk in the Headquarters and began to gain much experience in the personnel field. I was promoted to Corporal not long after the transfer, and had a wonderful opportunity to go on R & R (Rest and Recuperation) in Saigon, Vietnam, one of the most prettiest places I have ever seen. Later that year, on November 16, 1951 while serving in North Korea, I reenlisted in the Army and began a twenty year military career. I deeply missed being away from my many friends in the 726th, but I had to do what I had to do.

During Christmas of 1951 I had a wonderful opportunity to be with my oldest brother, George A. Diggs, Jr., who was an infantryman assigned to the 24th Infantry Regiment, an all Black unit of the 25th Infantry Division. He had just come off of the front lines, and he thoroughly enjoyed a nice warm meal. and being able to sleep in a tent with some heat in it. My worst remembrance was talking to my first cousin, Vernon (Dukey) Williams who was escorting his brother, Donald Williams, body back to America. Donald died while serving in the Marine Corps in Korea. Because of the speed to return his brothers body back home, I only talked to Dukey by telephone. Actually, when Donald died, I had left Korea and was serving in the 24th Infantry Division in Japan.

After reenlisting, I had another scare come about, and that was desegregation of the military. It began in 1951 when the all African American units were broken up and we were assigned to various integrated units. In early 1952, I was transferred to the 1st Calvary Division. That was one of the worst units I could have been assigned to. When we encountered 1st Calvary tanks coming down the roads, we had to duck for cover, because they would shoot at us. Not a nice unit at all, but God was good to me because I had been in Korea too long, so I was transferred to the 24th Infantry Division, and off to Japan I went. Wonderful assignment. I remained in Japan until March of 1953 when I finally returned home. Here I was assigned to the 738th AA Gun Battalion in the Philadelphia area. During my twenty years military career I was assigned to Korea three times, Japan one time and Germany two time. During one tour in Germany, My family joined me in Stuttgart for four years, and my youngest son, Fredric, was born there.

My most prestigious assignment during my military career was serving as the Sergeant Major of the ROTC Detachment at Morgan State College from 1957 through 1964.

In 1954, I married Shirley Washington from Catonsville, Maryland. We have four sons: Louis S. Diggs, Jr., born in 1955; Blair Alexander Diggs, born in 1957; Terrance Carl Diggs, born in 1958, and Fredric Quentin Diggs, born in 1966.

In 1970 I retired from the United States Army and took a position as a teacher of Military Science in the District of Columbia Public School where I retired a second time as the Assistant to the Personnel Director for staffing in 1989. Since full retirement, I began an all new career of researching and writing books documenting the histories of many of the forty historic African American communities in Baltimore County, Maryland. I was most surprised to learn that many history books about Baltimore County failed to reflect the histories of thise African American communities. It was as if there were never any African Americans residing in the county. To date, I have published six books documenting the historis of many of these communities and have received another grant from Baltimore County to publish my seventh book, and I have amassed in excess of 8,000 photographs reflecting life in the historic African Americans in Baltimore County.

## Gets ROTC post at Morgan

*SUN 1957*

Sergeant First Class Louis S. Diggs of 315-B Winters Lane, has been assigned as Sergeant Major, ROTC Instructor Group, at Morgan State College, it was announced this week at U.S. Army Military District of Maryland headquarters at Fort Holabird.

Prior to his new assignment, Sergeant Diggs was Post Recruiting Sergeant of the Headquarters and Headquarters Garrison at Fort George G. Meade.

Sergeant Diggs, who attended Douglass High School in Baltimore, served in Korea from December 1950 to February 1952, entered the Army on June 20, 1950 and has successfully completed the Army GED test for high school.

* * *

AMONG HIS decorations are the Good Conduct Medal with two clasps; the National Defense Service Medal; the Army of Occupation Medal; the Korean Service Medal; the Army of Occupation Medal; the Korean Service Medal with five Bronze Stars, and the United Nations Service Medal.

He resides at the Winters Lane address with his wife, Shirley C. Diggs. His mother, Mrs. Agrada C. Diggs, lives at 4311 Dewey Avenue, in Baltimore.

1957 Baltimore Sun Newspaper article that reported SFC Louis S. Diggs as Sergeant Major of Morgan State College's ROTC Program. He served as Sergeant Major from 1957 until 1964, with another tour to Korea in between.

SGT Louis S. Diggs. After leaving the 726th Trans Truck Co in Korea in 1951, Louis was assigned to the 70th Trans Truck Bn in Korea until 1952 when personnel assigned to all African American units were transferred to integrated units. He was assigned to the 1st Calvary Division, but had been in Korea too long, and was immediately transferred to the 19th Infantry Regiment of the 24th Infantry Division and was sent to Japan for another tour of duty.

**Information provided by the son of an individual who was assigned to the 726th Transportation Truck Company in 1953 after the unit was integrated**

I received an e-mail from an individual named John Chambers who had responded to a notice that I had placed on one of the Military web sites as I was seeking to make contact with any members who had served with either Headquarters and Headquarters Company, 231st Transportation Truck Battalion, or the 726th Transportation Truck Company when both units were stationed in Korea during the Korean War.

Mr. Chambers indicated that his father, Private First Class William (Bill) Chambers from Philadelphia, Pennsylvania, joined the US Army in September 1951, and after completing his basic training at Fort Dix, New Jersey, he ended up being assigned to the 726th Transportation Truck Company in March 1953. He recalled his father saying that the 726th Transportation Truck Company was one of the only all Black company until everyone got to Korea. His father was White.

He does not have much information on his father, except that he served as a driver of a heavy truck with the 726th Transportation Truck Company in Korea and that he distinguished himself in that capacity and was awarded the Commendation Ribbon by the Commander of the 70thj Transportation Truck Battalion.

His father named his truck "The Irish Rose" or "Irish Rose"

He tried to learn more about his father, but his military records were lost in a fire.

Mr. Chambers was kind enough to share some of the photographs that his father shared with his family. These photographs are shown on this and the following page.

Part of a convoy of trucks, obviously from the 726th, hauling troops.
(Photo provided by John Chambers)

This is a photograph of William Chambers' truck which clearly highlights "726th" on the grill.
(Photo provided by John Chambers)

Motor Pool, 726th Trans Truck Co in Korea
(Photo provided by John Chambers)

Getting ready to make up a convoy in Korea
(Photo provided by John Chambers)

Probably the heavy duty truck driven by
PFC William (Bill) Chambers when he was
assigned to the 726th Transportation Truck
Company after the organization was no
longer an all African American Maryland
National Guard organization in Korea.
(Photo provided by John Chambers)

Lining up for a convoy, 726th
Trans Truck Co in Korea during
the Korean War
(Photo provided by John Chambers)

On of the wreckers assigned to the
726th Transportation Truck Company
when in served in the Korean War.
(Photo provided by John Chambers)

**Persons assigned to the 726th Transportation Truck Company in October 1950. Official copy of unit roster cannot be located. These names came from the unit photograph taken at Camp Edwards, Massachusetts in October 1950**

Captain Bedford T. Bentley
1st Lt. Joseph Bracy
1st Lt. William Harris
2nd Lt. Emerson Brown, Jr
M/Sgt Albert Brooks
M/Sgt Samuel Wilson
SFC L. Bradford
SFC J. Cutts
SFC Lloyd R. Scott, Sr.
SFC J. Lee
SFC L. Lee
SGT J. Duckett, Sr
SGT B. Young
SGT E. Horton
CPL E. Kearsey
CPL J. Queen
RCT J. Beckwith
RCT L. Travis
RCT C. Rice
SGT George Thomas
SGT Charles Gilmore
SGT S. Tillman
SGT Frank Palmer
SGT W. Frazier
RCT W. Corbin
RCT J. Easterling
CPL Paul Milburn
PVT H. Matthews
RCT J. Graham
PVT H. Corbin
PVT J. Harris
PFC H. Cofield
RCT R. Sparrows
RCT H. Graham
PVT J. Graves, Jr.
PVT J. Ray
PFC C. Palmer
RCT R. Craig
RCT A. Reid
SGT E. Williams
PFC A. Burman
CPL J. Cole
PVT W. Gray

PVT L. Williams
PFC Louis S. Diggs
CPL C. Jones
PFC Claude Urquhart, Jr.
CPL Percy Lambson
PVT J. Newby
RCT J. Janey
PFC E. Jones
PVT J. Jones
PVT Lester Bey
RCT N. Hawkes
RCT W. Simmons
RCT H. Coleman
CPL G. Wilson
RCT R. Corbin
PFC G. Braxton
CPL B. Parsons
RCT H. Savage
RCT E. Smith
PFC W. Miller
PFC Jeffery Carey
CPL J. Hopkins
RCT G. Plowden
PVT J. Douglass
PFC N. Nickings
PVT F. Williams
PVT Sidney Dorsey
PFC C. Bowman
PFC H. Jones
PFC H. Wilson
CPL J. Washington
RCT J. Hance
PFC H. Collins
PFC L. Robinson
RCT I. Powell
PVT V. White
PFC B. Shields
CPL R. Williamson
PVT O. McMilliam
PVT W. Brooks
PVT E. Haste
RCT H. Ramsey
CPL R. Jones

PFC W. Saunders
RCT W. Harris
PVT W. Smith
CPL W. Anderson
PFC V. Marshall
PVT R. Wallace
PVT L. Reaves
CPL J. Hill
PVT C. Hardy
PFC L. Morse
RCT C. Jones
PVT P. Wallace
RCT R. Parker
PFC L. Parker
CPL R. Denton
PFC P. Bright
RCT W. Littlejohn
PFC L. Parker
CPL R. Denton
PFC P. Bright
RCT W. Littlejohn
PVT J. Jayson
RCT L. Brown
RCT C. Clairborne

# Photographs provided by member of the 726th Transportation Truck Company

726th Transportation Truck Company of the 231st Transportation Truck Battalion, Maryland National Guard. They were ordered to active duty in August 1950 to support the Korean War. By December 31, 1950, the unit was in Korea, and was the first US National Guards unit to arrive in Korea to support the war.
(Photograph provided by ret SFC Louis S. Diggs)

The converted Liberty Ship, "Sergeant Sylvester Antolak," that took Headquarters and Headquarters Company, 231st Transportation Truck Battalion & the 726th Transportation Truck Company to Korea in 1950.
(Photograph provided by ret SFC Louis S. Diggs)

One of the platoons of the 726th Trans Trk Co in formation in Camp Edwards, Mass in 1950.
(Photo provided by ret 1SG Lloyd R. Scott, Sr.)

l to r: SGT Bradford, SFC Lloyd Scott, and 1SG Brooks, of the 726th Trans Trk Co in Korea in 1951
(Photo prov by ret 1SG Lloyd R Scott, Sr)

Newspaper photo showing men from Hq & Hq Co, 231st Trans Truck Bn, 147th and 726th Transportation Truck Companies being sent to Camp Edwards, Mass after 1950 activation. Name and date of paper is not known. Believed to be the Baltimore Afro-American. (Article provided by ret MSG Nathaniel Pope)

In the Motor Pool of the 726th Trans Truck Co in Camp Edwards, Mass. Unit is preparing to go to Korea. 1950 (Photo provided by ret 1SG Lloyd R. Scott, Sr)

In Camp Edwards, Mass, 1950, l to r: Jeffery Carey, Leon Haste, Richard Wallace, unknown, and Roy Burroughs, all members of 726th Trans Truck Co. (Photo provided by ret 1SG Lloyd R. Scott, Sr)

L to r: Leon Haste, Lt. Joseph Bracy and Roy Burroughs, all of the 726th Trans Truck Co in Camp Edwards, Mass. 1950 photograph (Photo provided by ret 1SG Lloyd R. Scott, Sr.)

Left is Lt. Joseph Bracy with Sgt Lloyd R. Scott, Sr, both of the 726th Trans Truck Co in Camp Edwards, Mass. 1950 photo. (Photo prov by ret 1SG Lloyd R Scott, Sr.)

L to r: Cpl Lambert, Lt Box Harris, Lt
Joe Bracy and Sgt Charles Gilmore, 726th
Trans Trk Co in Korea 1951.
(Photo provided by ret 1SG Lloyd R
Scott, Sr.)

Callisah Jones on left, 726th Trans Truck Co on
way home from Korea, probably 1952
(Photo provided by ret 1SG Lloyd R. Scott, Sr.)

726th Trans Truck Co area in Korea in 1951.
(Photo provided by ret 1SG Lloyd R. Scott,
Sr.)

Left is possibly Callisah Jones with Louis
Diggs is 726th Truck Company area in 1951.
(Photo provided by Ret 1SG Lloyd R. Scott, Sr)

L to r: Unk, 1SG Brooks and SFC L. Scott, Sr.
726th Trans Truck Co enroute home from
Korea, 1951 or 1951.
(Photo prov by ret 1SG Lloyd R. Scott, Sr.)

1st Sgt Albert Brooks, 726th Trans Truck
Co in Korea, 1951
(Photo prov by ret 1SG Lloyd R. Scott, Sr.)

1st Sgt Albert Brooks, 726th Trans Truck
Co in Korea, 1951
(Photo prov by ret 1SG Lloyd R. Scott, Sr.)

Left is Louis Diggs with believed to be SGT Sam Wilson in the 726th Truck Company area in Korea in 1951.
(Photo provided by ret SFC Louis S. Diggs)

Sgt James Newby, 726th Trans Truck Co in Korea in early 1950.
(Photo provided by ret 1SG Lloyd R. Scott, Sr.)

Louis S. Diggs, 726th Trans Truck Co in Korea. Photo taken in early 1951.
(Photo provided by ret SFC Louis S. Diggs)

Members of the 726th Trans Truck Co that were picking up and transporting members of the US Marines in Korea in 1951.
(Photo provided by Willie Horne)

Cpl Louis Diggs, Center, of the 726th Trans Truck Co in Korea, with several of the Korean soldiers in the company. (Photo provided by ret SFC Louis S. Diggs)

One of the trucks of the 726th Trans Truck Co in Korea moving Korean refugees. 1951 or 1952. (Photo provided by ret SFC Louis S. Diggs

The 726th Trans Truck Co area in Korea in 1951 or 1952. (Photo provided by ret SFC Louis S. Diggs)

Several of the guys from the 726th Trans Truck Co in Korea, 1951 or 1952. Names are not known. (Photo provided by ret SFC Louis S. Diggs)

In formation, 726th Truck Co in Korea in 1951 or 1951. (Photo provided by ret 1SG Lloyd R. Scott, Sr.)

# Interview - Ret SFC Elgia L. Butler, Jr. , a member of 147th Transportation Truck Company, when they were activated for the Korean War, and served in Europe.

Ret SFC Elgia Butler who served with the
147th Trans Truck Company in Germany

My name is Elgia Littleton Butler, Jr. I was born on April 13, 1923 in Daisy, Maryland which is located in Western Howard County. My father was Elgia Littleton Butler, and my mother was Mamie Snowden Butler. My father was from Montgomery County, and my mother was from Howard County. I was reared by my grandmother, Ida Snowden, in Howard County. I began elementary school in Daisy, Maryland, and in Baltimore, Maryland. I attended a school on Dolphin Street and Pennsylvania Avenue while I lived with a lady on Druid Hill Avenue named Mamie Gray. My next school was at Division Street near Lafayette Avenue, then I went to the African American high school in Cooksville. I had returned to Howard County by that time. I even attended school in the Reisterstown area near Glydon for a while when I lived with the Gaskins family. I left high school early because I had to go to work. While living in Daisy, there were no buses, and Mr. Wise, the principal of the school, lived on the Eastern Shore, in Princess Anne, but he came up here to teach school because he had his own car. He eventually married one of the Dorsey girls who was a cousin of mine, so the first year he drove us down to the school, and the way I had to pay him, I worked after school doing janitorial work. I walked from Daisy to Cooksville because I knew the back roads and back paths. I stopped school when I was sixteen or seventeen years of age, and went to work in the Washington, DC area as a laborer.

In 1942, I put my age up to nineteen years of age because the draft age was from nineteen years old to forty five years old, and I was only eighteen years old, which caused me to be drafted. The first place I went to in the military was at Fort George G. Meade, Maryland. My next assignment was at Fort Devens, Massachusetts; when we arrived at Fort Devens, it was cold, and Colonel Hyman Chase met the group, and the first thing I remember him saying as he was cussing, "Get these G.D. men inside before they freeze to death," and the officers in the 366th were wearing those big fur caps like the Russians would wear. I did my basic training with the 366th which at that time had a lot of officers from the old Black outfit down in Georgia, and they were sent to the 366th because the 366th and the 372nd were both Black outfits. These were both Infantry Regiments. We had three battalions in our Regiment. We had about 3,400 men. I stayed at Devens for almost a year, as we were doing all sorts of things there, like guard duty on the outlining sections of Massachusetts, and they finally started talking about sending us overseas, so they sent us to A.P. Hill, Virginia. The first weekend down there, the guys had to go to Fredericksburg to get the train, and at that time, they had one little coach for Black people. Heck, there was about 150 more soldiers there, and the guy was telling us that in this coach only Blacks could sit, and the next thing you knew, the guys picked him up, and he was crying, when we got to Washington, DC, there were Blacks all over the train. From then on, they gave us a separate train! The same thing happened in Richmond with buses. When the guys would go to Richmond, the guys had to sit in the back of the bus, so that time there were a lot of guys that would go to Richmond, and with the amount of men that would go at one time, maybe twenty or twenty-five men, how were all of them going to fit in the back of the bus, so there were quite a few incidents on the bus. It was not long before we got special buses. We didn't stay at A.P. Hill very long, from there we went to Atterbury, Indiana because it was too hard to deal with so many of us in the south. I was in the group when we went to draw the payroll in Richmond at the federal reserve. We had six jeeps with thirty caliber machine guns mounted on them, in a convoy, we drove down to Richmond, and the people looked at us, and couldn't get over seeing "Niggers" with all these weapons. From Indiana we went overseas, leaving from Hampton Roads, Virginia, and from there we took a troop transport that was on it's second maiden voyage, and we went to Casablanca, North Africa. It took us eight days to get there. On that ship was the 99th Pursuit Squadron of the Tuskegee Airmen. The whole ship was made up of all Black troop. There were 3,400 of us from the 366th Infantry Regiment alone.

We stayed in Casablanca for about six weeks or so, then we went to Oran, a small city, where we set up our bivouac area. God! we would burn up during the day and freeze during the nights. We remained there for several months, but we did not see any action at that time. We then went on a British ship from North Africa to Naples, Italy, and it's amazing, the difference is when you come across the Atlantic the water is so extremely rough, but the Mediterranean Sea was so calm; it was as smooth as silk, and when we got into Italy, they hadn't started the invasion yet. They had finished the battle for Angio, so what they did with us, they sent us as a unit to Southern Italy, around Forga, as we did guard duty for the fifteenth Air Force Group. We stayed there for eight or nine months, then, all of a sudden, the combat team, 370th Infantry Combat Team of the 92nd Infantry Division (Buffalo Division) came, and began fighting just above Rome, and they did so well, they sent them to Pizza and other areas. Most of the unit was Black, except for the White officers. During that time, the Afro Newspapers said the 366th Infantry was a fully qualified outfit to fight, and how come they were not in combat? So, they moved us from guarding the air base when the 92nd Infantry Division came in and went into a staging area below Veregio. Joseph Bracy was the first sergeant in D Company of the 370th Infantry. He ended up as an officer with the 726th Transportation Truck Company of the Maryland National Guard. Also with him was Thomas Briscoe and James Gilliam, all were part of the 92nd Infantry Division, and ended up in the Maryland National Guard.

I remained overseas for about twenty-six months. When I returned to America, they had a point system, which caused some of the guys to be sent to the South

Pacific when the war ended with Germany in 1945. The guys that did not have enough points to rotate back home, were sent to the Pacific, but I had enough points, so in 1945, in the middle of November, I was in the middle of the ocean on my way back home. I was discharged on December 2, 1945. I was a T-5, Technical Corporal, when I was discharged. After I was discharged, I went to work at Fort George G. Meade, Maryland. I worked there for a couple of years. I was called by the Post Office to come to work there. I remained in the Post Office for thirty-three years.

I recall when a group of us were working on the mid-night shift, and a fellow named Warren Mason said to us to come with him over to the Richmond Market Regiment Armory to go to the NCO Club over there, which we did. It was Roland Ball, Ernest Garner and myself, we all went over there and enjoyed ourselves, and one thing led to another, and Mason tried to talk us in joining the Guard. We were all World War II veterans. We all thought about it, and all three of us signed up. That was in July of 1950, just before they were activated for federal service. I didn't go to summer camp with them that year. I had no idea that the unit was being activated. I was assigned to the 147th Transportation Truck Company of the 231st Transportation Truck Battalion. Captain Cade was the commander of the company at that time. On August 19, 1950, or shortly thereafter, we were shipped out from the Richmond Market Armory to Camp Edwards, Massachusetts. We remained at Camp Edwards until the Spring of 1951 while the Headquarters and Headquarters Company, 231st Transportation Truck Battalion and the 726th Transportation Truck Company left for duty in Korea in November of 1950. We were sent to Camp Drum, way up in New York, to support a Southern troop from Tennessee, I think it was the 27th Infantry Division. We came back to Camp Edwards pretty close to summer when we got the orders to be transferred to Europe. By then, Captain James Gilliam was the Company Commander of the 147th Truck Company.

Life in Germany was not bad. By that time I was the Motor Sergeant of the company. There was no integration of the 147th at that time. The unit remained all Black. For a while, I had to leave the maintenance section of the company to take over one of the platoons in the company. There was a soldier named Sergeant Dennis who was selected for NCO school and left his platoon, so I was selected to replace him. While in Germany, the 147th Truck Company were supporting several Divisions, I believe the 28th Division was one. We would transport them to the bivouac areas in the field. We had to remain with them all during their training period. I remained in Germany for eleven months. I came back alone because my time was up. The unit did not return as a unit, rather the men came back when their time expired.

When I returned to America in July 1952, there was no place for any of us former National Guardsmen to go because some of the units were still in Korea, Germany or Virginia. When so many guys tried to get back in the National Guard, I recall many of the officers had rebelled from going back to the old segregated ways in the Guard. The Maryland National Guard was still a segregated organization, and the officers were determined they were not going back to the old ways. General Reckord, the Adjutant General of Maryland took Jesse Peaker, a former Warrant Officer in the 231st, and said to take a couple of the sergeants who would like to go back to the 231st Truck Battalion and make them lieutenants, and form an outfit, and that is what Jesse Peaker did. He took Scott, Coscoe Williams, Joe Mills, and another sergeant named Vaughn, and made them second lieutenants. They did form the outfit at the old Richmond Market Armory. The new outfit was still called the 231st Truck Battalion. I was one of the many guys that returned to the unit. Eventually, we moved from the Richmond Market Armory to Bentalou Street and Edmondson Avenue to an armory that was located right next to the fire station. I returned to the National Guard unit in 1953 as I recall that our first summer camp took place in Fort Eustis, Virginia. By then, one of my old friends, Warren Mason, had rejoined the unit as a Master Sergeant assigned to the 165th Truck Company. I think old Sergeant Nick was also assigned to the 165th. The second year under the new 231st we had our summer camp in AP Hill, Virginia and in Indiantown Gap Military Post, Pennsylvania.

When the 231st Truck Battalion finally integrated around 1955, the then Governor McKeldin had some thoughts of building a new armory for the 231st Truck Battalion, and the officers who were rebelling against going back to the segregated 231st Truck Battalion had returned to their old duties. Personally, I think the officers returned because the new unit headed by Captain Jesse Peaker was doing so well, but when they did return, it was agreed that the battalion would no longer be a segregated one. At that time, the building of the Cade Armory on Winchester Street was well underway. We were all very happy to see our own armory being built. It was very interesting to watch because the armory must have been built over a cemetery because you would often see bones emerge from the ground as the digging and construction went on. I stayed in the Maryland National Guard until around 1973 or 1974 when I retired as a Sergeant First Class with over twenty years of service.

Since retirement from the Guard, I joined the Veterans of the 231st Transportation Truck Battalion, with hopes of keeping the memories of our African American contributions alive. I recall that James Sommerville and Perry from the Eastern Shore, and Burton, all members of the old 147th Transportation Truck Company, actually started the Veterans of the 231st. As I can recall, I think that after they got several of the veterans interested in forming this group, they met at Tiffany's and got the unit started. That was around 1988 or 1989. The first president of the Veterans of the 231st was Claude Patterson, followed by myself. So far, we are the only presidents since I am still in office as president.

I was married previously to a lady from Cooksville named Ethel Miles, but I met another lady while working at Fort Meade named Amentha Hayes from Annapolis, and we eventually married. I met my current wife, Jackie, while I was residing on Walbrook Avenue. She was working at the Southern Hotel, and was truly a striking woman, and was always on the move. We just fell in love, and we eventually married. On January 24, 2003, we celebrated fifty years of marriage. We have no children.

I am very happy that a book on the history of the contributions of the African American men who formed the numerous Maryland National Guard units from 1879 through 1955, is being published because it is so needed for our current and future youngsters to know of the contributions we made from the Spanish American War through the Korean War.

# Interview - The late Cornelius Tillman, a member of 147th Transportation Truck Company, when they were activated for the Korean War, and served in Europe.

Cornelius Tillman

My name is Cornelius Tillman. I was born in Baltimore, Maryland on December 25, 1930. My mother was Lena Kess Tillman from Anne Arundel County, Maryland, and my father was Thomas Tillman who was from Columbia, South Carolina. My siblings were Nathaniel Tillman, Donald Tillman, and Maxine Tillman.

I was reared in Baltimore, Maryland, and first attended #122 Elementary School on Preston Street. I was one of those persons who did not take to education too well, so I was sent to a school on Biddle Street. The principal was Mr. White. This was sort of like a trade school on Biddle Street. I learned woodwork and other trades. When I turned eighteen, I did not graduate, rather I decided I had enough schooling. Thankfully, I learned a lot in woodwork. I can just about fix anything. I do a lot of work around my house. That was around 1937 when I stopped going to school.

A friend of mine came up from Virginia who was selling wood, coal, and ice, so I took a job with him hustling, arabing, until I was a bit over eighteen when my brother talked me into joining the National Guard. After I signed up for the draft, I went over to the Richmond Market Armory and joined the 231st Transportation Truck Battalion. They assigned me to the 147th Transportation Truck Company. I remained with the 147th throughout my entire career. That was around 1947. The Company Commander at that time was Captain Melvin Cade. Lt. Colonel Vernon F. Greene was the Battalion Commander. The first summer camp I spent with the unit was at Indiantown Gap in Pennsylvania. It was something really new to me because being a young man as I was, I didn't know anything about the military, but I was a bit on the rebellious side for a while, but they calmed me down. The next year for summer camp we went to Camp Pickett, Virginia. My duties all of the while was that of a truck driver. When I was working with John arabing, I used to drive his truck. My mother had signed for driving license for me when I turned sixteen, so driving was not new to me, and I always enjoyed driving.

During training at Richmond Market Armory, I recall there was a sergeant in our company who was very good at driving the 2 1/2 ton 6 X 6 trucks, so many of the guys new to the unit, including myself, learned how to drive those big trucks by him.

I wish I could recall his name, but that was a really long time ago. I was short, so I had to hold on to the steering wheel to pull myself up so I could change the gears, but I got real good with doing that. It wasn't long before I learned to change gears with my foot. I was never a hard learner.

In 1950, while still assigned to the 147th Transportation Truck Company, and we got word that the battalion was being activated for the Korean War. I was scared as the devil, not knowing what was in store for me getting ready to go to war. I wasn't married at the time, but I was very lucky because the battalion was in Virginia doing the summer of 1950, and we got the word while we were in summer camp. I missed going to Korea because I had been on a weekend pass and when I returned that Monday morning, the guys in my unit was loading up and being shipped to Camp Edwards in Massachusetts. At that time I had an old 1937 Chevrolet and had just driven back from Baltimore, and we who had cars were told that we could not go back to Baltimore to take our cars home, so they permitted some of us to follow the trucks that were enroute to Camp Edwards with our cars. When we finally arrived at Camp Edwards, we were indoctrinated for duty in Korea, and we knew in 1950 the Koreans were just chomping on the Americans, and all of us were scared as the devil.

I did get a leave to come home before being sent overseas, and I told my mother we were going overseas and that just worried her to no ends. I never will forget that she gave me a verse out of the bible that I wrote down, and instructed to keep it with me at all times, which I did. I don't recall exactly what happened when I returned to Camp Edwards, but luckily, my unit was sent to Camp Kilmer in New Jersey. It was in the winter of 1950 when the 726th Transportation Truck Company with the Headquarters and Headquarters Company, 231st Transportation Truck Battalion were sent to Seattle, Washington. We all knew where they were going. The guys were saying that when you were sent to Camp Kilmer in New Jersey, that was the departure point for duty in Europe. I said "Thank You, Jesus!" I really had no desire to go to Korea to fight in the war. I was only eighteen or nineteen years old at the time, and believe me, I was scared. I remember seeing the war movies from the Second World War, and I just knew the Korean War was much like it. I wanted nothing to do with it! My brother, Donald Tillman, got out of the unit when we got federalized. He was a family man with four children, so he was eligible to be released. He was assigned to the 726th Transportation Truck Company at the time.

The 147th was sent to Heilbron, Germany during the winter or early spring of 1951. Even though we drove our old trucks up to Camp Edwards, Massachusetts, we were issued new trucks that we had to learn to drive all over again, but we took them with us when we were deployed to Germany. Some of the guys were transferred to other units, but most stayed together. When we left for duty in Germany, the 147th was commanded by a Captain or Lieutenant Smith. I don't recall his first name. He didn't remain as the company commander for too long because Captain James Gilliam took command of the 147th not long after we arrived there. Some of the officers with us in Germany were Lt. Thomas Briscoe, and Lt. Wrenfro who was not a National Guardsman, and several other, but I do not recall their names. After we arrived in Germany there were several outside officers assigned to the company, some were

Regular Army, and some enlisted men who had been in Europe since World War II. All of the men in the 147th were African Americans. I recall that integration came to the military around 1951, but as long as I was assigned there, we never had any men other than African Americans. Most of the time the 147th Transportation Truck Company was in Germany, we were hauling troops. I recall many times when the battalion would call down and put our company on alert, and we'd fall out in formation, then we'd get our gear, and our trucks and head for the mountains. We'd remain out with the troops for a week, two weeks, or sometimes even a month. Some of our drivers would haul gasoline to the tankers near the border where the Russians were located, and it was then that they would be involved in running "The Red Ball Express." I remained in Germany for about seven months. In our Kasern, we had Germans hired to do a lot of the domestic work for us, like cooks, waiters, maids, barbers, shoe repairmen, etc. They made life very nice at that time. My enlistment was just about up, as a matter of fact, it had expired, but because of the Korean War, I was extended for an additional year. I returned to America in 1952, and was discharged in May, 1952. I did not return to the Maryland National Guard. I liked my independence, and the military just did not fit in the scheme of things. After getting out of the service, I went to work for Mace Produce Company as a chauffeur, then went to work for Fred Rual Produce Company on Hanover Street as a driver, then to the Maryland Cup Company, then when a friend of mine got a job at the Bethlehem Steel Company, and I found out they were paying a dollar more than I was earning; I was earning $2.25 an hour at the Maryland Cup Company, and Bethlehem Steel Company were paying $3.25 per hour, so I went to work for Bethlehem Steel, where I worked for about twenty-eight years before retiring. I was a painter at Bethlehem Steel. I retired from Bethlehem Steel Company in 1996.

I was single the entire time that I was in Germany. I didn't marry until the 1970s. I was going to marry early, but my girl friend found out that I was being shipped overseas, so she called the marriage off. I met my wife, Harriet Steward, in the 1960s while she was working for Maryland General Hospital. We were together for about ten years, then in the 1970s, we married. We did not have children together, but she had three children from a previous marriage.

I must say, however, that by being in the 231st Transportation Truck Battalion, and spending time in Europe, really made a man out of me. I was not a very active person before joining the Guard, but all that quickly changed. My best remembrances when I was a member of the 147th Transportation Truck Company were driving those big trucks. I was always a bit "gas happy," and those big 2 1/2 ton trucks just made me feel so good when driving them, especially in Europe where they have those little small towns with their narrow roads, we'd make our trucks backfire when riding though those little towns and would scare the devil out of the people that lived there. However, I do have nice remembrances of life in Germany, and especially the way the German people received us. After they got to know us, they accepted us very nicely. One of the saddest remembrances of my life in the National Guard was to see the hungry people in Germany dig through the wasted food we would take to the dump. It was enough to hurt you to your heart.

## Interview - Ret SSG Douglass Montague, a member of 147th Transportation Truck Company, when they were activated for the Korean War, and served in Europe.

Retired SSG Douglass Montague

My name is Douglass Montague. I was born on October 21, 1932 in Baltimore, Maryland. My parents were Lillie Montague Robinson and Robert Hines. I have no siblings.

I grew up at 565 Dolphin Street in Baltimore. I went to Samuel Taylor Elementary School, Booker T. Washington Junior High School and Douglass High School, graduating in 1948 or 1949. After I graduated, I took a job as a meat cutter in Lafayette Market, from there I joined the Maryland National Guard. I had a couple of friends who were members of the National Guard, Ronald Brooks, and one other friend whose name slips me now. They encouraged me to join, saying it was a fine organization and they had been in the unit for several years. That was in 1950, just about a month before the unit was activated to support the Korean War. I was assigned to the 147th Transportation Truck Company of the 231st Transportation Truck Battalion. I actually joined the unit after they had returned from summer camp, which I think was in early August or late July 1950. I joined the unit about two weeks before they were activated on August 1950. To be honest, I was very frightened about being activated so quickly after I joined. It was not what I was looking forward to. During the time when I joined, the draft was in effect, and I felt that by joining the Guard would help me avoid the draft, which at that time if you were in the National Guard, you were not subject to the draft, and I did not want to be drafted.

It ended up that I was eventually comfortable with the unit being activated, and being sent to Camp Edwards, Massachusetts. Of course, since I was relatively new to the unit and to the military, I had to go through all the basic training. We did physical education training, going through various training like on the rifle range. When we found out our unit was being transferred to Germany, I felt a little uncomfortable because I thought for sure that our unit was just being activated to stay in Camp Edwards, but when they told us we were being shipped to Germany, I simply was not prepared to go. Being a single man, when we did arrive in Germany, I really had myself a ball. I remember when we left to go to Germany, we sailed on the General Grettle, a troop ship that took us eleven days to get to Bremerhaven, Germany, and it had its problems going over the Atlantic Ocean. We slept down in this little hole in a hundred degree temperature. It was really frightening, but we made it. Not only was it rough going through the English Channel. I'll never forget that raggedy boat.

When the unit was activated, I was classified as a truck driver, but as time went on, I played the bugle for the 147th - I was the Bugle Boy. At that time, it was the bugle that told you what to do and when. I played the wake up call in the morning, I was playing the work call, the mail call, the end of the day call, I played them all. I also played the Officers' Call. I would go over to the Officers' area and play the Officers' Call to get them up in the morning. That was what I did until the bugle calls were eliminated, then they made me the Company Mail Clerk. Very rarely did I drive a truck, because I was more involved in handling the mail. I was traveling from Heilbron, Germany to Stuttgart twice daily to pick up the mail for the unit. It was a full time job. My mail room was located inside the orderly room.

The 147th spent their entire time in Germany transporting troops from one area to another. In fact, I was not with the company when they were doing a lot of transporting because of me being the mail clerk. I recall going to Stuttgart every morning, passing German Police on the autobahn, and that was kind of frightening because I was in this little jeep by myself, but I eventually got over it. It eventually became a pleasure trip for me. It was a thirty-five or forty mile trip, twice a day.

The social side of being overseas was tough because you didn't know the language of the people, and back then the people were very friendly, but they were frightened of us because we were American soldiers, but eventually, they got to the point where they began to admire us and we ended up meeting a lot of very nice people. I had no problem as time went on. I really began to become very pleased with being assigned in Germany. I met a German family that lived in downtown Heilbron that I became very friendly with. The last name of the family was Wolf, and there was a German girl that I admired named Myra La Wolf. Really fine people. Our unit sort of took care of them. They didn't have anything, they were hungry, very little clothing, so we did everything for them to help them out because they were truly beautiful people. They treated the members of the 147th like we were kings. People in general were so nice to us. It just made for a pleasant tour of duty.

Our unit was located in a Kasern, a new building that was set up like a hotel. Unfortunately, I do not recall the name of the Kasern. We had private rooms and all. It was like being in a hotel. The German people kept the place clean, and they worked practically for nothing. They kept our place spotless. I recall the Wolf family always kept all of my clothes cleaned for me. I tell you, when I took a shirt off in the evening, by the next morning that shirt was cleaned and pressed. Some of the members of the unit had to pull the normal GI duties, like KP, etc., but I was the fortunate one, being the mail clerk and the company bugler, I never had to bother with those kinds of assignments. I remember when some of my friends would not get mail and they would get pretty sad, and I used to joke with them and I'd say "I tell you what, you don't have to worry about mail tomorrow because you will get some mail - I will be the one writing to you, so you won't be left out on mail call."

Some of the members in the 147th that I recall were Captain Melvin Cade who was the commanding officer, Lt. Thomas Briscoe, Lt. Bryant, Warrant Officer Gunther, First Sergeant Scott, and Sergeant Gardner are the only ones I can recall right now. While in Germany I was not able to do a lot of travel. My job really kept me tied down. I was the only mail clerk and the only bugler, so I was not free to just take off on leave. It was work, work, work every day. It was fine with me because I didn't have to worry about KP duty, guard duty, or any kind of duty. Heck! I basically stayed in Class A uniform every day. I ended up as a Private First Class and I wasn't too unhappy about that because I was so satisfied with my job. I was afraid that a promotion would take me out of the nice soft job I had. I was in Germany for one year. I never will forget when I returned home on the Maurice Rose, which was a real luxury liner. It took us eleven days to get to Germany and it only took us seven days to return to the states.

After being discharged, I eventually returned to the National Guard for a couple of months, then I got out and stayed out for about four years, then I returned back to the Guard. I then joined another National Guard unit that was stationed in Parkville, a medical unit, the 136th Combat Support Hospital unit where I served as the retention NCO and the unit recruiter, plus I was a community worker for the unit. By then, the 231st Transportation Truck Battalion, an all Black unit, no longer existed. Everything in the Maryland National Guard was integrated. I remained in the National Guard for twenty-six years. I retired from the Guard, but I do not remember exactly when I retired, but it was probably in the 1980s. I retired as a Staff Sergeant.

I retired from the Veterans Administration Hospital on Loch Raven Boulevard. I started at Fort Howard where I worked until they opened the one on Loch Raven Boulevard where I transferred to. When I reached age fifty-five, I retired from the VA after twenty-eight years. I was one of the emergency technicians, which a lot of that training came from being assigned to the Combat Support Hospital.

I married Dorothy Yates Montague, and we only remained married for two years. We had no children. My second marriage was to Alice Brown Montague. We have no children together, but I am the father of Ellestine Montague, Douglass Montague, Jr., Maureen Montague, Daryl Montague and Angela Montague.

My best remembrances of being assigned to the 147th is that I never had any bad experiences while assigned there. I always got along with everyone. I think the thing that I enjoyed the most was being the mail clerk for the unit. That was truly a pleasure. The next best remembrance was during the time I was playing the bugle. That was really a lot of fun. I think I enjoyed the best when I would stand on the hill in the Officers' area waking them up in the mornings. I also enjoyed playing taps at night, and believe it or not, I played taps from my bathroom window every night. I learned the skill of playing the bugle when I was in the Pride of the Baltimore Elks as a child where I played in parades, etc.

I joined the Veterans of the 231st Transportation Truck Battalion after I met Orville Perry when I was at the Cactus Willie's Restaurant one Sunday when he mentioned to me about the Veterans organization. He said there was a lot of my friends in the group, and he encouraged me to join, and that was in 2003.

**Interview - Robert Dunton, Jr., a member of 147th Transportation Truck Company, when they were activated for the Korean War, and served in Europe.**

Robert Dunton, Jr.

My name is Robert Dunton, Jr. I was born on March 14, 1931 at 1404 Bond Court in Baltimore, Maryland. My parents were Mildred Mills Dunton and my father was Robert Dunton. My father was born in Baltimore, Maryland, and my mother was born in Richmond, Virginia. There were nine in our family who were Dorothy Dunton, Leroy Dunton, Earl Dunton, Clarence Dunton, Raymond Dunton, Charles Dunton and then there were two twin sisters who are Ernestine and Geraldine Dunton.

I went to elementary school at #130 on Carrolton Avenue and Saratoga Street, then I went to Trade School #176 on Franklin Street. I didn't go any further in school. I dropped out of school when I was fourteen years old. I had to put my age up to go to work. When I was fifteen years old I got my drivers license and began to drive trucks. I've drove trucks until I joined the National Guard in 1947. My initial assignment was in the 147th Transportation Truck Company. I was in the boy scouts at the time, and after I left the boy scouts someone mentioned to me about the National Guard and said where it was located, so I went over there, which was the Richmond Market Armory, and that was when I enlisted. I think Colonel Brady was the battalion commander. In 1947 there were only two truck companies under the 231st Transportation Truck Battalion which were the 147th and 726th Transportation Truck Companies. Everyone in the battalion were African American. I think it was about a year later when the 165th Transportation Truck Company came into being. When I first joined, I was a truck driver, then I became a truck driver trainer. I became a Private First Class. That was all I ever did was carry the MOS of a truck driver.

In 1950 our unit was activated from Richmond Market Armory. By then I was a T-5. The battalion was split. The 147th went to Germany, 726th went to Korea, the 165th stayed in the United States assigned to Fort Eustis, Virginia, and the Headquarters and Headquarters Company of the 231st went to Korea. I was then assigned to the 147th, and was sent to Germany with the unit. When we got to Germany, I did not stay with the 147th, they needed truck drivers in another company, and they drafted me from my company for assignment to the 447th Transportation Truck Company which was also in Germany. Our unit was over strength, so some of us had to be transferred to companies that were under strength. I stayed in the 447th for eighteen months. The 447th Transportation Truck Company had a different make up from the 147th that I left from. All of the enlisted men in the unit were African Americans, but all of the officers were White Americans. After I left the 147th I lost all contact with the guys in the unit until I returned to the United States. While in Germany, all we did was haul troops around, cargo, ammunition, food, machinery, etc, that we had to use strip maps to locate our delivery areas, and how to get there. I returned to the United States in 1952. I tried to get back in the National Guard, but the way things were during those years, we didn't appreciate what was really going on, so we just decided not to return to the unit. I never returned to the Guard. During that time the unit was located in an armory on Edmondson Avenue.

I did not associate myself with the unit until I joined the Veterans of the 231st Transportation Truck Battalion in 1997. When I got out of the army, I returned to driving a truck until a few years later I went to the shipyard on the Key Highway to work. Jobs were not too hard to find. From the shipyard I went to the B&O Railroad and worked for them for a while. I went to numerous jobs. Discrimination was pretty rampant during those years, and it was hard for me to cope with it. Eventually I retired from the Pierce Ica where records are stored. I was a motor operator down there, which was in Jessup, and I retired from there.

I really did enjoy my years with the National Guard. I came up through the cub scouts, the boy scouts, then eventually I went on to the National Guard and finally to the regular army. It really was a nice life. Some of my best remembrances of things that happened to me in the National Guard were going away to summer camp every year. We went to Virginia, Pennsylvania, and Maryland, just different camps. It was some great two weeks. We all had our ups and downs, but everyone got along, which made life pretty good. I enjoyed driving the captain around picking out different routes for motor marches. I was picked because I was one of the better drivers.

There was lots of discrimination when we would go to Virginia for our summer camps, especially at Camp Pickett because we were not allowed to go to certain places in the area, we were not allowed to eat with the White troops. The White troops always ate first, and we had to wait until they finished before we ate. stuff like that we had to put up with. Then we had problems in Annapolis because if you wanted to go into town you had to sit in the back of the bus, and if you wanted to go to a movie, you had to go upstairs where they made the African Americans sit, all that stuff was going on during those times. When we went to Germany we had social problems in the Stuttgart area, but none of that existed in the Korenwestheim area where I was station, that is after I left the 147th. Actually, there was no segregation in dealing with the German population, racial problems came when dealing with other Americans, White American troops. We were never put on equal basis like the White troops. Of course, we were quite accustomed to segregation because right here in Maryland we faced it all the time, including being a military unit. Right here in the Richmond Market Armory was segregated. Though we were in the shadows of the hugh 5th Regiment Armory, we could not soldier there, but we did leave quite a few of our trucks in their motor pool area. Heck, they even made us march over to the

5th Regiment Armory to get our trucks, stuff like that. In the Richmond Market Armory, it was not a full armory, the 231st was headquartered over top of a actual market, located on the corner of Linden Avenue and Howard Street. Believe me, the Richmond Market Armory was designed strictly for a young persons. You had to go up these real steep steps to get into the Armory, an older person would have a devil of a time going up and down those old wooden steps. There was nothing to hold on to either, no bannister. There was a hugh drill floor that we drilled on.

I actually enjoyed my years with the National Guard, it was a very exciting, close knit organization, then, too, being in the Guard added a little more money in my pocket, plus having to go to summer encampment every two weeks a year added much more money in my pocket. I was pleased.

I never will forget when our unit was federalized and we marched down Howard Street. We were marching to the train to go to Camp Edwards, Massachusetts. I recall many pictures were taken, but no one can find any of those pictures today.

I met my wife when I got older. Her name was Rachel Thomas, and we married in 1977. We had no children. Unfortunately, my wife died in 2001.

My uncle was a member of the First Separate Company. His name was Albert Dunton, a brother of my father. He didn't stay with the First Separate Company very long, as a matter of fact, when the draft was going on for World War II, he volunteered for the Navy. You know, the 231st Transportation Truck Company was the old First Separate Company, who, like the 231st, had all African American men, officers and all.

## Interview - Raymond C. Jackson, a member of 147th Transportation Truck Company, when they were activated for the Korean War, and served in Europe.

Raymond C. Jackson

My name is Raymond Clarence Jackson. I was born on November 14, 1932 in Baltimore, Maryland. My parents were Anna Mae Bolden Jackson and Meredith Jackson. My oldest brother was Meredith Jackson, then Robert Jackson, and Glenwood Jackson. That was all of my siblings.

I attended School #132, Old Coppin up on Mount Street, then to #112 on Laurence Street, then to #456, a junior high school on Lafayette and Druid Hill Avenues, then I went to Carver Vocational School on Carrollton and Lafayette Avenues. I did not graduate, rather I quit in the eleventh grade. After that I just went to work, and joined the Maryland National Guard. That was in 1948.

My oldest brother was going into the service, and I was thinking of joining the service myself, but I was not quite eighteen years old, I remember my cousin, Corky Harden, was a member of the National Guard and he used to tell me how nice it was, and when they were scheduled to march, and I'd go and watch them, and I then found out that I could join the National Guard even though I was not yet eighteen years old, which is what I did, and was then assigned to the 147th Transportation Truck Company. That first year I went to Camp Pickett in Virginia to attend summer camp with the National Guard. It really was nice, and by me being a new soldier, I had to learn the basics of soldering. I was a good experience. It was to my advantage that I could drive a little bit, so it was not too much to learn to drive those big trucks. I recall on Sundays when we were back at our home base, which was the old Richmond Market Armory, on Sundays we would be driven to the motor pool area which was located in Pikesville, to learn to drive the trucks. We would bring the big trucks back down to the Richmond Market Armory where instructors would teach us how to drive them.

When I first joined the National Guard, I really don't remember the name of the company commander of the 147th Transportation Truck Company, but I know not long after I joined Captain Melvin Cade was the company commander. In 1950 when the entire battalion came back from summer camp, we were all shocked to find out that our battalion had been ordered to active duty to support the Korean War, but we were not told where exactly we were going. Most of us were just young kids, excited to learn of this, but not sure what the future would bring. I recall that I was very excited.  At that time I was just a private first class, but I was an acting corporal, a squad leader, and shortly after returning to the Richmond Market Armory, I was made a full corporal.  My platoon sergeant, who recommended me for the promotion was Sergeant John Teaker.

When our unit went to Camp Edwards, Massachusetts, life was really pretty nice.  We did a lot of basic training and training on those big 2 1/2 ton 6 X 6 trucks.  The new guys who came to the outfit to bring the unit up to its authorized strength had to go through the basic training, while the older guys concentrated on enhancing our driving skills since we had our basic training by attending numerous summer encampments.  We were teaching the new guys how to go through infiltration courses, driving, firing their weapons, etc.  We remained at Camp Edwards for almost a year.  The 147th was transferred to Pine Camp, New York, while the Headquarters and Headquarters Company, 231st Transportation Truck Battalion and the 726th Transportation Truck Company were shipped out to Korea.  We had quite an experience at Pine Camp, which was later changed to Camp Drum, because we did quite a few things up there that a lot of the other units did not do, such as in our mess hall we had curtains at the windows, the floors were well sanded, we ate off of real dishes instead of mess kits, then we had people from the Army who would come in and inspect us, and we always looked really good.  It was like being at home.

Later in 1951 the 147th got orders to be deployed to Europe, and we all were quite happy about it because it was a lot better than going to Korea.  Actually, while we were stationed in Camp Edwards, Massachusetts, the battalion headquarters and the 726th Transportation Truck Company had already received orders for them to be deployed to Korea, so we figured we did not have to worry about going to war.  Many of the older men from the 147th were transferred to the 726th in order to bring their company up to authorized strength.  I was on the list to go to Korea with the 726th, but instead they put me on temporary duty and pulled my name off the list, so I stayed with the 147th.

Life in Germany was really not all that good.  You see, we were the only Black soldiers in the area, and the German people hadn't seen too many Black American soldiers, and they were a little shy of us, they didn't know how to take us for one thing, but eventually, they came around and found out that we were people just like them, only different colors.  I did not stay with the 147th long after they arrived overseas.  I was sent on TDY to Kornwestheim, Germany above Stuttgart to serve on the Army boxing team.  When I stopped boxing, I became a trainer or boxing instructor.  I went all over Germany serving in that capacity.  During my boxing career, I was a light-middle weight boxer, and though I did not become a champion, I think I won something like eight out of ten matches, somewhere around there.  I thoroughly enjoyed that duty.  I had enlisted in the Regular Army after the National Guard unit was activated in 1950.  I stayed in the military for six years.  I stayed in Germany from 1951 until 1954.  I recall that the guys from the 147th began to rotate back to the United States in 1952.  I remained on the boxing team until all of the men from the 147th were returned home, and was then transferred me to the 32nd Transportation Truck Company in Viagan, not too far from Stuttgart, Germany.  In 1954, I was rotated back to the United States. I was then assigned to the Army Transportation Center in Fort Eustis, Virginia where I served as an instructor of driving until my discharge date in 1955. I had strong feelings about staying in the Army, but I got out. Often I wished I had remained in the Army and made it a career. When I got out of the Army I really had no desire to return to my old National Guard unit, however, Captain Jesse Peaker tried to get me to enlist back in the 147th when they had been relocated to an armory on Edmondson Avenue. I declined and never got involved with the National Guard again. I joined the Veterans of the 231st Transportation Truck Battalion after seeing Albert Sommerville who talked about starting the veteran's group. I remember when Sommerville and some of the old guys from the Eastern Shore met at Sommerville's home and started the group. We started off with only the guys from the old 147th Transportation Truck Company. We really talked first about having some type of reunion, but ended up as a veteran's unit. I am a charter member. Tilman, George Burton, Orville Perry, Sommerville and I were the charter members. Our first reunion we had was at Tiffany's on Lombard Street, which was when a lot of the fellows that we hadn't seen came in. The majority of the guys were still from the old 147th. We didn't have a name at the time, and after we began to reach out for guys from all of the units, we called ourselves the Veterans of the 231st Transportation Truck Battalion. We were able to pull in guys from Headquarters and Headquarters Company, 231st Transportation Truck Battalion and from the 165th and 726th Transportation Truck Companies.

I retired from the Teamster's Union in 1985. I am divorced. My wife was Margaret Jackson, but I do not recall her maiden name. We had no children. That is I had no children with Margaret as it was my second marriage. I was first married to Geraldine Turner Jackson, and we had no children together. I have a son that was born in Germany who now lives in Omaha, Nebraska. His name is Raymond Seawell. His mother is a German. Then I have a daughter named Raynette Noel. I also have a son named Tyrone Jackson.

My best remembrance of the National Guard was marching with the unit and having the opportunity to go to different places. I always did like to see soldier's marching, plus it was something that I always wanted to do. I thoroughly enjoyed my years with the 147th Transportation Truck Company.

# Interview - Kedrick W. Powell, a member of 147th Transportation Truck Company, when they were activated for the Korean War, and served in Europe.

**Kedrick W. Powell**

My name is Kedrick William Powell. I was born on September 3, 1930 in Baltimore, Maryland. My parents were Alfred John Powell, who was a member of the First Separate Company here in the Maryland National Guard, but I cannot find the literature to back that up, but he was the one who was instrumental in me joining the guards in the first place, and my mother was Edith R. Clary Scott, she remarried. Both of my parents were born in Maryland. I have no siblings.

I attended Samuel Corage Taylor Elementary School #122, Booker T. Washington Junior High School #130, and Frederick Douglass High School #450, and I also attended Baltimore City Community College. I did not graduate from high school with my class, rather I came out in 1949. graduated in 1964 with an evening certificate.

In 1948, while I was still in high school, I joined the Maryland National Guard. My father talked me into joining the guard because of the experience I would gain and the possibility of going overseas. He was telling me about his experiences when he served in the First Separate Company when he went to France during the First World War. He has the French award that was given to his unit for their participation in the war over there, and he was very enthusiastic about that, and me being a futuristic type of person, always visualizing things, I could just picture myself being in the same type of situation that he was in, and that sort of encouraged me to join the guard. It wasn't the fact that I loved the army so much, to be honest, they were talking about a draft during that time, and I said to myself that maybe if I joined the guard I would not have to go into the service, but after joining, the whole situation changed. I was assigned to the 147th Transportation Truck Company. Back in 1948, some of my friends in the 147th were Vernon (Boo) Carter, Charles Watkins, Hugh Williams, Herman Smith, Wellington Dickey, and several others whose names slip me at the moment. When I joined the guard, the 231st Transportation Truck Battalion, with its companies, were located in the old Richmond Market Armory. It was a real experience after joining the 147th because I never had regimentation during my life, being disciplined the way they were, but being militarily regimented, it was quite an experience. We learned the difference in coordination, drills, discipline, camaraderie among the troops, and just being away from home because at the times we were drilling we would go on two weeks maneuvers during the summer. My first maneuver was in Indiantown Gap, Pennsylvania, and that was the first time I had ever been away from home for a period of time, camping out in the woods and barracks, eating in mess halls, just experiencing the regime of the army. Everything being uniformed, clothing had to be in uniform, and just everything being so regimented, and I really did enjoy it. Plus, I learned to drive. We used to go every Sunday to Pikesville to the armory where we kept our vehicles, and I learned to drive the big 2 1/2 ton trucks. I recall I stripped many gears learning to drive. It was fun and quite an experience. I was a truck driver with an MOS of 0345. In 1949 we camped at Camp Pickett, Virginia.

On July 1, 1950 I got married to Evelyn King. We have three children who are Veronica Deborah Powell, Lydia Rozell Powell, and William Kedrick Powell. We had just returned from summer camp at Camp Pickett, Virginia, and it was quite a shock to discover that the entire battalion had been activated to support the war in Korea. I didn't quite know how to handle the situation right away, me just being married. I would have been all right if I was by myself. I was only nineteen years old then, and I did not know how long I would be gone. We crowded our honeymoon into just a couple of weeks and we really wanted to get a place for ourselves, but we decided to live with my mother on Eutaw Street which was right around the corner from the Richmond Market Armory. I had to leave the Richmond Market Armory long before the entire unit left. I was chosen as one of fifty people from the unit to be in the advanced party, and I was promoted to private first class. We left Baltimore before the end of August in 1950 on a cargo train with all of our equipment to take to Camp Edwards, Massachusetts. We had to get our area on the post ready for the remaining troops . I had to resolve myself to the fact that I am now in the army. In Camp Edwards I met some of the old soldiers in the train station where we were coming out of, and they were using terms that I was totally unfamiliar with, and in a week or so I began to get comfortable with this new situation as we were accepted as comrades coming into the service. They knew that we were National Guardsmen but they still accepted us. It did not take me long to realize that there is a distinct difference between a draftee, a National Guardsman and a Regular Army person.

While assigned to Camp Edwards, we had to get the barracks prepared for the incoming troops, get the trucks moved from the train area to the company motor pools, transferring material and equipment, and just getting the area ready. My platoon leader was Lieutenant Thomas Briscoe. Captain Melvin Cade was our company commander. Before we were deployed overseas, the entire battalion was transferred to Camp Drum, in upstate New York to serve as the post transportation. Our base was still at Camp Edwards; we were just placed at Camp Drum in Watertown, on TDY. I had never seen so much snow in my life. The snow was so deep 'til you couldn't see your barracks. We stayed up there for the entire winter of 1950 and part of the summer in 1951. As I can remember, we were there during the summer to support the local National Guard during their summer encampment. I recall how much we all enjoyed going to Syracuse, New York where all of the entertainment was. At that time Lt. Gardner was the company commander of the 147th. He was quite the disciplinarian. A phrase that he used was "Soldier, who did it to you?" and you'd say "Sir, I did it to myself," and his response was always "I have nothing else to say." He forced us to believe in self-evaluation. He made us make choices in life, right or wrong. I carried that discipline throughout my life. We lost one of our comrades up there who drowned, a fellow by the name of Brooks. There was a swimming pond in the area that we used for recreation purposes, that had a platform in the middle of it that you used for diving. I recall that one evening we all swam out to the platform for fun, and when it was time to return to the beach, we all dove in and swam for the shore. When we got there, we noticed that one of the guys was missing, and that's when we found out that he had drowned.

Around the fall of 1951, the 147th was notified that it was being transferred to Germany. We took a troop ship to Bremerhaven, Germany and was stationed in Heilbron, Germany. While there we were attached to a battalion that was station in another part of Germany. History had a way of opening my eyes. All of my life, I pictured life in Germany after the war being very terrible, and then I saw much of the devastation with my own eyes. In 1951, Germany was still in a shambles. You could see the rebuilding taking place, but not fully. The buildings were full of bullet holes, there were plenty of bombed out buildings from the air raids, and the inhabitants were still begging for food. Hunger was rampant. Many Germans hung around our barracks begging for food. In my childhood, we knew about poverty and segregation, but at the same time, we saw hunger, but never like I saw it here. It was terrible to see women and children sleeping in bombed out buildings.

While the 147th was in Germany the units went to many places. Germany is about the size of a country that you could sit inside the state of New Jersey. France, blended with Germany, could probably be set inside Texas. Italy was another small country that you could probably sit inside the state of Texas or California. All of these countries combined in Europe would probably take up just a small part of the United States. It is important that we realize the fact that once people start saying that they are French or German, or Italian, or English, as opposed to saying he is African. Africa is a continent; Germany, France, Italy, etc., are countries in a continent. People don't address them as being European, they distinguish the difference, like if someone is saying they are going to visit Europe, they don't say that, they individualize it by saying I'm going to France, or I'm going to Italy, or Germany, but when they say they are going to visit Africa, they say I'm going to visit Africa, not Nairobi, not Kenya, not Uganda, etc., so you have a point of geography there.

We were instructed to transfer troops from that particular area in Germany, along with another brother company, 747th Transportation Truck Company, to the various bivouac areas. We had bivouac area in Ohlm, New Ohlm, Stuttgart, Karlsruh, Munich, Mannheim, etc., and we traveled to all of those places from Heilbron. We did not carry our old truck overseas, all of the old GMC's were discarded completely. We were issued new trucks called Reo's. We were fascinated with them because they had this long water spout that came out of the side of the truck, which made them amphibious. They could go through very deep water, as long as that spout was out of the water. They were very easy to drive, so a lot of retraining was not necessary. They were larger with closed in cabs, which was a good factor compared to the old GMC's. During my period of time in Germany, the army was still segregated, this was 1951. There were all Black units and all White units. We hauled White troops all over Germany, but we were never housed with them. Captain Gilliam was our company commander at that time, and by that time I had made corporal. Only so many promotions could be made at any given time, and I assumed that I was on the list for promotion to sergeant, but it never materialized. There was an NCO Academy in Munich, Germany. I was one of three chosen from the 147th to be represented at the NCO Academy. It was Sergeant First Class Arthur Jones and Sergeant First Class James Sommerville and myself. It was a six weeks TDY at the academy. It was known then as "The West Point of Europe." Getting there was when we were integrated, Whites and Blacks were housed in the same barracks. I recall that rank was never mentioned there, we were all in the same training. We were all awarded certificates of training, completion of training in Administration, leadership and tactics, that we carried on our discharge. We were also given rights to wear the green leadership tabs on our uniforms. Because the quota system was still in place, I was not able to receive a promotion to sergeant, and it was time for me to be rotated. I remained in Germany for about nine months. I think those that were married would be the first to be returned home, and being that I was married with a child, I was one of the first to leave Germany. Quite a few of the guys in the 147th decided to remain in the military and reenlisted and were subsequently transferred to units throughout Germany. While I was in Germany with the 147th, our unit was never integrated.

When I returned to the states, I did have a desire to remain with the National Guard on one hand, and did not on the other hand. Of course in 1952, the 231st Transportation Truck Battalion was not under state control. They were still in Korea, and to my knowledge the unit did not return to state control until around 1955, but by that time, my mind was not on rejoining the National Guard. I stayed out, but still remember the good times with the unit that I was assigned to. Until 1999 when Malcar Waters approached me about joining the club that had just started of veterans of the 231st. I liked the idea of seeing some of the old guys, but at that time there were only eight or ten guys in the group, all from the 147th. That was the first time I had any relationships with the old guys since leaving Germany. The president of the Veterans of the 231st when I first joined was Colonel Claude Patterson. Sergeant Elgia Butler was the Vice President, Sergeant Cornish was the Treasurer, Vernon Carter was the Secretary Treasurer, and Sergeant Riley was the Secretary. I have been with the Veterans Club ever since. In 2000, Sergeant Elgia Butler became the President and I became the Vice President, and the other officers remained the same.

During my work years, I was with the Veterans Administration where I worked since 1952 when I got out of the service. I retired from there in 1985. They were located at Fort Howard, Maryland, and my duties at the end of my employment was transferable between Fort Howard and Loch Raven. I retired as a Physical Therapist Assistant, so we transferred from clinic to clinic.

Before closing this interview, I would like to encourage people to consider service in the military, be it in the regular army or the national guard, or the Army, Navy, Marines, Air Force, or whatever branch. It is an experience for a young person. Our crime rate is getting out of hand, and discipline is sorely needed, there is no respect for a lot of things, and consequently this will enable the youth of today, male and female, to get an overall picture of the discipline and education afforded those in the armed services.

**Interview - Vernon J. Carter, Jr. , a member of 147th Transportation Truck Company, when they were activated for the Korean War, and served in Europe.**

Vernon J. Carter, Jr., as a Lieutenant Colonel
in the Maryland State Guard

My name is Vernon Joseph Carter, Jr. I was born on May 4, 1931 in Baltimore, Maryland. My parents were Viola Boone Carter Green and Vernon Joseph Carter, Sr. I had a sister who passed when she was only two years of age. Her name was Doris. I had a step-brother who passed when he was nineteen years old named Archie Boone.

I attended School #112 on Calhoun and Laurence Streets, then at School #119 on Gilmore and Mosher Streets. After elementary school, I went to School #130A on Saratoga Street and Carlton Avenue. You went to the seventh grade there, then you were transferred to Booker T. Washington Junior High School where you went to the eighth grade. After Booker T. Washington Junior High School, I went to Frederick Douglass High School where I played football, baskerball, did some boxing, and played the saxophone. I did not graduate because the National Guard unit that I was assigned to was activated in 1950, so I decided to go into the service because I was an acting sergeant in my unit. I figured I would have to go into the service in another six months or so, and I might as well go now since I had some stripes on my arm.

I joined the National Guard in January of 1948 and was assigned to the 147th Transportation Truck Company. The company commander at that time was Captain Melvin M. Cade. That was part of the all-Black 231st Transportation Truck Battalion that was commanded by Lieutenant Colonel Vernon F. Greene. I learned to soldier in the Richmond Market Armory. The whole reason that I enlisted in the National Guard was that you played basketball and all kinds of sports, and I liked sports, but of course, I found out after I enlisted that the only time you played basketball or any sports was after drills, and the drills were from eight to ten, and sometimes ten thirty, so then we played basketball and didn't get home until close to midnight. The Richmond Market Armory was called the Fourth Regiment Armory at one time, but I guess it was changed to Richmond Market Armory because we were housed there, right over top of the Richmond Market. We drilled on the large drill floor on the second level of the armory. There was a balcony that ran around the entire armory, and you could look down on the armory.

When we were activated, I never will forget many officers came to the armory, stood on the balcony and called each of our names as we stepped forward. I learned to become a truck driver, but before that we learned the basics of soldiering like marching, etc., then came the training on the trucks, and we had to go out to Pikesville Armory to do that on Sundays where we learned to drive the jeeps and the trucks. My first summer camp was at Camp Ritchie, Maryland. I think I went there twice.

In 1950 when I found out that the 231st Transportation Truck Battalion was being activated for the Korean War, we were in Camp Pickett, Virginia, undergoing our annual summer encampment, and when we returned back to Baltimore around July 6, 1950, and everyone knew that the Korean War had broken out and the word was out that we should not unpack our bags. It wasn't a confusing situation, but everybody was wondering what was going to happen, and we were always called to the armory about things that we could do, and instructing us on the possible moves that we may make, how many more people do we need to bring our companies up to full strength, and recruiting plans, and things like that. I was still a single person then and still enrolled in high school. When August 19, 1950 rolled around, sure enough we were activated, and the word was out that we were going to be transferred to Fort Sill, Oklahoma. There were lots of rumors around that we would be going to different military posts, so we remained right there in Richmond Market Armory for at least a month. During that time we soldiered continuously at the 5th Regiment Armory. Every morning we would march up to the 5th Regiment Armory where we soldiered. The soldiers that resided in Baltimore or in the Baltimore area were permitted to return home after training, but had to report back to the armory in the morning for the daily training. The guys that lived on the Eastern Shore or Annapolis or wherever far away from Baltimore had to be quartered at the Richmond Market Armory. Finally, the word came that the battalion was being shipped to Camp Edwards, Massachusetts, so we dodged the bullet as for going to Fort Sill, Oklahoma.

On the morning we were to leave Baltimore, we all met at the Richmond Market Armory where we were in mass formation, and Sergeant Lloyd R. Scott, Sr. from the 726th Transportation Truck Company marched the entire battalion which then consisted of Headquarters and Headquarters Company of the 231st Transportation Truck Battalion including the 147th and 726th Transportation Truck Companies to the train station. He marched us up Linden Avenue or Howard Street over the Howard Street Bridge to North Avenue, then turned left heading up North Avenue over the North Avenue Bridge to the freight train station that was at the end of the bridge. There we boarded the train. The word was out that we would be at Pennsylvania Station, but that was not true, so a lot of our family members missed our departure from Baltimore. The train did stop at Pennsylvania Station, and I never will forget because my family was there and my girlfriend, Tena, and quite a few other people, including reporters from the Afro American Newspapers. I was so happy because I had a chance to say good by to my family.

Life at Camp Edwards for me, at the beginning, was nice. I still thought of military life as a step up from boy scouts. However, we were quite busy training, but what happened, our unit had an excess of some two hundred men in our company that came from New York and New Jersey, and even New Mexico, and the rest of them came from the South. The army didn't know what to do with them, so they assigned them to our company. They were all African Americans. We never had any White troops in our outfit until we were sent overseas. At that time I was an acting section sergeant. We trained all those men that came from different states. We gave them their basic training, and their truck training. We took them through the infiltration course, first aid, gas chamber, and training with the weapon. It was a bit difficult putting a lot of these guys through training because many were twenty-five and twenty-six year olds, and I think they resented the younger guys being superior to them. They were drafted just before they reached the non-draft age, but we all got along pretty good. We were sent to Camp Pine, New York to support other National Guard troops. I think it was during their summer encampment.

We eventually got orders to ship out to Germany. The other two units had already been shipped out to Korea - Headquarters and Headquarters Company of the 231st Transportation Truck Battalion and the 726th Transportation Truck Company, so our unit had to leave New York very quickly to return to our home base which was Camp Edwards, Massachusetts. We left by truck convoy. We drove all night long to get back to home base. I recall that it was so cold that one of the guys in the unit, I believe his name was Carter, had to be hospitalized from exposure to the cold. There was another guy in the company that was also taken in by the cold weather. He, too, was sent to the hospital, and we never heard from him. I don't recall his name.

When we got to Germany, we were all quite happy about it because we were not sent to Korea. We had a right nice time on the ship because they had WACs on the ship, and we made a stop in Bordeau, France, and also in England. I recall I took pictures of the White Cliffs of Dover at that time. We had no trucks when we finally arrived at our destination in Germany, so we spent a lot of time just soldiering and doing a lot of class work. We were located in Heilbron Germany. About three months later we received our brand new trucks, which were REO's. Of course no one knew how to drive them right away, so we had to take truck driving training all over again. Once we learned how to drive them, we were the fastest things in Germany, and we had some young boys that had gas on their chests. When we hit the autobahn, they were gone. I remember one day when the MPs had to come down to our Kasern and govern our trucks down. We were always in the woods, but sometime we would be in the garrison. In the woods we would support the infantry units. During those times it was right nice being a non commissioned officer because when all the trucks were on the road, we had nothing to do around the base, so we all just took life pretty easy until they returned. Before arriving in Germany our company commander was Lieutenant Owens. Captain Burgess ended up being our company commander. He made out pretty good with the unit and caused the unit to receive a commendation. When he left we got Lieutenant Hardner as commander. He was pretty hard. He made Captain when he was with our unit. Eventually, Captain Gilliam took over the company. Captain Gilliam came to us from our other unit, the 165th Transportation Truck Company which had been activated and stationed in Norfolk, Virginia.

Life Germany was very nice. It was almost like being on a college campus. We had hard wood floors, we had a barber and a tailor. We even had German women come in to do the cooking for us, and the Germans did the KP duty. There were six men to a room. There was still our Mess Sergeant who was in charge of the kitchen. I stayed in Germany for eleven months. When I returned to the States, the 231st Transportation Truck Battalion had not yet returned from Korea. I did like the army life and I had applied to reenlist in the regular army, but it took so long for the paper work to be completed, and all of the guys in the unit was returning home, so I just forgot reenlisting and went on home. I was discharged at Fort Meade, Maryland on July 12, 1952. Right after that, I began college education at Morgan State College.

We were not able to return to our National Guard home. A military police unit had taken over the Richmond Market Armory. I recall some of the officers in the unit were fighting to get our space back. I recall Captain James Gilliam and Lieutenant Thomas Briscoe were two of them. Word came from Washington that the unit had to be put back together in the National Guard, then the Adjutant General of Maryland picked Captain Peaker to head up the organization. Captain Peaker has been a master sergeant. We eventually got an armory on Edmondson Avenue at Bentalou Street. I think it was called the Edmondson Avenue Armory. It was then that I returned to the Guard, but we were having meetings before that started. We were meeting at homes to put the plan together for the new unit. I recall they gave some sort of aptitude test, and four or five people were selected to become officers. I recall there was Lt. Coscoe A. Williams, Lt. Carroll, Lt. Scott, and one other. I went back to the 147th. I think I stayed with them for six more years, until around 1959, almost 1960. They brought in a Lt. Leaf from Ohio, and we not see eye to eye, so I was discharged.

The state was thinking of having a unit to take care of things militarily in case the National Guard was pulled away, or activated, so the state guard was re-formed. I joined them in 1981 or 1982. I started out as a second lieutenant because I had a college degree from Morgan State College. I rose to the rank of lieutenant colonel in the state guard. I ended up as the G1 (Adjutant) in the battalion. I am now on the Minuteman status. I only have to make muster once a year.

My wife is Ruth Butler Carter. I am the father of Vera Jean Carter, and she has a daughter who has four children. I have two step children named Nathaniel E. Green and Darryl S. Green. Nathaniel has a son, and one grandson. My wife and I have a daughter together, who is Vernishia Yolanda Carter. I got married on August 29, 1964. I brought a new car in 1962, a house in 1963, and got married in 1964.

I am one of the charter members of the Veterans of the 231st Transportation Truck Battalion. I started off as the Financial Secretary. I am a 33 degree Mason, a life member and past District Commander of the VFW, Past President of the Baltimore Cossock, Inc., Sergeant at Arms in the Morgan State University Varsity "M" Club, and a life member in the Morgan State University Alumni Association.

**Persons assigned to the 147th Transportation Truck Company in October 1950. Official copy of unit roster cannot be located. These names came from the unit photograph taken at Camp Edwards, Massachusetts in October 1950**

CAPT Melvin Cade
!ST LT L. Bryant
WOJG T. Owens
1SG A. Golden
SFC J. Teagle
SFC C. Branch
SGT C. Martin
SGT W. Carter
SGT C. Dennis
SGT V. Carter
SFC A. Jones
SGT C. Owens
SFC T. Scott
CPL C. Watkins
SGT O. Harley
CPL J. Watts
SGT R. Watkins
CPL K. Powell
SGT J. Sommerville
CPL J. Paylor
CPL O. Brown
PFC W. Tutman
CPL Ernest Soden, Jr.
CPL J. Young
PVT D. Monteque
RCT Orville Perry
RCT I. Brown
RCT A. Sivel
RCT R. Austin
RCT R, Gillard
RCT D. Jones
RCT E. Ragins
RCT G. Hawley
CPL W. Akrey
CPL H. Williams
CPL C. Gibson
RCT Robert Dunton, Jr.
CPL W. Dickey
CPL F. Carter
CPL Raymond Jackson
RCT A. Myers
RCT J. Colbert

RCT W. Hilliard
RCT K. Jackson
RCT J. Rainey
RCT S. Chase
RCT G. Freeland
RCT J. Crenshaw
RCT W. Cornish
RCT J. Jayson
RCT L. Brown
RCT C. Clairborne
RCT M. Weaver
RCT G. Thomas
RCT P. Holden
RCT S. Stanley
RCT N. Ellis
PFC E. Livers
PFC Cornelius Tillman
RCT E. Garner
RCT C. Broadard
RCT A. Preston
RCT S. Christian
RCT J. Lapaley
RCT L. Thompson
RCT J. Williams
RCT O. Watson
RCT J. Keaton
RCT W. Richardson
RCT T. Harris
RCT R. Ball
RCT C. Morton
RCT G. Walter
RCT A. Summerville
PFC W. Johnson
RCT L. Phillips
PVT T. Whitehead
RCT C. Jones
RCT F. Keyes
PVT G. Davis
PVT L. Hall
PFC R. Paxton
RCT K. Dickerson
RCT W. Jordan

RCT J. Smith
RCT J. McDonald
RCT E. Kirton
RCT L. Smith
RCT A. Wainwright
PFC H. Johnson
PFC D. Evans
RCT D. Vaden
RCT T. Harmon
RCT J. Rogers
RCT G. Burton
RCT J. Watson
RCT I. Thompson
PVT W. McLugan
RCT J. Whittington
RCT J. Jones
RCT J. Massey
PFC J. Williams
RCT G. Cutts
RCT C, Williams
RCT R. Brooks
RCT C. Mobray
RCT R. Boyd
RCT L. King
RCT R. James
RCT M. Rhodes
RCT W. Armstead
RCT R. Farmer
RCT W. Green
RCT N. Johnson
RCT A. Ashby
RCT S. Watkins
RCT L. Gaines
RCT R. Watkins
RCT R. Sharpe
RCT R. Bennett
RCT B. Williams
PVT Ernest Diggs
RCT J. Thomas
PFC R. Alexander
RCT R. Kennard
PFC A. Williams

RCT P. Deshields
PVT W. Brooks, Jr.
RCT  Spotswood
RCT G. Mosley
RCT C. Gray
RCT J. Mayfield
RCT H. Davis
RCT R. Watkins
RCT W. Watkins
PFC C. Carter
PFC Malcar Waters
RCT H. James
RCT E. Butler
RCT M. Collins
RCT W. Walker
RCT J. Reid
RCT L. Carter
PVT L. Garvin
RCT W. Wormley
RCT V. Grimes
RCT J. Cannon
RCT T. Fitzgerald
RCT W. Pearson
RCT C. Hall
RCT R. Enoch
RCT C. Smith
RCT B. Lane
RCT T. Lofton
RCT N. Collins
RCT H. Brooks, Jr.
RCT J. Fuller

# Photographs provided by member of the 147th Transportation Truck Company

Company photograph of the 147th Transportation Truck Company right after they were activated and stationed at Camp Edwards, Massachusetts, 1950.

One of the platoons of the 147th Transportation Truck Company when it was in Germany. 1st Lt. Thomas Briscoe, front row, center, was the Platoon Leader. 1951 photograph

Another one of the platoons of the 147th Transportation Truck Company when it was in Germany. 1951 photograph.

One of the drivers in the 147th Transportation Truck Company when it was stationed in Camp Edwards, Massachusetts.
(Photo provided by an Unknown member of 147th)

Compny area of the 147th Transportation Truck Company in Germany. 1951 photo
(Photo provided by Malcar Waters)

In the motor pool of the 147th Transportation Truck Company when it was in Germany. R to L: Ernest Soden, Otis Williams, Raymond Jackson, and Walter Akery. Others are not known.
(Photo provided by Malcar Waters)

Members of the 147th Transportation Truck Company when it was in Germany. L to r: Hugh Williams, unknown, and Roy Kinnard.
(Photo provided by Malcar Waters)

In the motor pool of the 147th Transportation
Truck Battalion when it was in Germany.
Names of soldiers are not known.
(Photo provided by Malcar Waters)

PFC Ernest Diggs, a member of the 147th
Transportation Truck Company when it
was in Germany.
(Photo provided by Malcar Waters)

Some of the members of the 147th Trans Trk
Co when it was in Germany.  L to r:  Unk,
Albert Summerville, Unk, Unk, Ernest Livers,
Unk,. Unk,. Unk, George Thomas, Raymond
Wallace and Roy Kinnard.
(Photo provided by Malcar Waters)

Some of the members of the 147th Trans
Trk Co in Germany.  Names are not known.
(Photo provided by Malcar Waters)

Standing is CPL Ernest Soden, and an unknown member in the
truck.  They are members of the 147th Trans Truck Co in Germany.
(Photo provided by Malcar Waters)

CPL Raymond Jackson, a member of the
147th Trans Truck Co in Germany 1950s.
(Photo provided by Raymond Jackson)

PFC Robert Dunton, Jr., a member of the
147th Trans Truck Co in Germany in 1950s.
(Photo provided by Robert Dunton, Jr.)

Special Orders from the Battalion that
the 147th Trans Trk Co served under
in Germany in the 1950s.

Some of the members of the 147th Trans Trk Co
when it was in Germany in the 1950s. Names are
not known.
(Photo provided by Malcar Waters)

Some of the members of the 147th Trans Trk Co in Germany
working at the Railroad Station in the 1950s.
Photo provided by Malcar Waters

**Interview - Ret Lt Colonel Lorenzo (Bus) Felder, a member of 165th Transportation Truck Company, when they were activated for the Korean War, and served in Fort Eustis, Virginia and in Europe.**

Lorenzo (Bus) Felder when he served in the US Marine Corps during World War II. He was a member of the Montford Point Marines.

My name is Lorenzo (Bus) Felder. I was born on August 15, 1922 in St. Petersburg, Florida. My parents were Nola B. Chatmon and Reces Felder. My mother was born in St. Petersburg, Florida, and my father was born in Okela, Florida. I had one sister, LaReesa Felder. My sister was first married to a Mr. Rice, then re-married to Mr. Rogers, then re-married to a Mr. Matthews, and then re-married to Pinky Clark. She had no children. I have a step brother named William Chatmon, and a step sister name Tyler Chatmon. Both are from Baltimore, Maryland. I came to Baltimore, Maryland when I was fifteen years of age, and resided at 1537 Lanvale Street. I attended the old Booker T. Washington Junior High School, PS #130 on McCullough Street, and when I graduated from there in 1938, I attended and graduated from the old Douglass High School, PS #450. I graduated in 1942. I attended Morgan State College in 1942, but cut my education short because I enlisted in the Marine Corps in 1942. I served in World War II until the war ended, when I returned to Morgan State College, and graduated in 1949. I majored in Political Science and History. I did not take ROTC at Morgan because back then this program was not offered there. After graduating from Morgan, I attended Law School at the University of Maryland.

I met my wife, Norma Lewis, while we were both attending the old Booker T. Washington Junior High School in Baltimore, Maryland. We married on October 5, 1950, while I was on a four-day leave from Fort Eustis, Virginia. We first took up residence with her mother on North Avenue. During my assignment at Fort Eustis, we were pretty close to Baltimore, and quite naturally, everyone wanted the week ends off so they could return home. I was not an exception. The only way such weekend leaves were distributed equitably was that one weekend one half of the company was off, and the other weekend, the other half of the company was off. We had a bus that would bring us to Baltimore, at the YMCA on Druid Hill Avenue, and on Sunday evenings, we would meet back at the YMCA for a bus ride back to the base. During this time, the 165th was transferred from Fort Eustis to Fort Story which is also in Virginia. It was very nice to be home every other weekend. My wife and I never had children.

I first became associated with the Maryland National Guard in 1948 when I got a commission as a second lieutenant in the 231st Transportation Truck Battalion that was located at the old Richmond Market Armory in Baltimore. I was assigned to the 165th Transportation Truck Company. In those days the Transportation Battalions belonged to the US Army, not to the Divisions, but attached to the divisions. We were attached to the 29th Division of the Maryland National Guard. The one thing that sticks to our mind was during the summer encampments when we would participate in the Division Reviews. By being a service unit, we were always at the end of the massed formation, and I will never forget, when we would come up to the reviewing stand, the band would stop playing the marching music, and when we marched in front of the reviewing stand, the band would play "I Wish I Was In Dixie" or "Old Black Joe," rather than play the traditional military marching music. You would hear mumbling throughout the battalion as we marched, and you could imagine what they were saying. Though every African American in our battalion was highly ticked off with the way we were treated as we marched, of the young men who had warm blood flowing through their veins, but it never reflected on the professionalism in our marching. We always marched past the reviewing stand like the true professional American soldiers that we were. This happened to our unit many times during our years of summer encampment wherever the 29th Division went, which was usually Camp A.P. Hill in Virginia or Indiantown Gap Military Reservation in Pennsylvania. In many ways, we as an all-Black unit were segregated against, both at home in Baltimore and away during summer encampments, one has to realize that since we were never treated equally throughout the many facets of life, missed being equally treated. It is like soldiering in the 5th Regiment Armory. We never, ever soldiered in there, so how could we miss it! Or for that matter, any of the ways we were treated in everyday life - when one asked if you were bothered about drinking in a segregated water fountain, or eating in a segregated restaurant, how could you respond negatively if you never drank out of a White only water fountain, or never ate in an integrated restaurant. Segregation was just a way of life back then, and we as a race, made the best of it. It was this mind-set that the old all-Black Maryland National Guard units, from the days of the Monumental City Guards in the 1800s, through the Spanish-American War, World War I, World War II, and in the Korean War soldiered so well, and fought so bravely.

I do recall how the old Richmond Market Armory was used by the 231st and its companies, which really was not too bad. We had to use the upper level of the armory as the lower level was used as a market. The armory was an extremely sturdy, strongly built building, without air condition, though it was heated. We had a very large drill floor. Our trucks were maintained in the Pikesville Armory on Reisterstown just a block or so up from Slade Avenue in Pikesville. It is a hugh facility with a big rectangular yard with many garages. We practiced driving and maintaining our assigned trucks there.

In 1950 when we were called to active duty, we were not ready for such call up. I will never forget, it was a Sunday afternoon when the 5th Regiment sent out a call for muster at the 5th Regiment. We were all rounded up, and we met at the

Armory that we were called up for active duty as a battalion. The powers to be recognized that the 165th Transportation Truck Company was the youngest company, and we needed both more men and more training. Actually, the truck companies all needed more men to fill many of the vacancies, so recruiting teams were developed, with an officer heading each team. We spread out throughout Maryland, mostly on the Eastern Shore to recruit. It was years later that I recognized that it was much more to recruiting than to sign men up for the units. None of us really had the knowledge and skills as recruiters, and as a result, many of the young men who came up to Baltimore for their physical examinations and other qualifications, such as academics, did not qualify and had to be returned home. I recall on my team was Lt. William A. (Box) Harris, and several of the enlisted men, whose names I cannot recall. We went to Easton, Cambridge, and other units on the Eastern Shore. We had trucks that we took with us to transport the newly recruited men up to Baltimore. Just about every lieutenant assigned to the battalion was assigned to a recruiting team. These teams only lasted for a couple of weeks. We were moving so fast on these recruiting team that we simply overlooked some of the required qualifications. The Maryland National Guard headquarters had to look upon our battalion as one of their units because they wanted Maryland to look upon our Maryland National Guard unit as being filled with Maryland men.

As to the 165th Transportation Truck Company, we had high ranking non-commissioned officers who had never been to boot (basic) training, so they pulled us out of the battalion structure, and sent us to Fort Eustis as a separate company, while the Headquarters and Headquarters Company, 231st Transportation Truck Battalion, the 147th Transportation Truck Company and the 726th Transportation Truck Company, were sent to Camp Edwards in Falmouth, Massachusetts. The commander of the 165th at that time was Captain James Gilliam, but he was pulled from the company, and I, as a second lieutenant, had to command the unit while we were enroute to our active duty post in Virginia. At that time there were only three other second lieutenants assigned to the 165th. As soon as were arrived at Fort Eustis, we were assigned a Regular Army captain as the company commander and a Regular Army Warrant Officer as the maintenance officer. The flavor of the unit changed drastically because these Regular Army officers did not care to be assigned to a National Guard unit, and there was a camaraderie among the troops of the 165th because we all had close relationships with each other since we were all from the same home town; even when we spoke to each other, it was more or less on friendly terms. Of course salutes were always the order of the day, but, for example, one day I recall reporting into the orderly room when the First Sergeant greeted me as "Good Morning, Lieutie!" and the company commander overheard it. He called me into his office and wanted to know what the hell did the first sergeant mean by addressing me as "Lieutie?" Shortly after that situation, I was transferred out of the company, and was sent to a transportation unit in Germany. The entire company was broken up like that. Many of the men from the unit were cut from the company and transferred to other units. I stayed with the 165th at Fort Eustis for about six months before I was transferred. In Germany, I was assigned to the 37th Highway Transport Division in Mannheim, Germany. This division was made up of several trucking battalions. I was assigned to an all-Black outfit that was integrated after 1951. You know, I never will forget when integration took place in the part of Germany that I was stationed. The all-Black units were stationed in Mannheim, and the all-White units were stationed in Heidelberg. When it was time for integration, and it was decided how many Blacks would be transferred to Heidelberg, and how many Whites would be transferred to Mannheim, they crossed each other on the autobahn as the transfers took place. I remained in Germany for about three years.

There is another point I need to bring out about the 231st Transportation Truck Battalion when we were activated in 1950, that is the social life we all had to experience. When we were on active duty, we as Black officers were not permitted to use the Officers Clubs. I recall at Fort Eustis, the Army gave us a little wooden shack for use by the Black Officers to socialize in, and they would send over a couple bottles of liquor on the weekends, and there were many other Black officers stationed at Fort Eustis in 1950.

By the time I returned from Germany, the Battalion from Korea had also returned. The 231st Transportation Truck Battalion officers, when we were all regrouped in Baltimore, demanded to the National Guard Headquarters, that we not go back to our old segregated ways. At that time, Jesse Peaker, who was a Captain at the time, was the commander. Colonel Vernon Greene, as well as the other ranking officers from the Battalion had returned, but they would have nothing to do with the unit going back to its old segregated ways. Their demand for an integrated unit was so great that the news media picked up on it, and the National Guard relented and gave in to the demands. After that, all of the old officers assumed their positions within the battalion and companies. The regrouping of the battalion did not happen at the old Richmond Market Armory, rather they were stationed in an old, very large garage on Edmondson Avenue at Bentalou Street. There was a fire station next door. The garage was renamed at the Edmondson Armory.

I was then assigned to Battalion Headquarters as the S3 Officer where I was eventually promoted to Lieutenant Colonel. After Colonel Green served as the battalion commander in the Edmondson Avenue Armory, and took the unit to the newly built Westchester Street Armory, he retired from the Guard, and it was then that Major Melvin Cade took over the unit.

Lorenzo (Bus) Felder when he was stationed at Camp Lejune, Montford Point, NC in WWI. 1944
(Photo provided by Ret LTC Lorenzo (Bus) Felder)

110

On the right is Lt. Lorenzo (Bus) Felder, working with other officers of the 231st Trans Truck Bn when they were activated to support the Korean War. Left to right: 2nd Lt. Thomas Briscoe, 2nd Lt. William A (Box) Harris, 2nd Lt. George M. Brooks, and 2nd Lt. George E. Dawson. Photo came from an article in the Baltimore Afro American Newspaper in 1950 that was provided by ret LTC Lorenzo (Bus) Felder.

Botom of photograph on the right is 1st Lt. Lorenzo (Bus) Felder in 1951 when he was assigned to the 37th Highway Division's 70th Heavy Truck Company in Nance, France. (Photo provided by ret LTC Lorenzo (Bus) Felder

Interview - William S. Adams, a member of 165th Transportation Truck Company, when they were activated for the Korean War, and served in Fort Eustis, Virginia.

William S. (Bill) Adams

My name is William S. Adams. I was born on May 23, 1933 in the historic African American community of Lutherville, Maryland

My parents were the late William and Mary Adams. My siblings are: Thomas C. Adams Sr., Mary Adams Cooper (Deceased), Sarah Peggy Adams (Deceased), Grace Adams Matthews (Deceased), Allen L. Adams, Celeste Kathleen Adams, and Maynard Adams.

I attended Lutherville Colored School #24, and Carver High School in Towson, Maryland. I received a Bachelor of Science Degree in Commerce and Social Studies from LaSalle University in 1981, and a Masters Degree in Martial Science from Rockwell Euro technical University in 1994.

My wife is Carolyn Greenfield Adams. My children are William S. Adams, Jr., Reginald Adams, Montressa Evans Clarke (Deceased), Bryan Adams, Ali Hassan and Yolanda Robinson.

I joined the all African American Maryland National Guard's 231st Transportation Truck Battalion, 165th Transportation Truck Company on June 19, 1950; approximately two weeks before the beginning of the Korean War. I was extremely proud of the fact that 165th had been selected to serve on active duty. It was especially gratifying to learn that the 231st Trucking Battalion was the "only" Battalion under the 29th Division to be placed on active duty. It affected me greatly; I was finally going to get a change to fulfill my patriotic duty.

I was disappointed that the 165th Trucking Company was separated from the rest of the Battalion and sent to Fort Eustis, Virginia where we received basic training. After basic training for a short while we were stationed at Fort Story, Virginia. In January 1951, approximately twenty individuals of the company were transferred to various units and sent to Korea. Their replacements were new draftees from Fort Jackson, South Carolina and other units. Our company was nicknamed "The 165th Double Clutchers"

I returned to Baltimore Maryland on June 19, 1952. After separating from the military in 1952, I was carried in reserve status until being discharged 1956. I worked for General Motors, Fisher Body Chevrolet Division on Broening Highway as an assembler, and Baltimore Transit Company as a bus operator.

For approximately thirty years, I worked for the Baltimore City Public Schools, retiring from the position of Director of School Bus Operations in 1997.

William (Bill) Adams from Lutherville, Maryland, when he was assigned to the 165th Transportation Truck Company in 1950.

One of the platoons of the 165th Transportation Truck Company. Not sure when the photograph was taken.
(Photo provided by ret LTC Lorenzo (Bus) Felder

Following has been extracted from an article from the Baltimore Afro-American Newspaper that appeared about the 165th Transportation Truck Company on Sept 9, 1950. The article contain the names of persons assigned to the unit:

## 165 Truck Co. Departs
## Kin See Loved Ones
## Off in Murky Dawn

Silhouetted against a dusty grey September morn, 18 vehicles bearing men of the 165th Transportation Truck Company rolled from the outfit's home headquarters at the Richmond Market Armory, Thursday, headed for Fort Eustis, VA.

A ghostly silence covered the armory as the wheels of the last six-by-six, carrying members of the last component of the 231st Truck Battalion, rolled down Linden Ave.

Brides, fiancées, sweethearts and mothers still waved as the police-escorted convoy merged and faded into the breaking dawn.

### Bleak Weather, Bleak Hearts

It was a brisk morning and these women who were sending sons, husbands, brothers and cousins to answer the call to duty were wearing toppers. Many had the collar turned up.

At 5:30 a.m. as the men lined up in the makeshift drill hall at the armory, for the final roll call before leaving, these women huddled until the last man was accounted for and the soldiers grabbed their equipment and headed for the trucks.

There were no tears. Wives kissed their husbands tenderly-mothers touched sons, ladened with barracks bags- sisters reminded, "Don't forget to write"- an overnight bride repeatedly kissed a corporal, her husband of a few hours.

### Captain Gilliam Busy Man

Walking fast, jogging, and often running throughout the predawn embarkation, which began at 3:30 a.m. was the company's 29-year-old commander Capt. James Gilliam of 1813 Madison Ave.

Captain Gilliam was serious and there were tight lines about the corner of his mouth, as he directed the proceedings, which included:

A caterer-served breakfast at 4 a.m. the roll call, dispatching of correspondence, loading of trucks and inspection of the armory building by a major from the

Maryland Military District.

## Moved Like Clockwork

At 6: 20 a.m., riding the lead jeep, Captain Gilliam made a broad sweeping movement with his arm- the truck motors roared and the 165th was off. There was a broad smile on Gilliam's face.

Bidding 1st Lt Roland Rogers good by were his wife, Mrs. Josephine Rogers, mother, Mrs. Etta Rogers, sisters, Mrs. Reva Spencer and Mrs. Rosalind Lee and brother-in-law, Carol Lee.

Saying farewell to Cpl Walter Reddick of 339 Hillen Rd. were his bride of a few hours, sister, Mrs. Marion Clinton, and mother Mrs. Laura Reddick.

Two cousins from Lutherville 1st.C Sgt James W. Brown and **Pfc. William Adams**, said so long to Mrs. Gertrude Pitts, Mrs. Mary Cooper, Mrs. Elizabeth Adams, Mrs. Mary Adams and Mrs. Doris Brown, the sergeant's wife.

## Wife Leaves Tots at Home

While her two sons, ages 5 and 10, respectively slept at home at 1817 Smallwood St. Mrs. Clinton Nichols came down and said goodbye for the family to the father Sergeant Nichols.

Mrs. Marie Farrell, Mrs. Monica Cross and Mrs. Marie Murry wished luck to Pvt. Columbus H. Ferrell, his mother, grandfather and sister respectively.

Mrs. Muriel Weeks of 1530 McCullough St whispered parting words to her brother Pvt. Eldridge DunnMoodie.

## Korea Not To Be Forgotten

The most confused party was a few weeks old puppy - "Korea" Clutched tightly in his master's arms, he seemed to wonder just where he was going.

The other three companies of the 231st are now training at Camp Edwards, Mass. They are the 147th 726th and Headquarters companies which left town last Wednesday.

The 231st was the only Maryland National Guard unit called to active duty since the war in Korea. On Sept. 3, the 165th was federalized and became a part of the U. S. Army.

Company Roster listed the members of the 165th:

1. Capt.  James  Gilliam
2. 1st Lt.  Roland Rogers
3. 2nd Lt.  Lorenzo Felder
4. 2nd. Lt.  Nathaniel Young B
5. W/O.  Nison Miles C
6. Sgt.  Warren Mason
7. Sgt.  Clinton Nichols Sr.
8. Sgt.  James Brown M
9. Sgt.  James Brown W
10. Sgt.  William Wax
11. Sgt.  Joseph Weeden
12. Sgt.  Joseph Mills H
13. Sgt.  William Cotton H
14. Sgt.  Vincent Kellum T
15. Sgt.  Roosevelt Davis
16. Sgt.  Elmer  Rice C
17. Sgt.  Robert Vaughn A.
18. Sgt.  James Waters
19. Sgt.  Warren Tilley L
20. Sgt.  Clarence Ingram H
21. Cpl.  William Barnes
22. Cpl.  Leonard Bruce
23. Cpl.  Robert Jones L
24. Cpl.  Ernest Gaines
25. Cpl.  Calvin  McFadden
26. Cpl.  Edward Parago
27. Cpl.  Maxie Roe P
28. Cpl.  Franklin Simms T
29. Cpl.  Edward Watties N
30. Cpl.  James Wiggins I
31. Pfc.  William Adams S.
32. Pfc.  Benjamin Bonds Jr.
33. Pfc.  Thomas Carey I
34. Pfc.  Rudolph Hayes D
35. Pfc.  Henry Jackson
36. Pfc.  Charles Murrill L
37. Pfc.  Henry  Pleasant
38. Pfc.  Thomas Ross F
39. Pfc.  Robert Stevenson L
40. Pfc.  Nathaniel Butler
41. Pfc.  William Debnam
42. Pfc.  Irvin Fraction
43. Pfc.  Howard Graham Jr.
44. Pfc.  Walter Reddick

| | | |
|---|---|---|
| 45.Pfc. | Wilson Thornton J | |
| 46.Pfc. | William White R | |
| 47.Pfc. | Cosco Williams Jr. A | |
| 48.Pfc. | Thomas Brown G. | |
| 49.Pfc. | Sandy Gregory | |
| 50.Pvt. | Melvin Simpson | |
| 51.Pvt. | Thaddeus Townsend G | |
| 52.Ret. | Russell Allen | |
| 53.Ret. | Jennifer Carroll | |
| 54.Ret. | Wellford Fields | |
| 55.Ret. | Melvin Griffin C | |
| 56.Ret. | George Mondie H | |
| 57.Ret. | Clarence Sanders | |
| 58.Ret. | Robert Williams | |
| 59.Ret. | Rudolph Woods V | |
| 60.Ret. | James Wooden A | |
| 61.Ret. | William Burke | |
| 62.Ret. | David Ford | |
| 63.Ret. | Calvin Payne M | |
| 64.Ret. | Jack Johnson R | |
| 65.Ret. | Louis Carter Jr. C | |
| 66.Ret. | John Fowles R | |
| 67.Ret. | William Hamilton C | |
| 68.Ret. | John Parker | |
| 69.Ret. | Charles Powell H | |
| 70.Ret. | William Lewis | |
| 71.Ret. | James Royster D | |
| 72.Ret. | Thomas Carroll L | |
| 73.Ret. | Jerry Johnson T | |
| 74.Ret. | James Smith | |
| 75.Ret. | Arthur Fowles | |
| 76.Ret. | Nathaniel Long | |
| 77.Ret. | William Fields J | |
| 78.Ret. | Charles Johnson A | |
| 79.Ret. | Lawrence Bell Jr. | |
| 80.Ret. | Elderidge Dunn-Moodie | |
| 81.Ret | Millard Edwards | |
| 82.Ret. | Melvin Brashears | |
| 83.Ret. | Leonard White W | |
| 84.Ret. | Charles Stevenson A | |
| 85.Ret. | Thomas Green L | |
| 86.Ret. | Macon Stith L | |
| 87.Ret. | Samie Wright | |
| 88.Ret. | John Purdy L | |
| 89.Ret. | William Walker A | |
| 90.Ret. | Harvey Blair L | |
| 91.Ret. | Carl Stokes S | |

92.Ret.     Frank Ellis Jr
93.Ret.     Calvin Tilghman F
94.Ret.     William Seaberry   J
95.Ret.     Wilbur Thompson  W
96.Ret.     Irdell Matthews Jr
97.Ret.     Charles Reynolds
98.Ret.     Wilbert Brown
99.Ret.     Rudolph Smith
100.Ret.    Edward Jacobs J
101.Ret.    Charles Bell  J
102.Ret.    Columbus Ferrell H
103.Ret.    William Brown Jr
104.Ret.    Donald Jackson S
105.Ret.    Albert Redd
106.Ret.    Emory Cotton B
107.Ret.    Willie Robin B
108.Ret.    Albert Corbin L
109.Ret.    Nathaniel Baker

165th Transportation Truck Company trained along with other reserve units at Fort Eustis. Upon completion of basic training the unit transferred to Fort Story V.A.

In January 1951 approximately thirty privates were transferred and assign to other units enroute to Korea. Newly trained draftees from Fort Jackson South Carolina replaced them. 165th Transportation Truck Company went back to Fort Eustis and stayed for the entire 21 months. During the summer of 1951 the company participated in Exercise Southern Pines in Fort Bragg, North Carolina. In March 1952 the company went to Fort Hood Texas for Exercise Longhorn. On June 19, 1952 the company was disbanded from active duty status.

**Interviews of members who Joined the 231st Transportation Truck Battalion after the unit was reorganized after the Korean War, in the mid-1950s, and while the unit was still segregated.**

**Interview of Ret SFC Timothy Lee Riley, former member of the segregated 726th TransportationTruck Company who joined the unit after it returned home from Korea**

Ret SFC Timothy L. Riley

My name is Timothy Lee Riley, and I was born on June 29, 1938 in Baltimore, Maryland. My father was William Robert Riley and my mother was Sarah Flemings Riley. My siblings are Camelia Ellen Ann Riley, Patricia Eleanore Riley, William Robert Riley Jr., III, Arno Quincy Riley, Gary Guy Riley, and Renee Claudine Riley.

For elementary school attended PS#138 that was located on Harlem and Monroe Streets, and I went to PS#130 Annex which was a Junior High School, and I went to the old Douglass High School PS#450 that was located on Calhoun Street and from there I was transferred to Gwynns Falls Parkway where Douglass High School is located now. I graduated in February 1957 from high school. After graduation, I worked for several odd jobs at the telephone company, but prior to that I joined the Maryland National Guard on November 29, 1955. I was still in high school when I joined, because all my life I wanted to be in the military. I always thought a soldier was somebody. Some of my family members and friends that I knew in the military were real heroes to me, and they inspired me to be like them.

At the time I joined the Maryland National Guard, the unit was located in a armory on Edmondson Avenue at Bentalou Street, right next to the fire station. The 231st battalion had returned from duty in Korea with their colors. There was a fall out with the officers in the battalion who refused to return to the unit because, I think it was because they did not want to serve again in a segregated organization, so General Reckord, the Maryland Adjutant General asked Captain Jesse Peaker to form a company of men. At that time, the men were meeting in homes, then when the Edmondson Avenue Armory came into being, we met there instead of in homes, and recruitment of men began. There were some of the sergeants in the old 231st who were made officers on the spot. It was then, in 1955, when I joined this newly created 231st. At that time all of the units had been returned to Baltimore. I don't know about all of the units, but most of the men that were assigned to the 726th before and during the Korean War returned to their unit. A lot of the guys that were assigned to the 147th before and after their Germany assignment, did not return. When the 165th returned from duty in Fort Eustis, Virginia, many of those guys returned to their unit. I was initially assigned to the 726th Transportation Truck Company. Captain Jesse Peaker was in charge of the armory at that time. The company commander of the 726th was 1st Lieutenant William A. (Box) Harris. It really was a nice assignment, although we got paid every three months, we didn't mind that. We went to Tuesday night drills, we also went to drivers training on Sunday in Cooksville, we would go to Fort George G. Meade, Maryland for training in driving the trucks. We used to meet at the armory, go to Pikesville to pick up the trucks and then we would go to either Cooksville or Fort Meade for training every Sunday for the longest time. That's where I learned to drive the big 2 1/2 ton 6X6 trucks, a tractor and trailer, a fork lift, and lots of other equipment. The military taught me well. It was real fun. This is what we need to day. I am so sorry we got rid of the draft because the young people today have no where to go, nothing to do, and it's sad, but that's the way it is.

I thoroughly enjoyed out summer camps, it was just like a vacation to me. We trained, we learned how to shoot our weapons, we learned how to bivouac in the field. The first summer camp I went to I was really on the lonely side, but I eventually got used to it. Some of the non-commissioned officers that I remember who were in the unit when I first started were Sergeant Lloyd R. Scott who was the Field First Sergeant; our First Sergeant was Sergeant William R. Durant at that time, and then we had Sergeant Pope, Sergeant Peacock, Sergeant Joseph King, and Sergeant Jennings. They were all in the 726th. When you saw one, you saw them all, they really stayed together. I am one of the fellows that, I didn't go on active duty with the Maryland National Guard, because at the time I joined it was not required. Most of the soldiers in the 726th when I joined had been with the 726th in Korea during the war, and I learned a lot from those experienced soldiers. Those were my idols like Sergeant Butler, Sergeant Jim Brown, Sergeant George Thomas. I really loved to march, and I never will forget Sergeant George Thomas, who we called "TNT" who taught us all the marching skills. There was stiff competition between him and Sergeant Scott. I still think today that Sergeant Lloyd R. Scott is the best cadence calling soldier I have seen in my life. I used to love to hear him call cadence. I was a proud young kid, and I'm sixty-five now, and I'm still proud. The National Guard has been really good to me.

I eventually made a career in the National Guard. I was an E-4 for fourteen years, a Specialist Fourth Class. I was a truck driver and like a handy man all those years. I could operate just about any equipment, I was even a typist. When I made Sergeant, then I started to move up the ranks very quickly. I retired as a Sergeant First Class, but I was in the First Sergeant's slot for about a year, and I went to a lot of military schools during my career. I attended the NCO Academy in Pikesville, then to Towson for the First Sergeant's School, and others. I excelled in every thing I did in training. I feel that I have made significant contributions to the military. I retired with twenty-seven years with the Guard. I left the guard for a while and took a job driving a tractor and trailer, but eventually returned to the unit. I am glad that I remained with the guard because there are many benefits secured from that service, like when my regular job shut down at Bethlehem Steel Mills, and then when the insurance was taken from us with the health benefits, and thanks to my service in the Maryland National Guard, I am in Tricare for life, which doesn't cost me anything, and my family and I get good medical coverage.

I am married to Doris Cunningham Riley. We married on January 20, 1968. We have six children who are Tony Keith Riley, Thomas Kenneth Riley, Cheryl Juanita Riley, Perry Thomas Stanfield, Jeryl Renita Riley and Sarah Zerita Riley. My wife did not care that much for me being away so much in the guard, she wanted me home all the time. I had a hard time staying in the guard, but I enjoyed the service so much, and I knew of the benefits after reaching age sixty, that regardless of the situation, I was going to hang in there with the unit, and I did. My children loved the idea of their father being a soldier. My wife eventually came around, it just took some time.

Back in 1959, or around that time, we were still a segregated military unit, we moved back to the Richmond Market Armory for a while, then we went into a brand new armory on Winchester Street called the Cade Armory. One of the less memorable things that I recall from being a member of the National Guard was being activated for the riots in Baltimore City and the Cambridge riots, and that was a little rough service. Things were so segregated that you could cut it with a knife, it was very tense. The soldiers who were with us, and some were White went along with us, and it was rather odd duty being with those guys. In Cambridge we were not allowed to go into any of the stores or facilities down there, we just had to stay inside the armory, and that was it. During that time I was the jeep driver for the company commander of the 726th, Lieutenant William (Box) Harris. The only thing I didn't like about it, me being young, I wanted ammunition for our weapons. We had fixed bayonets, but empty rifles. First we had the shields and batons for riot control purposes, but later we were issued weapons because of the incident that happened at Kent State University. Only the platoon leader had ammunition in his weapon. It was quite an experience. I recall when Dr. Martin Luther King was killed and there were riots in Baltimore, we had to handle that also. If you lived in East Baltimore, you had duty in West Baltimore, and vice versa. The National Guard did not want any conflicts of the soldiers running across people that they knew. I was stationed in the Druid Hill Park area myself. I was afraid because it was just like wartime, only wartime with your own people, but we got through it. I was a corporal at that time.

When the 231st Transportation Truck Battalion with its companies became in integrated unit, we were no longer a trucking unit, rather we were converted to the 229th Supply and Transport Battalion. We had been so used to being a segregated unit, we actually resented the White soldiers who were assigned to make up our new unit. Our units mixed right away, and eventually, we all adjusted to the new situation. The 726th became Company A in the maintenance area. We had a few White soldiers in our company. There was a White company assigned to the battalion that was located somewhere in Virginia. When we were first integrated, the battalion commander was Lieutenant Colonel Hudgins who had been with the 231st Battalion. He succeeded Colonel Cade when he passed in the 231st. I think he did a very good job.

I actually retired from the 229th.

Most of my memories of military duty with the Maryland National Guard were truly beautiful, but there were times when segregation would rear its ugly head, like once we were on a commitment hauling troops from the 175th at the 5th Regiment Armory, and they would not permit us to eat with the troops, we had to either eat our meals outside of the armory or return to our own armory. Times were pretty rough back then, but we did what we had to do. We obeyed orders. I recall when we went to a couple places down in Virginia and North Carolina, we had to go to the back doors of eateries to get something to eat, and that was in the latter part of the 1950s and early 1960s.

My best remembrances of life in the National Guard is the way military life helped to make me a man, especially from the guidance from non-commissioned officers like Sergeant Lloyd R. Scott, Sr., a darnn good man, and a soldiers soldier. It built my image up, my self esteem, my spirit, and that's what I can say to every young man today, he needs that training, that discipline. The army taught me well.

SP4 Timothy Riley when he was assigned to the 229th Transportation Battalion in the 1960s.
(Photo provided by ret SFC Timothy Riley)

# Interview of Ret MSG Nathaniel Pope, former member of the segregated 147th Transportation Truck Company who joined the unit after it returned home from Germany

Ret MSG Nathaniel Pope

My name is Nathaniel Pope and I was born on June 25, 1935 in Rocky Mount, North Carolina. My parents were James Pope and Rosalee Summers Pope, both of whom were from North Carolina. I have five siblings, who are: James Pope, Hattie Pope, William Pope, Johnny Pope, and a sister named Fannie Pope.

I attended school at PS#123 for my elementary schooling, then went to Briscoe School and PS#452, a Vocational School. I came out of school in 1952 and went to work. I began my working career in at the Monroe Upholstery Company on Franklintown Road. From there I went to Western Electric where I remained for twenty-seven years before retiring.

I got involved with the National Guard because of hearing about the 231st from all of my friends in my block. They were part of the unit and they talked about the unit being activated. I remember going down to the Richmond Market Armory because they were recruiting, but I was turned down because I was too young. That had to be in 1950, so when the unit went away and returned, I then joined the 231st Transportation Truck Battalion. As a matter of fact, there were about four guys from my neighborhood who joined at the same time. At that time the battalion was located at the Edmondson Avenue Armory. When I joined, I was assigned to the 147th Transportation Truck Company. I was one of the first privates that joined the unit when they were re-organized after the Korean War era. It was not long after joining the guard that the unit was returned to the Richmond Market Armory on Linden Avenue. It was at the Edmondson Avenue Armory where we learned dismounted drill, how to wear the uniform, first echelon maintenance on the truck, how to put the top on, top off, different things like that. At that time I really don't remember who the company commander of the 147th was, but the first sergeant was Sergeant Cotton. He wasn't first sergeant too long, Sergeant Harley took over as first sergeant. Company commanders came and went. I really don't even recall the names of the platoon leaders, and that was because when we would fall out in formation, the area was very small, and the platoon leaders never fronted their platoons. When I did get a platoon leader that I remembered, it was Lieutenant Cosco

Williams. I think he was a sergeant in the 165th Transportation Truck Company, and was one of the newly appointed officers when the unit was reformed under Captain Jesse Peaker. I really did not know the circumstances of what happened to the original 231st when they returned from the Korean War. I heard the guys talk about the situation, but I really did not know what they were talking about. All I knew was that I wanted to become part of the unit.

I liked the military at that time because my thoughts of a soldier were about the discipline and getting a job done, and these guys were professional from World War II and the Korean War, and they knew what they were talking about when they were teaching us, and they also taught us about everyday life, which meant a lot for an eighteen year old. Back then, some of my role models were the field first sergeant named Sergeant James Brown, who was my truck master for as long as I can remember. Lieutenant Cosco Williams, was one of the persons who really kept me in the National Guard. He was the first one to talk to me about remaining with the unit when my first enlistment was up. I was his jeep driver, then I became his platoon sergeant, and he would teach me all the things that he knew about the military. Then there was Lieutenant Howard, the old Judge Howard. He joined us when he came here from Ohio. He was my platoon leader, and a very good man. When I got married, it was him that helped me through those trying times, he helped me to buy a house, being a lawyer, he was extremely helpful to me.

I got married in 1957. My wife is Shirley Mondowney, and we had two children, but one died at a very young age. My daughter's name is Dawn Pope. My wife hated the idea that I would make a career of the National Guard. That was all the way through, but it's amazing because I met her in the armory. Some of the ladies used to come to the Armory on Friday evening, then she and her girlfriends used to type for Sergeant Harley. He paid them to help him keep his paperwork straight.

While in the National Guard, I rose in rank pretty quickly. I remember when I first made Private First Class, and that was all I wanted because I thought that one stripe really looked good. With me, lacking what was going on, I got promoted to corporal pretty quick. At that time they came out with a six month program for the reserves and national guard. Anyone who came in during that time had to go away for training, so I took the training in Fort Knox, Kentucky, then transferred to Fort Jackson, South Carolina for further training. After this training for the light vehicle training course, they shipped me back to my unit. I was actually on active duty for six months. When I returned to the National Guard, I was promoted from corporal to sergeant. Actually, the regular army does not recognize reserve and national guard rank, so I went on active duty as a private. I don't recall my first summer camp, but I do remember others. We used to go to Indiantown Gap Military Reservation, Pennsylvania and it was a little exciting to me because what you hear and read about the army and what you see on television, it really was somewhat the same, we had to pitch tents and other various military duties. Now you take the World War II sergeants, they helped a lot. I can remember a Sergeant Summerville, he would show you had to put down your poncho on leaves, etc., and make yourself comfortable in those little tents. He was good, but it would get really cold at night. Also, at that time, I did not realize that things were segregated, and while we attended summer camp. We were an all Black unit, and you know I didn't realize that. It became a reality to me when we began to transport troops from the 29th Division, and I can recall one case that comes to mind. I had a fifteen truck commitment to take one of the brigades of the 29th Division to camp. Lieutenant Cosco and myself met with the major and he told us the amount of trucks that we had to send to each company, and after all of the information was secured, he said that he would see me in the morning. I asked the major about where we could go inside to the latrine, and he said he was sorry, but you cannot go inside because you are Black. That was one thing, but when we got to the camp, Lieutenant Cosco and I had to go around and retrieve all of the vehicles that we had dispatched to these different units, and most of the guys would mentioned that they haven't eaten, so when we told the company commander and the first sergeant that we had no food for our troops, and we were informed that they did not have food for us, so that is where the old soldiers that came from Korea would talk about "brown bagging it!" Bring your brown bag, and that's when we realized that we always had to bring our own food when hauling the 29th Infantry Division, and that is when I realize the full situation as far as being a Black soldier. That was in the late 1950s. Before those types of terrible incidents, I was just having fun soldiering with the 231st. Actually, these experiences made me train the troops under me just a little harder, especially to always be prepared.

I remained in the Maryland National Guard for thirty-eight years. Of all of those years, I only went on active duty once, and that was for training purposes. When I first joined the National Guard in the early 1950s, the entire 231st Transportation Truck Battalion with its three truck companies were still an all Black unit. Integration did not come to our unit in the National Guard until the 1960s. When we did integrate, they brought a company of White troops and took the same amount of Black troops from our unit and put them in the White units. This particular White unit was from Annapolis, and the same amount of Black troops were transferred throughout the Maryland National Guard. I can remember my friend, Joe King was transferred to the 5th Regiment Armory to a unit, as a matter of fact, most of the guys from my unit were transferred to other units located in the 5th Regiment Armory. I believe that was the very first time in the history of the Maryland National Guard that African American soldiers were assigned to White units at the 5th Regiment Armory. It wasn't too bad serving with White troops. After the 231st Transportation Truck Battalion was re-organized to the 229th Supply and Transport Battalion, the White unit was supply, and we were still transportation, so they did their thing and we did ours. We were separate, but if we had to deal with the supply end of commitments, we all worked together, besides, we also had White troops in the transportation unit. I do recall the NCO's from the White unit were great. They came right in and mixed in well. We even had summer camp together. Of course in the early days, we were always separated from the larger unit. If the division was located in one area, we'd be located in another area quite a distance from the division. With our integrated unit, it seems like we were put much closer to the division. I had a paper clipping of an article written about us in Indiantown Gap Military Reservation in Pennsylvania about how after parades on Saturday when the units would go back to their respective areas, the other units got their medals and awards on the parade field, and when it was time for our troops to be recognized in the same way, they would send the Assistant Division Commander to our area to make the awards to our troops. By then I was an E-6 Staff Sergeant, the Platoon Sergeant. Actually, our unit was one of the best in a lot of aspects of soldiering. Our rifle team was the second in all of Maryland, just to give you an idea of our proficiency.

I ended up as a Master Sergeant, E8. My assignment at the time of retirement was the Transportation Operations NCO with the battalion. I left company assignments quite a few years before retirement. I had been in the National Guard for over twenty years when I made Master Sergeant, and that was when I left company assignments. I was an E-6, Staff Sergeant for eighteen years. I could not transfer out of the 231st because the Maryland National Guard was segregated. I recall when I was offered a new assignment beyond the company level when a colonel desired my services, and the only way I agreed to go was if he made me a Master Sergeant before going on to the new assignment. At that time I was a Sergeant First Class. He agreed, and off I went to Division Supply in Towson, Maryland. I switched military career from maintenance to supply. This was the only way that I could gain additional promotions. I encountered big problems, not only going from transportation to engineers, to maintenance, all in the Cade Armory, before going to the new assignment in Towson as a Senior Supply Sergeant in Class Nine. There were a few Blacks already there when I got there, with quite a few of them being females. My problem was with the section office of the Class Nine Section, they indicated that they did not send for me and he did not need me, but I knew how the system worked, and I overcame it. That was the reason I told the colonel that I did not want the assignment, unless I was promoted before going to the Class Nine Section. There were many, many problems long before I was assigned there, but the Colonel promoted me to render some leadership to overcome some of those problems. The unit had flunked their inspections, weapons training was on the decline, etc., it just lacked leadership there. I was not really recognized until we got the unit back to top notch status and they began passing their inspections. A lot of my problems ceased after that. I remained there for about ten years. I was given the job as Sergeant Major at Towson, Maryland Armory. I turned it down because I was moving to Richmond, Virginia, and at the same time the Lieutenant Colonel I was working for was given the task to reorganize the 229th Supply and Transportation Battalion. He asked me to come with him to help in the reorganization. I accepted and ended up as the Battalion Transportation Operations NCO. I retired on January 19, 1992.

Of all of the years I spent in the National Guard, my best remembrances were the many things I learned in life. When you take courses and listen to some of the old soldiers, you learn a lot, and if you applied this knowledge, you can go far in the Guard, which was what I did. I applied this learning in all of my assignments over the years, as a matter of fact, my nickname was "Policy," because I wrote the SOP for transportation operations here and everything I did, I had a policy, with some type of publication to back it up. Good memories. I never had any regrets of spending so many years with the guard. My wife hated every bit of my being in the military until after twenty years when they gave the wives a class on what they could encounter after retirement, then she became interested.

# Chapter 7

(The End of the Segregated "Monumental City Guards" and it's succesor all-African American Maryland National Guard Organizations)

In our society, usually only members of combat units receive honor, glory and recognition participating in the wars of this country; however, many people do not understand the roles of many of the Army units that participated in our wars from the first conflict through the current wars and conflicts. The brave African American men from the Maryland National Guard who participated in combat during World War I as Company I, 372nd Infantry should be applauded and recognized for their service; and so should the brave African American men from the Maryland National Guard who participated in service to their country during World War II when they participated in guard duty at strategic points along the shores of New Jersey and New York, and their overseas duty in the Hawaiian Islands as Service Company, 372nd Infantry. In 1947 when this unit from the Maryland National Guard was redesignated as the Headquarters and Headquarters Detachment, 231st Transportation Corps Truck Battalion with its assigned three truck companies, entered into a service field, but just as important as any other unit in the U.S. Army. The definition of Koger on this field of labor clearly notes the importance of service and labor units: "As important as our fighting forces, we know that no army has won by its men at the front alone. The supplies must reach the soldiers; they must be fed and the troops and supplies must be transported to them......"[22]

From 1950 until their inactivation in 1955, the men of Headquarters and Headquarters Company, 231st Transportation Truck Battalion and 726th Transportation Truck Company, functioned as one of the service units Koger noted. Many times, under small arms fire, attacks from above, and during the extreme cold temperatures doing their share in moving supplies, arms, and men, make all of these men heroes. Had they not been redesignated in the service field from a combat infantry unit, and ordered to active duty to support the Korean War, then from the authors view who participated with the 726th, there would have been many decorated African Americans returning to Baltimore after their tours of duty. Unfortunately, during the tours of duty of all of their units, they were functioning in an extreme segregated society, both on the home front at well as on the war front. It was not until 1951 when true integration of the army units became a reality. This author can attest to this situation himself, because when he enlisted in the Regular Army, as a members of the 726th Transportation Truck Company deep into North Korea in 1951, he was transferred out of the 726th to an all-African American unit with White officers, which was been typical of American army units for hundreds of years.

By 1955, the 231st saw all of it's units deactivated and reinstated in the Maryland National Guard as the 231st Transportation Battalion (Truck) with four (4) companies: Headquarters and Headquarters Company, 147th Transportation Company, 165th Transportation Company, and 726th Transportation Company; however, in 1953, General Reckord, the Adjutant General of Maryland ordered the 231st to be reinstated in the Maryland National Guard as a segregated battalion of African Americans, but because the officers from the old 231st were protesting being reinstated as a segregated unit, General Reckord promoted Warrant Officer Jesse Peaker to Captain and ordered him to recruit for officers and enlisted men for the old 231st, which he did. When the units were returned to Maryland State control, they were relocated in Baltimore at an armory located next to the old fire station on Edmondson Avenue at Bentalou Street. The building was called the Edmondson Avenue Armory. Eventually, the 231st was reorganized as the 231st Transportation Battalion (Truck), they were subsequently reorganized many times as noted:

From 1953 to 1955 they were called the Headquarters and Headquarters Company, 231st Transport Battalion (Truck) under the command of Captain Jesse P. Peaker.

From 1955 to 1960 they were called the 231st Transportation Battalion (Truck), back under the command of Lt. Colonel Vernon F. Greene.

From 1960 to 1968 they were called the 229th Transportation Battalion and the 229th Supply and Transport Battalion under the command of Lt. Colonel Melvin H. Cade, Lt. Colonel Lester C. Hudgins, and Lt. Colonel George M. Brooks.

From 1968 through 1975 they were called Company C, 103rd Engineer Battalion under the command of Major Wayne Thompson and Major Roland Evans, Company C, 728th Maintenance Battalion under the command of Lieutenant Alex Bishop and Captain Rudolph Walters, and 2nd Platoon, Company B, 728th Supply and Transport Battalion and FASCOM, Company A, 728th Supply and Transport Battalion under the command of Lieutenant Herbert Parker.

Also from 1975 to 1976 they were called the 734th Maintenance Company under the command of Captain Rudolph Walters.

Also from 1975 to 1985 they were called the 243rd Engineer Company under the command of Captain Joseph Mills, Major Joseph Bradley, Major Bruce Blanchard, Major Dee Humphrey, and Major Albert Schwietezer.

Also from 1975 to 1985 they were called Company C, 58th Support Battalion under the command of Captain Charles Sigmund, Captain Edward H. Ballard and Captain Walter Hurt.

From 1985 to 1993 they were called the 229th Supply and Transport Battalion under the command of Lt. Colonel Michael N. Scheupner, Jr., Lt. Colonel Michael P. Tangzyn, and Lt. Colonel Edward H. Ballard.

From 1993 to 2002 they were called the 229th Main Support Battalion under the command of Lt. Colonel Donald M. Choate, Lt. Colonel Joseph Blume, Jr., and Lt. Colonel Donald Krebs.

From 2002 to date the organization is known as the 229th Support Battalion under the command of Lt. Colonel Wayne Johnson, Sr.

For many years, the men of the 231st requested an armory of their own, and finally later in 1959, the state built the Winchester Armory located on Winchester and Braddish Avenues. In 1965, the armory was renamed The Melvin N. Cade Armory in honor of the Commander of the 229th Supply and Transpoprtation Battalion. Lieutenant Colonel Cade assumed command in 1961, and in the same year was promoted to Colonel. Along with other members of the 229th, Colonel Cade led the move to have the National Guard integrated. Integration of the 231st Transportation Truck Company did not come easy. Most of the officers of the 231st Transportation Truck Battalion, including the officers assigned to the truck companies within the battalion, objected to returning to the segregated situation it left in 1950. From 1951 on, all of the units were integrated, and felt that it was better to have an integrated National Guard unit because it promoted better efficiency and better morale. These officers elected to remain in an inactive status until Governor McKeldin agreed to let the battalion enlist anyone into the unit irrespective of race, creed, or color. The following officers and warrant officers filed a petition to have the 231st Transportation Truck Battalion and its companies integrated:

> Lieutenant Colonel Vernon F. Greene
> Major Melvin H. Cade
> Major Donald C. Parker
> Captain Bedford T. Bentley
> Captain George Brooks
> Captain James Gilliam
> Captain Lester Hudgins
> First Lieutenant Joseph Bracy
> Warrant Officer Joseph Armstead
> Warrant Officer Earl Jackson

Trying to integrate the 231st Transportation Truck Battalion did not come easy at all. In 1955, when the colors to the Battalion was returned to Maryland State control from their tour of duty in the Korean War, General Milton Reckord wanted to have the battalion reactivated in their old segregated way. The officers and enlisted men were all in an inactive status. Most of the personnel assigned to Headquarters and Headquarters Company, 231st Transportation Truck Battalion, 147th Transportation Truck Company, 165th Transportation Truck Company, and the 726th Transportation Truck Company had already completed their tours with their units. All were activated in 1950, and it was not 1954, which obviously meant that all of the men had returned to civilian status in Maryland, with the exception of persons like myself who opted to reenlist and remain in the Regular Army.

It is my understanding after talking with members of the 231st, Officers and enlisted men, that in 1953 when the battalion with its companies, were to be reinstated with the Maryland National Guard, the officers approached General Reckord to permit the battalion to allow them to enlist anyone in the 231st who desired to be a part of the organization, without regard to race, color, creed, etc. General Reckord was not in favor of having the Maryland National Guard integrated, therefore, the officers remained in an inactive state and the battalion was not reinstated.

General Reckord then took a bold step and found some of the enlisted men of the unit willing to accept commissions and on December 16, 1953 had four previous enlisted men commissioned with forty three enlisted men inducted into the newly activated 147th Transportation Truck Company. There were insufficient personnel to activate the battalion because it took something like 100+ personnel per company, or 300 to 400 personnel to form the battalion with the three truck companies. Also, it is my thoughts that the colors of the 231st Transportation Truck Battalion had not yet been returned to Maryland State control as the battalion was still functioning in Korea as late as 1954. Most likely, the 726th Transportation Truck Company was likewise still functioning in Korea in 1954. Several enlisted men of the 147th Transportation Truck Company indicated that the 147th had been returned from Germany before 1954. I was not able to find any information as to when the 165th Transportation Truck Company was released from its stateside assignment. Most likely the 147th Transportation Truck Company was eligible to be reactivated as a Maryland National Guard organization in 1954.

In the meantime, the inactive officers began action to bring the segregated situation of the 231st to the wider community. All of these inactive officers elected to remain in an inactive status until their request to enlist into their unit any applicant, not only African American.[23]

One of the major concerns expressed by the inactive officers is that they felt that it was better to have an integrated unit because it promoted better efficiency and better morale.[24] Further, each officer, from Lieutenant Colonel Vernon F. Greene, who was the commanding officer before and during the Korean War, down through the Warrant Officers, has sufficient military experience to become a vital and essential part of the National Guard.[24] At some point in time between 1954 and 1955, these inactive officers submitted a petition to the Governor of the State of Maryland, and solicited the help of the NAACP. According to an article that appeared in The Sun, Monday, November 21, 1955, Governor McKeldin ordered the end of racial segregation in the Maryland National Guard. Major General Milton A. Reckord, the Adjutant General of the State of Maryland, who had already reactivated the old 231st Transportation Truck Battalion as a segregated unit, indicated that he will comply with the order from the governor immediately, in which he did, and all of the inactive officers were reinstated to their formal position. This action made Maryland the first Southern State to drop racial barriers in its military service.

This action also made the Monumental City Guards, with all of their heritage and history come to a quick halt since the 231st was now an integrated unit within the Maryland National Guard. There were numerous African Americans who had a desire to maintain the 231st in its old way. To explain how they felt, and how General Milton Reckord was able to attempt not to change the status quo on the 231st, the following article appeared in a Baltimore newspaper that I believe to be the Sun, dated January 2, 1954 is quoted:

"New unit former; old officers quit. 4 officers, 43 enlisted men join segregated unit. Maj. Gen. Milton Reckord has finally activated his jim crow National Guard unit.

On December 16, four officers and 43 enlisted men were inducted into the newly activated 147th Transportation Company.

The State Adjutant General has been trying to re-activate the 231st Truck Battalion since September.

But the officers and enlisted men of the 231st had served honorably in the army in Korean War service as members of fully integrated units.

They wanted no part of a segregated National Guard unit and flatly told the General that.

When convinced that the officers meant business, General Reckord boasted that he would find some men who would serve in a separate trucking unit and not pay any attention to jim crow.

Two weeks ago in a building at 2237 Edmondson Avenue, which has been designated as their separate armory, the new Guard unit received official Federal recognition from Lieutenant Colonel J. Wright, a regular army officer.

Although only at company strength now, Guard officers hope enlistments will swell the outfit to its former battalion strength - when it will again be known as the 231st.

Commissioned as officers to the new unit was Warrant Officer (jg) Jesse Peaker, and 2nd Lieutenants Theodore Scott, Cosco Williams, and Lloyd G. Henderson, Jr.

Lt. Scott, son of a local policeman, has been designated the company commander. He joined the 231st before the outfit went on active duty in 1948, and served as an enlisted man.

Lt. Henderson, platoon leader, was formerly a sergeant major at the Edgewood Chemical Center.

Lt. Williams, a Morgan College student, joined the outfit in 1949 just before the group went on active duty.

Warrant Officer Peaker, who works in the comptroller's office at Morgan, is handling most of the administrative duties attached to the re-activation.

Mr. Peaker who has served with the 231st as a sergeant major, is well aware of the conflict between General Reckord and the officers of his outfit.

He asserts that the re-activation of the separate unit was necessary because the 231st gained world-wide recognition while fighting in Korea.

The unit has two unit citations and each man in has at least three battle stars.

With that rich heritage we feel that the 231st, as a unit, should not be allowed to die. Mr. Peaker also reasoned that he and the other newly appointed officers were afraid the federal government would take back the $90,000 allocated the 231st unless we re-activated.

Brigadier General Harry C. Ruhl, executive officer, Maryland Military Department, was well pleased with the re-activation of the unit and scoffed at the previous unrest among the officers with: 'As far as we're concerned, this is the outfit.'
Major General Reckord could not be reached for comment.

The high ranking officers who served with the 231st during the Korean War and refused to serve in a segregated unit included Lt. Col. Vernon F. Greene, who commanded the outfit, Major Charles Parker, Capt. Lester C. Hudgins, Lt. William A. Harris, Major Melvin H. Cade and Capt. James H. Gilliam.

Captin Jesse Peaker, who in early 1950s accepted an appoinment
to have the 231st Transportation Truck Battalion reinstated in
the Maryland National Guard as a segregated organization.
(Photo provided by ret MSG Nathaniel Pope)

# Chapter 8

(Life in the Units After Integration)

(Life in the numerous organizations that succeeded the segregated 231st Transportation Truck Battalion are shown in photographs shared by members of the various organizations)

# Photographs provided by member of the 231st Transportation Battalion (Truck) From 1953 to 1960 - After the Korean War

Some of the members of the 726th Transportation Truck Company after the unit was returned to National Guard status after the Korean War. The only identified person is SFC Wilson who is standing on top of the truck. Photograph was taken in the late 1950s when the unit was at summer camp in Camp AP Hill, Virginia.
(Photograph provided by ret MSG Nathaniel Pope)

SP4 Ernest Hargrove, a member of the 147th Trans Trk Co after the unit had returned from duty in Germany. Late 1950s photo. Photo taken at summer camp in IGMR, PA.
(Photo provided by ret MSG Nathaniel Pope)

One of the truck companies of the 231st at work. Late 1950s photo taken at a summer camp.
(Photo provided by ret MSG Nathaniel Pope)

LTC Lester Hudgins (right) watches CWO Jackson congratulate SFC Winkler at Camp AP Hill, VA in early 1960s photo.
(Photo provided by ret MSG Nathaniel Pope)

Platoon Sergeant Nathaniel Pope, 1960s
(Photo provided by ret MSG Nathaniel Pope)

Standing, l to r: SGT Nathaniel Pope, Unk, Unk, SGT James Peacock, and Unk. Kneeling is 1SG Lloyd R. Scott, Sr. All are members of the 229th Supply and Transport Bn, and the Rifle Team. 1960s photo.
(Photo provided by Ret MSG Nathaniel Pope)

Standing,, l to r: SSG Irvin Smith, SSG James Peacock, MSG James Brown, SSG Nathaniel Pope, and SGT Theodore Rice. Center, sitting is 1SG Lloyd R. Scott, Sr., all members of the 229th Trans Bn. 1960s
(Photo provided by Ret MSG Nathaniel Pope)

SSG Nathaniel Pope, a member of the 229th Trans Bn in 1960. Photo was taken in the Motor Pool at the LTC Melvin H. Cade Armory.
(Photo provided by ret MSG Nathaniel Pope)

Sitting, l to r: SFC Elgia Butler, SGM Nichols, 1st Lt Thomas Briscoe, 1SG George Coleman, and Warrant Officer Willie Horne. Standing, l to r: SSG Clarence Martin, unk; MSG Claude Patterson, Unk, Unk, Unk, Warrant Officer Edward Watties, SFC James Dunmoodie, and the last three are unknown. 1960s photo.
(Photograph provided by ret SFC Elgia Butler)

**Photographs provided by member of Company C, 103rd Engineer Battalion, Company C, 728th Maintenance Battalion, 2nd Platoon, Company B, 728th Supply and Transport Battalion, and FASCOM, Company A, 728th Supply and Transport Battalion from 1968 to 1975**

Warrant Officer Edward Watties who was assigned to Company C, 728th Maintenance Battalion. Photograph taken in the 1970s. (Photo provided by ret MSG Nathaniel Pope)

On left is SFC Joseph King observing members of Company C, 728th Maint Bn at work during one of their summer encampments at Camp AP Hill, Virginia.
(Photo provided by ret MSG Nathaniel Pope)

SFC George Hardy, a member of the Mech. Maintenance Section of Company C, 728th Maintenance Bn. He was stationed at Camp Pickett, Virginia during his summer encampment.
(Photo provided by ret MSG Nathaniel Pope)

Left is Vernon Hudson, with Robert Plato as they work on one of the trucks. They were in summer camp at Camp Pickett, Virginia. Both were members of Company C, 728th Maintenance Bn.
(Photo provided by ret MSG Nathaniel Pope)

# Photographs provided by member of the 734th Maintenance Company from 1975 to 1976

On left in front seat is Captain Walter Hairston, the company commander, with 1SG Lloyd R. Scott, Sr. driving. Seating in rear of jeep is SFC George Thomas. The company was in summer camp at Camp Pickett, VA. (Photo provided by ret MSG Nathaniel Pope)

Members of the 734th Maintenance Company at work during their summer camp at Camp Pickett, Virgininia. (Photo provided by ret MSG Nathaniel Pope)

L to r: Elgia Butler, Edward Watties, Willie Horne, James Evans, Nathaniel Pope, Joseph King, and James Peacock. They were at summer camp in Camp Pickett, Virginia. (Photo provided by ret MSG Nathaniel Pope)

# Photographs provided by member of the 243rd Engineer Company and Company C, 58th Support Battalion from 1975 to 1985

French Officer presenting a battle streamer on flag of Company C, 58th Support Bn at activity. CPT Edward Ballard, facing the French Officer, was the commander of Company C. 1980s photograph.
(Photo provided by ret MSG Nathaniel Pope)

Colonel William Bradley, one of the oldest living members of the old African American National Guard unit. Photo was taken during an activity by the 243rd Engineer Company in the LTC Melvin H. Cade Armory in 1979.
(Photo provided by ret MSG Nathaniel Pope)

L to r: SFC Ronald Anderson, Gen George Brooks and 1SG Lloyd R. Scott, Sr. Anderson ans Scott were assigned to Co C, 58th Support Bn. 1980s photo
(Photo provided by ret MSG Nathaniel Pope)

Members of the 243rd Engineer Company in a parade at Rash Fields in Baltimore. 1981 photograph.
(Photo provided by ret MSG Nathaniel Pope)

L to r: SFC James Peacock, SP4 Marvin McClain, SGT Timothy Riley, and unknown. They were members of Co C, 728th Maint Bn. Photo taken at one of the summer camps in the 1970s.
(Photo provided by ret MSG Nathaniel Pope)

L to r: Unk, WO Joe Locklear, Gen George Brooks, Capt Bedford T. Bentley, LTC Lester Hudgins, WO John Holt, SGT Wilson, Unk, MSG Claude Patterson, SGT John Blake, SGT Mason, Unk, 1SG Lloyd R. Scott, Sr., SFC Elgia Butler, and SFC George Thomas. Photo taken in the 1980s.
(Photo provided by ret MSG Nathaniel Pope)

# Photographs provided by member of the 229th Supply and Transport Battalion from 1985 to 1993

At one of the military balls. Top, l to r: SFC William Wilson, SFC David West, SFC Nathaniel Pope, SFC Eldridge Jones, SFC Joseph King, and SFC James Peacock. Bottom, l to r: SSG Harry Johnson, SFC Frank Palmer, and SSG Robert Belle. (Photo provided by ret MSG Nathaniel Pope)

On left is SSG Donald Smith with 1SG Lloyd R. Scott, Sr. They were assigned to the 229th Support and Transport Battalion. Late 1980s photo.
(Photo provided by ret 1SG Lloyd R. Scott, Sr)

Color Bearers from the 229th Main Support Battalion during a parade. 1990s photograph
(Photo provided by ret MSG Nathaniel Pope)

Left is COL William Brady, Mrs. Shirley Pope and wife of COL Brady. At one of the balls
(Photo provided by ret MSG Nathaniel Pope)

1SG and Mrs. Lloyd R. Scott, Sr., at one of the military balls.
(Photo provided by ret 1SG Lloyd R. Scott, Sr)

# Photographs shared by members of the Veterans of the 231st Transportation Truck Battalion

## (Celebrating a luncheon at the Old Country Buffet in Catonsville on January 17, 2004)

Ret SFC Elgia Butler, the Club President, greeting ret 1SG Lloyd R. Scott, Sr. 2004 photo.
(Photo provided by ret SFC Louis S. Diggs)

Kedrick Powell, the Club Vice President, enjoying the luncheon with his wife. 2004 photograph.
(Photo provided by ret SFC Louis S. Diggs)

Robert Dunton, Jr., on right and William Barnes at the luncheon. 2004 photo.
(Photo provided by ret SFC Louis S. Diggs)

Left is ret MSG Nathaniel Pope, with his wife, Shirley and ret SFC Timothy Riley.
(Photo provided by ret SFC Louis S. Diggs)

On left is ret MSG Nathaniel Pope with ret SFC Timothy at the luncheon.
(Photo provided by ret SFC Louis S. Diggs)

Ret SFC Louis S. Diggs enjoying the luncheon with his wife, Shirley. 2004 photo.
(Photo provided by ret SFC Louis S. Diggs)

# Other photographs shared by members of the Veterans of the 231st Transportation Truck Battalion

On left is ret SFC Elgia Butler, President of the Veterans of the 231st Trans Truck Bn with the daughter of the late LTC Melvin H. Cade, LTCl Wayne Johnson, Jr., current commander of the 229th Support Battalion and LTG James F. Fretterd, the Adjutant General of Maryland at a dedication Ceremony for the 231st Trans Truck Bn on December 14, 2002. They just uncovered a plaque dedicating the armory as the LTC Melvin H. Cade Armory. 2002 photograph.
(Photo provided by ret SFC Louis S. Diggs)

L to r:  Vernon (Boo) Carter, _____, George (Tony) Thomas; Robert Dunton, Jr., and Raymond Jackson.  They had a display at the 7th Annual Baltimore County African American Cultural Festival in Towson in September 2003.
(Photo provided by ret SFC Louis S. Diggs)

# Photographs at one of the meetings of the Veterans of the 231st Transportation Truck Battalion (2003)

One of the Club's meeting at Cade Armory in 2003. L to r: ret 1SG Lloyd R. Scott, unk, Kendrick Powell, Raymond Jackson and Vernon (Boo) Carter.
(Photo provided by ret SFC Louis S. Diggs)

Left is Robert Dunton, Jr talking with Vernon (Boo) Carter at one of the Club's meeting at Cade Armory in 2003
(Photo provided by ret SFC Louis S. Diggs)

Malcar Waters talking at one of the Vets of the 231st Club meetings in 2003.
(Photo provided by ret SFC Louis S. Diggs)

The Club's Historian, ret MSG Nathaniel Pope making a presentation at one of the meetings
(Photo provided by ret SFC Louis S. Diggs)

Ret SFC Timothy Riley, the Club's Secretary making a presentation at one of the meetings.
(Photo provided by ret SFC Louis S. Diggs)

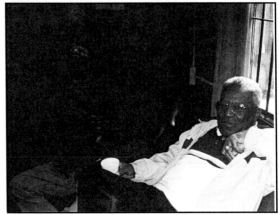

On right is ret SFC Montegue Douglass with one of the mmbers of the club.
(Photo provided by ret SFC Louis S. Diggs)

# Photographs at one some of the Veterans of the 231st at an activity at the Reisterstown Road Plaza (2003)

On left is ret MSG Nathaniel Pope getting displays of the Vets of the 231st set up at the Reisterstown Road Plaza and ret 1SG Lloyd R. Scott, Sr. (Photo provided by ret SFC Louis S. Diggs)

Left is ret 1SG Lloyd R. Scott, Sr., with ret SFC Louis S. Diggs, both of the Vets of the 231st. (Photo prov by ret SFC Louis S. Diggs)

The photo display of the Veterans of the 231st Trans Truck Bn at the Reisterstown Road Plaza. The display put up by ret MSG Nathaniel Pope. (Photo provided by ret SFC Louis S. Diggs)

An observer views some of the photographic display of the 231st Transportation Truck Battalion and the earlier units of the only African American Maryland National Guard at the Reisterstown Road Plaza. Ret MSG Nathaniel Pope is putting up the display on the right. (Photo provided by ret SFC Louis S. Diggs)

# Photographs at the display put up by the Veterans of the 231st Transportation Truck Battalion at th Mondawmin Shopping Mall (2003)

Left is ret MSG Claude Patterson with Kendrick Powell. Name of other person is not known. They were at the photographic Display the Veterans of the 231st Transportation Truck Battalion had in Mondawmin Mall
(Photo provided by Louis S. Diggs)

At left is ret MSG Claude Patterson, with Kendrick Powell and other members of the Veterans of the 231st Transportation Truck Battalion when they had a photographic display at the Mondawmin Shopping Mall.
(Photo provided by ret SFC Louis S. Diggs)

# Bibliography and Credits

[1] The Maryland Negroe in Our Wars by A. Briscoe Koger, 1942, Page 5

[2] Ibid

[3] Ibid

[4] Ibid

[5] Ibid

[6] Ibid, Page 8

[7] Ibid

[8] Ibid, Pp 8 and 9

[9] Ibid, pp 13 and 14

[10] History of the 229th S&T Battalion, date unknown

[11] Article written by Charles Johnson, Jr, Fayetteville State University, date unknown.

[12] Ibid

[13] The Maryland Negroe in Our Wars by A. Briscoe Koger, 1942, Page 14

[14] Article written by Charles Johnson, Jr.,Fayetteville State University, date unknown.

[15] Ibid

[16] History of the 229th S&T Battalion. date unknown.

[17] The Maryland Negroe in Our Wars by A. Briscoe Koger, 1941, Page 15

[18] History of the 229th S&T Battalion, date unknown.

[19] Freestate Guardian, article by Maj. John C. Andrews, HQ - STARC, Page 23, date unknown.

[20] Baltimore Afro-American newspaper, date unknown, but believed to be in July or early August 1950.

[21] Freestate Guardian, article by Maj. John C. Andrews, HQ - STARC, page 24, date unknown.

[22] The Maryland Negroe in Our Wars by A. Briscoe Koger, 1942, pp16 and 17.

[23] Baltimore Afro-American newspaper, November 22, 1959, page 1

[24] Ibid

# APPENDICES

R O S T E R

ORIGINAL ROSTER of the "MONUMENTAL CITY GUARDS"

mustered into the

M A R Y L A N D   S T A T E   M I L I T I A

15 MARCH 1882

CAPTAIN WILLIAM K. SPENCER

FIRST LIEUTENANT PETER WILSON                    SECOND LIEUTENANT JESSE L. DANDRIDGE

FIRST SERGEANT JAMES H. MOORE

SECOND SERGEANT CHARLES H. BROOKS               FOURTH SERGEANT WILLIAM WALKER

THIRD SERGEANT BENJAMIN R. DOUGLASS             FIFTH SERGEANT JOHN MITCHELL

FIRST CORPORAL JOHN RAY                         FIFTH CORPORAL STITH FURAHAN

SECOND CORPORAL HENRY B. EVANS                  SIXTH CORPORAL HENRY BROWN

THIRD CORPORAL GEORGE W. SCOTT                  SEVENTH CORPORAL JOSEPH H. WILSON

FOURTH CORPORAL EMORY R. JACKSON                EIGHTH CORPORAL MATTHEW M. MORTON

| | | |
|---|---|---|
| PRIVATE MOSES ASKINS | PRIVATE B. A. GATEWOOD | PRIVATE WASHINGTON OWENS |
| PRIVATE GEORGE ASH | PRIVATE THEODORE GASAWAY | PRIVATE NICHOLAS A. PIKE |
| PRIVATE LOUIS BURK | PRIVATE CLEMENTINE GASAWAY | PRIVATE JAMES P. PAUL |
| PRIVATE GEORGE W. BROWN | PRIVATE JOHN HURST | PRIVATE P. H. QUARLES |
| PRIVATE SAMUEL BROWN | PRIVATE SIDNEY JOHNSON | PRIVATE WILLIAM RAWSON |
| PRIVATE BENJAMIN BISHOP | PRIVATE DANIEL JOHNSON | PRIVATE WILLIAM ROBINSON |
| PRIVATE JOHN W. BISHOP | PRIVATE ROBERT JOHNSON | PRIVATE THOMAS STEVENS |
| PRIVATE BENJAMIN BURLEY | PRIVATE CHARLES JOHNSON | PRIVATE JOSEPH SHEAF |
| PRIVATE THOMAS BLACKWELL | PRIVATE SAMUEL JOHNSON | PRIVATE JOHN N. SMITH |
| PRIVATE LOUIS T. COLEMAN | PRIVATE DAVY JONES | PRIVATE JOHN S. SAVOY |
| PRIVATE HANDY COLEMAN | PRIVATE WILLIAM H. JONES | PRIVATE JOSEPH TURNER |
| PRIVATE JAMES COTTMAN | PRIVATE CHARLES H. JONES | PRIVATE RODERICK TWINE |
| PRIVATE JOSEPH H. COLLINS | PRIVATE LORENZO S. JONES | PRIVATE CHARLES TWINE |
| PRIVATE BASIL COWDY | PRIVATE WILLIAM JARDON | PRIVATE ARTHUR THOMAS |
| PRIVATE STEPHEN DICKERSON | PRIVATE ALFRED KELLY | PRIVATE JOHN S. THOMAS |
| PRIVATE WILLIAM G. DARBY | PRIVATE JAMES LA PRADE | PRIVATE JAMES WHITE |
| PRIVATE LOUIS DAVIS | PRIVATE ALFRED MACKEY | PRIVATE WILLIAM WELLS |
| PRIVATE GEORGE DEXTER | PRIVATE HEZEKIAH MAPP | PRIVATE ABRAHAM WILLIAMS |
| PRIVATE BUSH EVANS | PRIVATE FRANK MASON | PRIVATE JOSEPH WRIGHT, JR. |
| PRIVATE JAMES M. FREDERICKS | PRIVATE CHARLES MOSBY | PRIVATE HENRY WATTS |
| PRIVATE GEORGE GOODWIN | PRIVATE NATHANIEL NEVITT | PRIVATE THOMAS H. YOUNG |

Appendix A

# Md. National Guard's First Separate Company

Charles Johnson Jr.
Fayetteville State University

Since the forming of the First Separate Company in 1882, the Afro-American presence in Maryland's National Guard has been one that has been filled with controversy and humiliation. The history of the black Maryland Guardsman is also a tale of untinted patriotism, a love of country unhesitatingly given, but cruelly, a patriotic fervor and love of country only reluctantly received.

The narration which follows ever so briefly, a portion of the history of a band of determined men to serve as armed fighting men in the colors of their country.

Reconstruction was over in the South. Afro-Americans had served in several Southern state militias and had been a functioning segment of the United States Regular Army on the American frontier. Yet, it was not until February 20, 1879 that Maryland had a "recognized" force.

It was organized by Captain Thomas H. Lewis and was called the Monumental City Guards. Although the unit was a separate entity, its desire was to have it incorporated into the Maryland National Guard.

After several years pursuit of his aim, Captain Lewis and organization were accepted as a part of the National Guard and given the status of a separate company on February 20, 1882.

On the surface, the black men had achieved their purpose, but a cursory glance at the organizational chart for the National Guard in Maryland would suffice to convince the unsuspecting that the acceptance granted was not a full acceptance.

As proof of this contention a look at the chart for the period would disregular chain of regimental close in addition to the command a little line is drawn off to the side indicating the placement and position of the "First Separate Company."

Following shortly upon this snubbing of valor, the command of the all black unit passed to Captain Lloyd Young, who remained as the commander for a very short period, and then to Captain William R. Spencer, who received the credit for reorganizing the First Separate Company in 1883 as a field unit.

Under the leadership of Captain Spencer, the company developed into a more proficient group. The drills were standardized in accordance with army regulations and the seriousness of the men and the high standards set by the unit attracted men of high caliber.

The resulting increase in interest and the studied display of military bearing instilled a sense of pride in the men of the First Separate Company and occasioned many well-spoken words about the organization. Some indication of the esteem engendered by the "First" was the invitation extended the company

to participate in the Oriole's observation of Lord Baltimore's landing at Brown's Wharf in 1883.

The First Separate Company was never a large organization. Prior to its call to active duty in 1917, the actual strength for officers never exceeded three and the total strength of enlisted men reached a high of 70. The three officers for the company were:

Captain William R. Spencer, June 12, 1882;
First Lieutenant Henry Ryan Jr., Dec. 21, 1889; and
Second Lieutenant James T. Harris, Feb. 13, 1917.

It is interesting to note several points concerning the first two officers:

Both were the senior Maryland National Guard officers in their pay grade. The officer second in numerical sequence to Captain Spencer was Captain Edmond A. Munoz, who was white and had a date of rank of July 16, 1902. Likewise the officer second to Lieutenant Ryan was First Lieutenant Clifton A. Pritchell, who was also white and had a date of rank of March 26, 1913.

Neither of the two officers could be promoted due to the following reasons:

a. There was only one commander for the company and this was Captain Spencer.

b. Company commanders traditionally had the rank of captain. If a captain was not available, there were instances where Lieutenants had commanded comapnies until they were promoted or replaced by a senior officer.

c. Lieutenant Ryan could not be promoted unless the aforementioned occurred.

d. Afro-Americans were only assigned to the First Separate Company; therefore, Captain Spencer could not hope to be promoted or elevated into a staff position in the Maryland National Guard.

Thus, the First Separate Company was a "separate and supposedly equal company" inside the Maryland National Guard organization.

During the Shanish-American War of 1898, the company experienced several humiliating incidents when the military forces of the United States were called to active duty.

Maryland's National Guard was activated and the First Separate Company was the first to pitch its tents at Pimlico, where the Regiment was being mobilized. However, the First did not accompany the

Regiment to Cuba. It remained in Baltimore during the entire crisis. Perhaps its failure to move with the Regiment was due to the fact that it was not on the "recognized" list of the National Guard. A fuller recognition was not bestowed upon the organization until 1902.

Maryland's Guard was activated again on July 5, 1916 to help combat and effect the capture of Panco Villa. who was terrorizing the inhabitants along the Texas border. Again, the First Separate was not activated.

However, it should be mentioned that the First was not the only unit excluded because the Naval Militia was not ordered to move with the regiment.

However, reasoning for the latter exclusion is quite obvious since the Pancho Villa affair was one which required military forces and not naval units.

Even while the country was busy trying to capture the elusive Pancho Villa, it was beginning to realize that an even greater threat to its security was materializing.

President Woodrow Wilson and many of the nation's leaders were split over the issues of intervention and non-intervention into Europe's war. However, upon

the outbreak of hostilities in Europe the United States cast its lot with the Allies and this time the country

could ill afford to omit the band of determined fighting men to the Maryland First Separate Company.

Article written by Charles Johnson, Jr on the "First Separate Company" (Monumental City Guards) extracted from a book, title is unknown.

# MAGAZINE

**F**

The News American, Sunday, May 2, 1982

**"** It was like we were on one side of the street and they were on the other. If you stuck your helmet on your rifle and held it up above the trench, they'd blow a hole in it. **"**

— Harry Dorsey, 85

RED HAND DIVISION: Retired Lt. Col. William Brady remembers the bloody days of World War I from his easy chair at his west Baltimore home. Brady was a member of the much-decorated Company I, 372nd Infantry. The picture above, a fading relic dating to 1917, shows some of the members of that unit, dubbed "The Red Hand Division" for its courage during an intense nine-day campaign in September 1918.

# Old soldiers recall giving their all

Retired Lt. Col. William Brady and surviving members of the 372nd Infantry will be honored today for their heroic efforts in black National Guard units during World War I.

*My hope, when my eyes shall close in death, is that peace and truth shall live in generations to come. — Part of poem written in France in 1918 by Dough Boy Sumler Parran.*

**By Harvey Hagman**
News American Staff

When black National Guard units are honored today for their valor in World War I, World War II and the Korean War, 85-year-old William M. Brady will be there, still standing tall.

His comrades in arms, Harry Dorsey, 85, the Rev. Sumler Parran, 85, and Charles Wilson, 84, will be there with him. The four are the surviving members of Company I, 372nd Infantry, dubbed "the Red Hand Division" for its courage during a nine-day battle in France in September 1918.

"The Germans slaughtered us the same as cattle," Parran said, "but we kept on going. When we wouldn't retreat, the Germans got scared. Only 3 of us were left out of 250, most killed in hand-to-hand fighting, bayonet to bayonet, the best man wins."

One of four black American units assigned to the French Army by General John "Black Jack" Pershing in World War I, the 372nd became part of France's all-black 146th Brigade. The men wore American uniforms, but fought with French equipment.

The unit, which fought in the Argonne Forest, Verdun and Alsace-Lorraine, received the French Croix de Guerre with palms for bravery. The award will be re-presented by a military attache from the French embassy during the third annual Maryland National Guard show at 1 p.m. today at Rash Field near the Inner Harbor. The ceremony is part of the National Guard's effort to recognize the achievements of black units.

Recently, Brady, a retired lieutenant colonel, sat in his rubble-filled west Baltimore home and recalled the

wore his blue sweater with the gold American Legion emblem as he sifted through his memorabilia.

He pulled out a copy of an old letter from French General Goebek, commander of France's 157th Division. In it the general saluted "the dash, the heroic push of the Colored American regiment. The most formidable defenses, the best organized machine gun nest, the most smashing artillery barrages could not stop them. The Red Hand Division ... always held the lead in the historic advance ... After you have crossed the ocean anew, forget not ... our pure fraternity of arms has been sealed in the blood of the brave."

Brady also pulled out a yellowed newspaper clipping showing a granite monument standing alone in the French countryside. The obelisk was inscribed: "In memory of the members of the 372nd U.S. Infantry killed in action Sept. 20-Oct. 7, 1918."

Nearly 64 years later, the battles have faded into history with most of the men who fought them, but Brady still recalls the old unit. As a young man in 1916, his first attempt to enlist in the National Guard failed. Undaunted, "I put my age up two years the next time I went down," he said. "We were put on guard duty right away."

Soon, he was the all-black unit's company clerk, able to recall the names of the 68 men from the Baltimore area without checking his roster. Later, the unit was transferred to the old Allegheny Arsenal in Pittsburgh where it saw its first action — putting down a riot at a steel mill. From there, the unit traveled to Anniston, Ala., where it completed basic training before traveling on to Newport News, Va. There, I Company went into the federal service and boarded a troop ship for France.

"The colored sailors treated us all right," Brady said, "but the ship carried horses down below before us so you know how it smelled when the

**"** We had some tough guys, not bad guys, but tough guys. We moved up a couple times into German trenches when we had them on the run. **"**

— William Brady, 85

France, and marched outside of town to bivouac. Brady spent his first night in a stable, where he was given his first French food and a half loaf of French bread.

"When I went to sleep on a hay mound, I put the rest of my bread in my pocket," Brady said. "When I woke up the next morning a rat had eaten all around my pocket and eaten the inside of my French bread. That was my introduction to France.

"The next day, we started walking, and we walked and we walked and we walked. One night some of the boys found a barrel of wine down in the cellar where they were staying and they had a good old time," Brady said. Day after day the unit marched.

According to Parran, most of the company's losses came from German machine guns strategically situated

guns. But, when you're up against the wall, you do the best you can, say a little prayer, cuss a bit and keep on going."

I Company fought with the Senegalese and the black French. According to Brady, "They bowed to us and made a sign and we did likewise. Some of them could speak good and some couldn't. We got along all right."

The Senegalese didn't get along all right with the Germans. When they captured Germans, they'd cut off their heads and put them in a bag, according to Parran. "They were blood-thirsty men. The Germans would pile up the Senegalese six high with their machine guns, but they kept on going until they took the machine gun nest."

Brady called the French peasants "nice folks" who would wave to them from the fields as I Company marched past. Parran recalled the fear the black unit encountered in shops shortly after arriving in France. "French women were scared of us at first because they were told we were monkeys and had tails. I told the boys, 'Try to be gentlemen when we go into a town.'"

Later, the unit reached a French supply depot where the men turned in their U.S. rifles, helmets and sidearms. Initially, all American units in World War I fought under French and British command.

"In return they gave us a French rifle, a bayonet 18 inches long, which they called a French needle, and a small pack," Brady said. "But here's the best part. Our rifles shot five times, theirs shot only three times."

As I Company neared the front, Brady and the men watched French and German planes battle overhead during the day and marched at night. At the front, former guards from France's Devil's Island prison trained I Company to use their French rifles during lulls in the fighting. When an artillery barrage began, Brady said, "We'd run and jump into our trenches

Company could hear the Germans talking. "It was like we were on one side of the street and they were on the other," Dorsey said, adding that "if you stuck your helmet on your rifle and held it up above the trench, they'd blow a hole in it."

Behind the trenches, the first line of resistance, were machine gun nests. According to Parran, "We were the sacrifice men in the trenches. If it got too hot, you'd shoot off a pistol sending up a white star for machine gun fire and French artillery to come in."

I company suffered in the trenches for three months before being relieved. Life in the trenches was "pretty bad," according to Brady, but his unit was never overrun. "We had some tough guys, not bad guys, but tough guys. We moved up a couple times into German trenches when we had them on the run. Boys have told me they'd jump into those other trenches and as soon as the Germans saw the color of their skin they would surrender. Sometimes our boys wouldn't take prisoners. I've heard some stories about that, but I can't remember half the stuff."

When shells and gas bombarded I Company, the men in Brady's unit were ordered to stay in the trenches until long after the gas attacks had ended. During one attack, Brady inhaled too much gas. "My eyes were red and running and I didn't know what caused it. I woke up in a tent, then they took me to a French hospital with Catholic sisters and French doctors who told me I had been gassed."

To pass the time in the hospital, an Italian in the next bed, Martino Galucha, began teaching Brady Italian, while Brady taught Galucha English. They exchanged addresses. "Don't you know about a year after I got home, he came over here and married an Irish girl in south Baltimore. We became good friends," Brady said.

One battlefield scene is etched in

pieces, and to see it made you mad. There weren't many people left. What impressed me most was an old man and his young granddaughter walking up a hill to what was left of a church to ring the church bells. The church was torn to pieces. That really impressed me. I like churches anyway. I had the pleasure of telling the boys, 'Don't take nothing from a church when you see it all shot to pieces like that.'"

A hospital ship returned Brady to the United States, where he was sent to a hospital at Cape May, N.J. "When my father came to me, I couldn't see him," Brady said. "It took me quite a while to get my sight back and I don't do so well now. I only see out of one eye, but the VA takes care of that."

Following World War I, Brady worked at the old Baltimore Club at Madison Avenue and Charles Street, before joining the Veterans Administration, where he worked for 20 years before retiring.

During these years, Brady kept active in the military, founding a respected drum and bugle corps and serving as company commander, then commander of the 11th Battalion from 1941 to 1947. The unit provided security for critical civilian installations during and after the war. In 1946 he organized the 147th and 726th Transportation Companies of the Maryland National Guard and later was instrumental in organizing and obtaining federal recognition for the guard's Headquarters and Headquarters Detachment of the 231st Transportation Truck Battalion. During this period, he rose to the rank of lieutenant colonel.

Today, Brady lives with his wife Marie, 80, and their pet Great Dane. His adopted son, Emmett, followed in his father's footsteps, serving 20 years in Army. During World War II, his son-in-law served in Brady's unit.

As Brady walked to the door still lost in the memories of World War I,

Appendix C

Photographs of the First Separate Company
during World War II. The photographs
appeared in the Baltimore Afro American
Newspaper. Date is unknown. Article
provided by MSG (Ret) Nathaniel Pope

MEMBERS OF MARYLAND NATIONAL
GUARD march proudly along the Baltimore City

AFRO FILE PHOTO April, 1942
street during World War II.

AFRO File November 1940
Maryland National Guard — Armistice Parade.

Appendix D

MAGAZINE

# AFRO

## SECTION

**DECEMBER 31, 1974 - JANUARY 4, 1975**

brief history of the Monumental City Guard" that appeared in the Afro American Newspaper. Date is unknown. Article provided by MSG Nathaniel Pope

# The 229... Supply and Transportation

## 29th Infantry - founded 1879

Several hundred members of the old 29th Supply and Transportation Battalion, 29th Infantry are gathering from all over the United States for a reunion in Baltimore, Maryland this week.

If the original unit had not been disbanded in 1968, it would be 95 years old today.

The all-black unit served in four wars — Spanish-American War, World War I, World War II and the Korean War.

They were important in the war effort, they participated in and performed many deeds of heroism.

**History**

The unit is an outgrowth of the Monumental City Guards formed in Baltimore on February 20, 1879. It was an independent military organization under Thomas H. Lewis.

After two years, the unit was inspected by General Hubbard and staff. They made the recommendation that the Monumental City Guard be made part of the Maryland State Militia.

On February 20, 1882, the company became the First Separate Company of the Maryland National Guard.

In 1883, the company participated in the observation of the landing of "Lord Baltimore" in the city harbor. The company was the only black outfit in the parade.

The First Separate Company had a brief period of service during the Spanish-American War. It was the first to pitch tents at Pimlico, Maryland and stayed there for basic training for 31 days before entering active duty.

**World War I**

The company was the first to leave the state at the outbreak of World War I. The company was mobilized and mustered into Federal Service in July, 1917.

In January, 1918, it was reorganized and designated Company I 372nd Infantry.

As 'Company I, they arrived in France on April 4, 1918. They immediately entered into combat and were very active in Argonne Forest, Verdun, Sector 5 and Alsace-Lorraine.

When all the company officers were wounded in one of these engagements, Sergeant William Creigler, who later became Captain, commanding the company in 1943, led the men in attack. For this he was awarded the French Croix de Guerre with silver star, the highest French military honor.

The 372nd Infantry Regiment was awarded the Croix de Guerre with Palms by the French for the heroic method in which they accomplished their mission on the field of battle.

At the end of the war, the company was mustered out on March 3, 1919.

In June, 1922 the company was reorganized and federally recognized as Company A, 140th Auxiliary Engineer Battalion Maryland National Guard.

One year later it was redesignated as the First Separate Company, Infantry. It remained as such for 17 years.

**World War II**

In 1940, the company was redesignated 'Service Company' 372nd Infantry Regiment and seven months later inducted into Federal Service on March 10, 1941.

During World War II, the company received its basic training at Fort Dix, New Jersey and performed guard duty at strategic points along the Eastern seaboard adjacent to New Jersey and New York.

On May 3, 1945, the 372nd left for overseas duty in the Hawaiian Islands and received credit for participation in the Asiatic-Pacific Campaigns.

Inactivated at Oahu at the end of the war on January 31, 1946, the company was reorganized as Headquarters and Headquarters Detachment, 231st Transportation Corps Truck Battalion in April, 1947 in Baltimore under the direction of the Maryland National Guard.

The battalion was located at the time in the old Richmond Market Armory on Howard and Biddle Streets.

The 726th Transportation Truck Company, the 147th Transportation Truck Company and the 165th Transportation Truck Company of the Guard were assigned to the Battalion.

Three years later the Battalion was reorganized again as Headquarters and Headquarters Company, 231st Transportation Truck Battalion.

**Korea**

In August, 1950 the Battalion was mustered into Federal Service for the fourth time when the Korean War broke out. Before the year was out, the Headquarter and Headquarters Company, with the 726th Transportation Company was on its way overseas to Korea.

The 165th Transportation Company remained in the United States and the 147th Transportation Company went to serve in Europe.

The Company rendered a valuable contribution to the war effort. It was twice awarded for outstanding service, the Meritorious Unit Commendation.

It received the Republic of Korea Presidential Unit Citation and received credit for participation in eight Korean Campaigns.

When cease fire was announced on July 27, 1953, they began to stress other activities besides operations, the movement of supplies, troops, prisoners and the maintenance of equipment.

Some of these were extensive sports, educational building, and safety programs as well as the Armed Forces Assistance to Korea Program.

After service in Korea the unit was reorganized and redesignated as Headquarters and Headquarters Company, 231st Transportation Battalion (Truck) in April, 1954.

On February 21, 1955 the original unit was released from active military service and returned to State control.

They relocated in Baltimore at the Edmondson Avenue Armory on Edmondson Avenue and Bentalou Street.

On March 1, 1959 the unit again became an element of the 29th Infantry. The Headquarters and Headquarters Company, 229th Transportation Battalion, the 147th Trans. Co. was redesignated Company A, the 165th as Company B and the 726th as Company C.

For many years, the men requested an armory of their own and finally in 1959, the state built the Winchester Armory, located on Winchester and Braddish Avenues.

In 1965 the armory was renamed the Melvin H. Cade Armory in honor of the Commander of the 229th Supply and Transportation Battalion.

Lieutenant Colonel Cade assumed command in 1963 and that same year, was promoted to Colonel.

Along with other members of the 229th, Col. Cade led the move to have the National Guard integrated. They won places on the AFRO Honor Roll for this accomplishment.

In March of 1963 the organization was again reorganized and this time acquired from Annapolis, Maryland elements of the Division Quartermaster Company, which became Company A, Supply and Service Company. Company B of the Battalion became B Company of the 121st Engineer Battalion. As the 229th Supply and Transport Battalion, the former companies A and C became Company B, Transportation Motor Transport Company.

As a result of a reorganization of the Maryland National Guard, the 229th Supply and Transportation Battalion was disbanded in 1968. The colors were retired.

Members were reassigned to new units, Company C 103rd Engineer, 726th Maintenance Battalion.

Lt. Col. Melvin H. Cade

Capt. William Creigler and Lt. Le Roy Clay attending the national meeting of the National Guard Association of United States in 1939 in Baltimore.

# 231st Transportation Truck Outfit
# Conducting State-Wide Recruiting Drive

### First National Guard Unit Called to Colors; 20-Day Campaign Begun in N.W. Baltimore

1950s newspaper article on the 231st Transportation Truck Battalion as it prepared itself for active duty to support the Korean War. The unit was activated on August 19, 1950. Article provided by MSG (Ret) Nathaniel Pope

HEADQUARTERS
231ST TRANSPORTATION TRUCK BATTALION
APO [___] 301

| | | |
|---|---|---|
| SPECIAL ORDERS | | 16 Sep 1952 |
| NUMBER 239 | EXTRACT | |

1. Fol named EM (RCP) "reassignees" rel asg orgn indicated trf 8069th Repl Bn APO 301, for further transportation and reasg to 8056th Repl Depot AU, APO 27. Phys insp prior to departure will be accomplished as dir in App G, Cir 60, Hq, KUSAK, 52. DD Form 415 will be utilized by individuals to inform correspondents and publishers of a non-military address, a permanent military address, or to discontinue mail and publications until further advised as to new address. EDCSA: 22 Sep 52. WP o/a 21 Sep 52. TDN. PCS. USGAL. Tvl by RW auth. Auth: Cir 60, Hq KUSAK, 1952. 2-53010 1-10-210 P140, 02, 03, 07, S99-999.

| NAME | GRADE | SN | MOS | ORGN | RACE |
|---|---|---|---|---|---|
| BRADLEY, EARN T JR | PFC | RA14370972 | 4345 | 60th Trans Trk Co | Neg |
| EDD-FDC: Sep 52 | TOE: | 3 years | ETS: | Feb 54 | |
| BROWN, JAMES H. | PFC | US53085510 | 4345 | 60th Trans Trk Co | Neg |
| EDD-FDC: Sep 52 | TOE: | 2 years | ETS: | Feb 53 | |
| BROWN, JOHN C. | SGT | RA19242123 | 1931 | 40d Trans Trk Co | Neg |
| EDD-FDC: Sep 52 | TOE: | 6 years | ETS: | Aug 58 | |
| FOSTER, JAMES C. | PVT-2 | RA14399305 | 4345 | 60th Trans Trk Co | Neg |
| EDD-FDC: Sep 52 | TOE: | 3 years | ETS: | Feb 54 | |
| FREEMAN, EARNEST B. | PVT-2 | US53062331 | 4345 | 60th Trans Trk Co | Neg |
| EDD-FDC: Sep 52 | TOE: | 2 years | ETS: | Feb 53 | |
| GARDNER, ARTHUR B. | PVT-1 | US51064284 | 3060 | 60th Trans Trk Co | Neg |
| EDD-FDC: Sep 52 | TOE: | 2 years | ETS: | Sep 52 | |
| GEORGE, RAYMOND H. | PVT-2 | RA13336376 | 4345 | 514th Trans Trk Co | Cau |
| EDD-FDC: Sep 52 | TOE: | 3 years | ETS: | Jan 54 | |
| GIBBS, JAMES W. | CPL | RA34660374 | 4345 | 40d Trans Trk Co | Neg |
| EDD-FDC: Sep 52 | TOE: | 6 years | ETS: | Jun 56 | |
| GLENN, LEE W. | CPL | RA34744071 | 1931 | 40d Trans Trk Co | Neg |
| EDD-FDC: Sep 52 | TOE: | 6 years | ETS: | Jan 58 | |
| GOLDEN, EDDIE | SFC | RA33123104 | 1931 | 40d Trans Trk Co | Neg |
| EDD-FDC: Sep 52 | TOE: | 6 years | ETS: | Jan 58 | |
| HARRILL, WALTER A. | PFC | US53062402 | 4345 | 60th Trans Trk Co | Neg |
| EDD-FDC: Sep 52 | TOE: | 2 years | ETS: | Feb 53 | |
| HARRIS, LEO. | PFC | US53062422 | 4345 | 60th Trans Trk Co | Neg |
| EDD-FDC: Sep 52 | TOE: | 2 years | ETS: | Feb 53 | |
| HUTCHINS, L. V. | PFC | RA14380209 | 4345 | 42d Trans Trk Co | Neg |
| EDD-FDC: Sep 52 | TOE: | 3 years | ETS: | Jan 54 | |
| JACKSON, LAWRENCE UR | PVT-1 | US56053888 | 4345 | 42nd Trans Trk Co | Neg |
| EDD-FDC: Sep 52 | TOE: | 2 years | ETS: | Jan 53 | |
| JESSIE, JOHNNIE R. | SGT | RA34388160 | 1931 | 40d Trans Trk Co | Neg |
| EDD-FDC: Sep 52 | TOE: | 6 years | ETS: | Mar 57 | |
| KELLEY, ROBERT E. | SGT | RA17253227 | 1931 | 40d Trans Trk Co | Neg |
| EDD-FDC: Sep 52 | TOE: | 5 years | ETS: | Sep 53 | |
| KIDD, ALONZO | CPL | RA18090810 | 4014 | 60th Trans Trk Co | Neg |
| EDD-FDC: Sep 52 | TOE: | 3 years | ETS: | Dec 53 | |
| MALONEY, LLOYD G. | PFC | US55089706 | 4345 | 42d Trans Trk Co | Cau |
| EDD-FDC: Sep 52 | TOE: | 2 years | ETS: | Feb 53 | |
| MAANS, EDDIE J. | PVT-1 | US55060011 | 4345 | 42d Trans Trk Co | Neg |
| EDD-FDC: Sep 52 | TOE: | 2 years | ETS: | Nov 52 | |
| MUSE, JOHNNIE L. | PVT-1 | RA44154169 | 4345 | 665th Trans Trk Co | Neg |
| EDD-FDC: Sep 52 | TOE: | 3 years | ETS: | Jan 54 | |
| PEARSON, SAM | PFC | US55065582 | 4345 | 42d Trans Trk Co | Neg |
| EDD-FDC: Sep 52 | TOE: | 2 years | ETS: | Jan 53 | |
| PERKINS, BEN E. | PFC | US55045024 | 4345 | 60th Trans Trk Co | Neg |
| EDD-FDC: Sep 52 | TOE: | 2 years | ETS: | Jan 53 | |
| ROBINS, EUGENE | PFC | RA38500667 | 4014 | 40d Trans Trk Co | Neg |
| EDD-FDC: Sep 52 | TOE: | 6 years | ETS: | Aug 56 | |
| ROBINSON, THOMAS | CPL | RA14122215 | 3060 | 40d Trans Trk Co | Neg |
| EDD-FDC: Sep 52 | TOE: | 6 years | ETS: | Feb 57 | |
| SMITH, BERNARD P. | PVT-1 | RA31075458 | 4345 | 665th Trans Trk Co | Cau |
| EDD-FDC: Sep 52 | TOE: | 3 years | ETS: | Oct 53 | |

Appendix G

| NAME | GRADE | SN | MOS | ORGN | RACE |
|------|-------|-----|-----|------|------|
| SMITH, RILEY JR | PFC | US55041316 | 4345 | 60th Trans Trk Co | Neg |
| EDD-FLC: Sep 52 | TOE: | 2 years, ETS: | Feb 53 | | |
| SMITH, WILLIE | PFC | RA14308427 | 4345 | 60th Trans Trk Co | Neg |
| EDD-FLC: Sep 52 | TOE: | 3 years ETS: | Dec 53 | | |
| SPELLMAN, ALFRED | PFC | RA15295100 | 4345 | 665th Trans Trk Co | Neg |
| EDD-FLC: Sep 52 | TOE: | 3 years ETS: | APR 54 | | |
| SUGGERS, HENRY | PFC | US55106913 | 4345 | 80th Trans Trk Co | Neg |
| EDD-FLC: Sep 52 | TOE: | 3 years ETS: | Jan 53 | | |
| TANNEHILL, JOE H. | PFC | US53997207 | 4345 | 50th Trans Trk Co | Neg |
| EDD-FLC: Sep 52 | TOE: | 2 years ETS: | Jan 53 | | |
| TAYLOR, JESSE | N/SGT | RA361385 | 1302 | 43d Trans Trk Co | Neg |
| EDD-FLC: Sep 52 | TOE: | 6 years ETS: | Apr 58 | | |
| THOMAS, ROBERT L. | PFC | US53941851 | 4345 | 60th Trans Trk Co | Neg |
| EDD-FLC: Sep 52 | TOE: | 2 years ETS: | Feb 53 | | |
| TIBBS, WILLIE B. | PFC | US55078146 | 4345 | 60th Trans Trk Co | Neg |
| EDD-FLC: Sep 52 | TOE: | 2 years ETS: | Jan 53 | | |
| WALKER, TOMMIE L. | PFC | US56061395 | 4345 | 60th Trans Trk Co | Neg |
| EDD-FLC: Sep 52 | TOE: | 2 years ETS: | Feb 53 | | |
| WATKINS, WINSTON | PFC | RA54273073 | 4345 | 514th Trans Trk Co | Neg |
| EDD-FLC: Sep 52 | TOE: | 3 years ETS: | Feb 54 | | |
| WELLS, WALTER | PFC | US56068236 | 4345 | 60th Trans Trk Co | Neg |
| EDD-FLC: Sep 52 | TOE: | 2 years ETS: | Jan 53 | | |
| WHITAKER, GEORGE L. | PFC | US52961842 | 4345 | 60th Trans Trk Co | Neg |
| EDD-FLC: Sep 52 | TOE: | 2 years ETS: | Feb 53 | | |
| WRIGHT, THOMAS J. | PFC | US53044852 | 4345 | 60th Trans Trk Co | Neg |
| EDD-FLC: Sep 52 | TOE: | 2 years ETS: | Jan 53 | | |

2. Fol named EM (ETS) "separatees" rel asg orgn indicated trf 8069th Repl Bn APO 301, for futher transportation and reasg to 8058th Repl Depot AU, APO 27. Phys insp prior to departure will be accomplished as dir in App G, Cir 60, Hq EUSAK, 52. WD Form 415 will be utilized by individuals to inform correspondents and publishers of no permanent military address, or to discontinue mail and publications until further advised as to new address. WP o/a 21 Sep 52, EDDSA: 24 Sep 52. TDN. PCS. TICAM. Tvl by RR auth. Auth: Cir 60, Hq EUSAK, 1952. 2132020 1-40-210 P1410 02, 03, 07, 899-999.

| NAME | GRADE | SN | MOS | ORGN | RACE |
|------|-------|-----|-----|------|------|
| BROUGHTON, HERSHAL G. | PFC | US54003454 | 4345 | 20th Trans Trk Co | Cau |
| EDD-FLC: Sep 52 | TOE: | 2 years ETS: | Oct 52 | | |
| ELLIS, CHARLES A. | PFC | US55049645 | 4345 | 665th Trans Trk Co | Cau |
| EDD-FLC: Sep 52 | TOE: | 2 years ETS: | Oct 52 | | |
| GERLACH, LAURENCE F. | PFC | US55047230 | 4014 | Hq & Hq Co 231st T Trk Bn | |
| EDD-FLC: Sep 52 | TOE: | 2 years ETS: | Oct 52 | Race: Cau | |
| GUENTHER, JAMES P. | SGT | US56049555 | 3060 | 121st Trans Trk Co | Cau |
| EDD-FLC: Sep 52 | TOE: | 2 years ETS: | Nov 52 | | |
| KULICK, JOHN D. | PFC | US51025299 | 4345 | 60th Trans Trk Co | Cau |
| EDD-FLC: Sep 52 | TOE: | 2 years ETS: | Oct 52 | | |
| LANDRUM, CLARENCE E. | PFC | US53010796 | 4345 | 20th Trans Trk Co | Cau |
| EDD-FLC: Sep 52 | TOE: | 2 years ETS: | Oct 52 | | |
| SCHLEUSER, DALE A. | CPL | US55092074 | 4345 | 43d Trans Trk Co | Cau |
| EDD-FLC: Sep 52 | TOE: | 2 years ETS: | Oct 52 | | |
| SHEPARD, WILLIE | PVT-1 | US54030162 | 4345 | 121st Trans Trk Co | Neg |
| EDD-FLC: Sep 52 | TOE: | 2 years ETS: | Oct 52 | | |
| THOMPSON, LAWRENCE D. | SGT | US52615836 | 1014 | 20th Trans Trk Co | Cau |
| EDD-FLC: Sep 52 | TOE: | 2 years ETS: | Oct 52 | | |
| WAGNER, JOHN L. | SGT | US55051726 | 1931 | 42d Trans Trk Co | Cau |
| EDD-FLC: Sep 52 | TOE: | 2 years ETS: | Oct 52 | | |
| WELLS, ALFRED T | SGT | RA15044616 | 1931 | 514th Trans Trk Co | Cau |
| EDD-FLC: Sep 52 | TOE: | 3 years ETS: | Oct 52 | | |

(SO 239, HQS 231ST TRANS TRK BN, APO 301, DTD 16 SEP 53, CONT'D)

BY ORDER OF LIEUTENANT COLONEL SAYERS:

OFFICIAL:                              HAROLD O. WEBB
                                       Captain, TC
                                       Asst Adjutant

W. R. Fabinsky
W. R. FABINSKY
WOJG, USA
Asst Adjutant

DISTRIBUTION:

2-ea Indiv Conc
2-ea Unit This Comd
2-CO EPO, APO 707
3-PO APO 301
3-CO 351st TRT Gp
1-CG EUSAK, ATTN: KTR
1-ea Staff Sec This Hq
2-CO 8069th Repl Bn, APO 301
2-CO 8068th Repl Depot AU, APO 27
5-ea 201 File
10-ea File

*Handwritten at top:* THIS ARTICLE APPEARED IN DETROIT NEWS AFTER I CAME HOME. THOSE FELLOWS WERE ALL FROM THE 42N TRK. CO. THAT ARE LEAVING THE CHAPEL

## GIs' Devotion Builds Chapel

SOLDIERS at the front in Korea worship God as they can. Chaplains have conducted services from jeeps, trucks and tanks, usually out in the open and sometimes within the sight and sound of shooting war.

Sometimes to escape inclement weather, soldiers build modest churches like this "Truckers' Cathedral." Each man with a skill added his share, perhaps with hammer and saw or (left) creating murals and "stained glass" windows. Open to all sects, this religious haven is heated with an oil stove. Pews are wooden benches.

—UP Photos

Congregation includes Pfc. Duane Roeling, Clinton, Wisc., and an orphan he adopted.

Page 24—January 11, 1953 The Detroit News Pictorial

*Handwritten at bottom:* CHAPEL WAS AT UIJONGBU 231ST TRK BN

Appendix H

156

Partial article, with photographs, on several of the officers from the 231st Transportation Truck Battalion when they returned home from duty in Korea. Article provided by MSG (Ret) Nathaniel Pope.

# Korea Vets Home

### Gross Income $20,000

ferent attitude of the homefront toward the Korean war.

"The thing that struck me most is that people don't seem to be serious about the situation over there. Everybody is taking this thing like it was a neighborhood brawl.

"I haven't done much visiting yet, for I've stuck pretty close to home," remarked Colonel Greene.

Major Melvin H. Cade, 2300 block Madison Ave., has spent much of his time trying to get reacquainted with his 2 - year - old daughter, Deborah, and wife, Willie.

When Major Cade left Baltimore in August, 1950, his daughter was only 5 months old. "She was, naturally, too young to remember me.

"I'm still trying to realize that I'm back though.

### Thank God For Safety

"I was lucky enough to come out unscathed from World War II. When I was called to active duty again, I thought my number would surely come up.

"This is one time the law of averages failed, though, and I certainly thank God," he concluded.

Chief Warrant Officer John Holt, 1220 Druid Hill Ave., is another returning hero. "I just feel good, that's all, just very, very, good.

"It's better to be back home paying these taxes, than to be over there getting shot at all the time. With all its faults, this is still the greatest country in the world," declared the unit's personnel officer.

### Brothers Reunited

Capt. Lester Hudgins, 1500 block Pulaski St., had a joyous reunion with his brother, Cosmo, when he came home.

Both Capt. Hudgins and Sgt. 1st Class Cosmo D. Hudgins, served in Korea during the war. Because of battle conditions, however, the two brothers were never able to meet.

Sgt. Hudgins, 1121 Tiffany Ct., has been home from Korea several months. When his brother, Capt. Hudgins, came home Sunday, the long-awaited reunion occurred.

Recounting the odd round - the world reunion, Capt. Hudgins attributed it to the complexities "of a strange war."

### Captain Greets Dog

Like Lt. Dawson, Capt. Hudgins also had a new arrival to greet—his boxer dog, Prince. "My wife, Margaret, had written me about the dog, and when I came home we greeted each other just like old friends."

Capt. Bedford T. Bentley, 1900 block McKean Ave., has spent the better portion of his time "catching up with television."

Lounging around the house with his highball and pipe, Capt. Bentley said, "There weren't many daytime programs when I left, but now the air is cluttered with them.

"The biggest event in my homecoming, however, was the chance to see my son, Bedrod Jr., 4, and wife Barbara, again," declared Capt. Bentley.

### Anxious For Discharge ....

All of the officers express hopes of leaving the Army in short order, possibly in August. In fact, Lt. Dawson was the only person who mentioned even the remotest thought of making the Army a career.

The 231st left Baltimore in August, 1950 to undergo training at Camp Edwards, Mass. On December 6, 1950, the organization left Camp Edwards for Korea.

By Christmas, 1950, the outfit was on the front lines of Korea.

The present group of officers is the first contingent to return to this country.

Among the other servicemen reported homeward bound are CWO Wilbert E. Armstead, Sgt. James Hill, Cpl. James P. Hall, Cpl. Addison M. Williams, Sgt. William R. Floyd, Cpl. Henry Rawls, Cpl. William R. Bland, Cpl. Robert Goslee, Cpl. Arthur H. Griffin, Cpl. James Broaddus and SFC. Richard Dawson.

Appendix I

157

# A Combat Veteran Returns Home

Major Melvin H. Cade, Executive officer of the 231st, watches his daughter, Deborah 2, play with some Christmas toys she received while her father was fighting in Korea. His wife, Mrs. Willie Cade, watches the reunion. Although home just a few days, Major Cade, a former gym teacher at Douglass, has already journeyed to Druid Hill Park to watch his former charges participate in a track meet.

Appendix I (2)

158

# Father And Son — Together Again At Last

CAPT. Bedford T. Bentley who commanded a trucking company of the 231st Truks Transporta- tion Battalion in Korea was one of the returning Baltimore- ans last week end. Shown above with his son, 4-year-old Bedford Jr., Captain Bentley spent 15 months overseas. He expects to be discharged later in the year.

# A Returned Soldier Greets His Dog

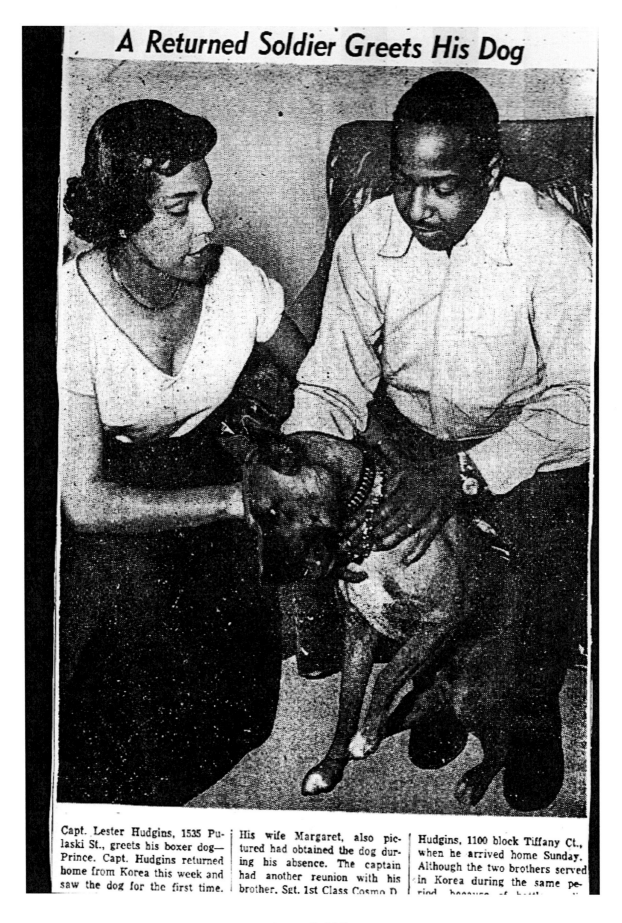

Capt. Lester Hudgins, 1535 Pulaski St., greets his boxer dog—Prince. Capt. Hudgins returned home from Korea this week and saw the dog for the first time. His wife Margaret, also pictured had obtained the dog during his absence. The captain had another reunion with his brother, Sgt. 1st Class Cosmo D. Hudgins, 1100 block Tiffany Ct., when he arrived home Sunday. Although the two brothers served in Korea during the same period, because of battle conditions...

⌐2 Year, No. 44     BALTIMORE, MD., JANUARY 2, 1954     28 Pages     Price 15 Cents

# Reckord Keeps Promise To Keep Guard Jim Crow

January 5, 1954 newspaper article About General Milton Reckord's efforts to reform the 231st Transportation Truck Battalion when its colors were returned from Korean duty, as a segregated unit. Article provided by MSG (Ret) Nathaniel Pope.

## New unit formed; old officers quit

### 4 officers, 43 enlisted men join segregated unit

By BUDDY LONESOME

Maj. Gen. Milton Reckord has finally activated his Jim-crow National Guard unit.

On December 14, four officers and 43 enlisted men were inducted into the newly activated 167th Transportation Co.

The State Adjutant General has been trying to re-activate the 231st Truck Bn. since September.

But the officers and enlisted men of the 231st had served honorably in the army in Korean war service as members of fully integrated units.

They wanted no part of a segregated National Guard unit and flatly told the General that.

**Made Boast Good**

When convinced that the officers meant business, General Reckord boasted that he would find some men who would serve in a separate trucking unit and not pay any attention to Jim-crow.

Two weeks ago in a building at 231? Edmondson ave., which ██████████████████ separate armory, the new Guard unit received official Federal recognition from Lieut. Col. J. Wright, a regular army officer.

Although only at company strength now, Guard officers hope enlistments will swell the outfit to its former battalion strength—when it will again be known as the 231st.

Commissioned as officers in the new unit were Warrant Officer (JG) Jesse Peaker, and 2nd Lts. Theodore Scott, Coree Williams, and Lloyd G. Henderson, Jr.

Lt. Scott, son of a local policeman, has been designated the company commander. He joined the 231st before the outfit went on active duty in 1948, and served as an enlisted man.

Lt. Henderson, platoon leader, was formerly a sergeant major at the Edgewood Chemical Center.

**Morgan Student**

Lt. Williams, a Morgan College student joined the outfit in 1948 just before the group went on active duty.

Warrant Officer Peaker, who works in the reregistrar's office at Morgan, is handling most of the administrative duties attached to the reactivation.

Mr. Peaker who has served with the 231st as a sergeant major, is well aware of the conflict between General Reck-

(Continued on Page 2)

ACTIVATING GUARD— Warrant Officer (JG) Jesse Peaker is handling the administrative details of the reactivation of the 167th Truck Co., a segregated National Guard outfit.

## Dr. Byrd talks to two clubs

### Candidate for Gov. is dinner host

Members of Monumental and Citizens Democratic Clubs were recently entertained by Dr. H. C. (Curly) Byrd at a University of Maryland dinner.

Their verdict: "He's a reasonable man."

Curly Byrd, outgoing president of the University of Maryland, filed as a candidate for Governor two weeks ago. He announced that he was in the race in 1887.

The gala dinner was held in the dining hall of the state university at College Park at 9 o'clock and lasted more than an hour.

## -Guard

(Continued from Page 1)

ord and the officers of his outfit.

He asserts that the re-activation of the separate unit was necessary because: "The unit gained world-wide recognition while fighting in Korea."

"The outfit has two unit citations and each man in it has at least three battle stars.

"With that rich heritage we feel that the 231st, as a unit, should not be allowed to die."

**Feared For Allocation**

Mr. Peaker also reasons that he and the other newly appointed officers were afraid the federal government would take back the $90,000 allocated the 231st "unless we reactivated."

Brig. Gen. Harry C. Ruhl, executive officer, Maryland Military Department was well pleased at the reactivation of the unit and scoffed at the previous unrest among the officers with: "As far as we're concerned this is the outfit."

Maj. Gen. Reckord could not be reached for comment.

The high ranking officers who served with the 231st during the Korean war and refused to serve in a segregated unit included Lt. Col. Bernon T. Greene, who commanded the outfit; Major Charles Parker, Capt. Lester C. Hodges, Lt. William A. Harris, Major Melvin E. Cole, and Capt. James H. Gilliam.

November 22, 1955 newspaper article about the African American officers from the 231st Transportation Truck Battalion's petition not to be reformed as a segregated military unit after the Korean War. Article provided by MSG (Ret.)Nathaniel Pope.

Newspaper article about Major General H. B. Powell, who supported having former all African American units integrated in the military. Article provided by MSG Nathaniel Pope

## This Is Prejudice

# Gen. Powell Says Integration Has Made Army A Better One

By WELDON WALLACE

(Continued on Page 4, Column 1)

PAGE 4

## This Is Prejudice

# Powell Praises Army Integration

By WELDON WALLACE

(Continued from Page 1)

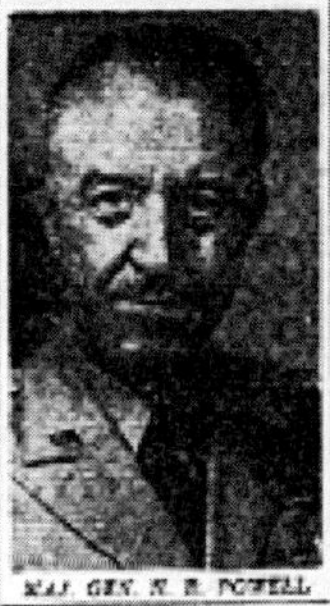

MAJ. GEN. H. B. POWELL

Two Reasons Noted

Accepted As Routine

Combat Line Took Precedence

All But Three Approved

Infractions Decrease

Thinks Morale On Upgrade

Some On Posts Segregated

Attend Same Dances

Article on banning segregation in the National Guard. Article provided by MSG (Ret) Nathaniel Pope

# SEGREGATION BAN IN GUARD INSISTED ON

## Mitchell, Of N.A.A.C.P., Opposes Any Reserve Bill Without Rule

Washington, June 27 (P)—A Negro leader told Congress today it would be national "suicide" if the proposed military reserve program fails to ban racial segregation in National Guard units.

He spoke out despite President Eisenhower's repeated plea against the segregation provision as extraneous. The President has said it would kill the legislation for a fourfold expansion of ready reserves, which he says is vital to national security.

The insistence by Negro leaders on the ban was renewed before a House Armed Services subcommittee by Clarence Mitchell, director of the Washington Bureau of the National Association for the Advancement of Colored People.

**"Not Even Our Great President"**

"We shall never agree with anyone, not even our great President, who tells us that we must not make an all-out effort to contribute our skills and abilities to the defense of the country in an emergency," he said.

After hearing Mitchell, the subcommittee scheduled a closed session tomorrow to act on the reserve program, which has long been hung up in the House by the segregation dispute. The subcommittee was expected to send it to the full committee without the anti-segregation provision. House action may come later this week.

Representative Powell (D. N.Y.) has said he is prepared to offer amendments from the floor to bar segregation, even though the President wrote him urging that he drop the fight.

**Said It Can't Pass Senate**

The President said the Senate would never pass a bill containing the anti-segregation provision even if the House does.

It was a similar provision by Powell tacked on an earlier reserve bill that stymied House action a month ago. The new compromise plan, designed to break the impasse, avoids all mention of the National Guard, although Guard spokesmen objected that they need additional manpower provided by the original bill.

Powell said his fight is based upon the expectation the Senate may put back features to which he objects, regardless of the final form of the House bill.

**"Guard Units Of Great Cities"**

Mitchell, in his testimony before the subcommittee, assailed the President for implying "that he is willing to settle for using all white manpower in National Guard units of great cities like Charleston, S.C., Birmingham, Ala. and Atlanta, Ga."

He contended that under the plan the United States would have two armies—an integrated one run by the Defense Department and a segregated one administered by the states.

Declaring this would be a "gross violation of the civil rights of colored people" he said it would be "an attempt to have the nation commit suicide."

**Guard's Role As State Militia**

Mitchell said most Americans do not want a "white army on the front lines," with Negroes relegated to the rear even though they want to fight.

Representative Winstead (D. Miss.), replying to Mitchell, said the National Guard amounts to "State militia." He said the founding fathers wanted them to be under state jurisdiction.

House leaders say the provisions of the new bill, plus President Eisenhower's strong support for it, will make it difficult for Powell to get the votes to tack on his new anti-segregation amendment.

The reserve bill is designed to reserve to 2,900,000 men by 1960, expand the 700,000-man trained. It includes stiffer enforcement provisions designed to require reservists to meet training obligations.

# Vets Say State Guard Fights Integration

By Eric Fleetwood

Korean war officer veterans have accused the Maryland Adjutant General of practicing race segregation in the State's National Guard at the expense of a strong force. They further claim that, up till now, Governor McKeldin has backed his actions.

The accusations were made by fifteen Negro officers, all inactive staff members of the 231st Truck Transportation Battalion which, they say, was the only Guard unit recalled during the Korean conflict.

All the officers have "elected" to stay in inactive positions until their request to enlist into their unit any applicant, White or Negro, is allowed.

### Major's Version

According to Major Melvin R. Cade, who was executive officer just before the unit returned to Maryland, all-Negro battalion became integrated during active service.

When it returned home once again it became all Negro and the officers requested Maj. Gen. Milton A. Reckord to allow them to enlist anyone into the unit irrespective of race, creed or color.

"This General Reckord refused to do then and has refused to do ever since," Major Cade said.

"We felt that it was better to have an integrated unit because it promoted better efficiency and better morale," he said.

The major pointed out that the battalion as presently constituted in the Maryland National Guard is commanded by a captain and although it is doing a good job the officers do not have the military experience of the inactive veterans.

### Stresses Experience

"Each officer, from Lieut. Col. Melvin F. Green—who was the commanding officer before and during the Korean war—on down through our warrant officers, has sufficient military experience to become a vital and essential part of the National Guard," he added.

The unit had one lieutenant colonel, three majors, five captains, four lieutenants and two warrant officers, all of whom saw active service in 1950-1952.

"Let a war come and let the unit be recalled it would be completely unprepared without the veterans," Major Cade said.

"We have written to Governor McKeldin," he continued, "seeking action against segregation, but we have been told only that he would seek a definite decision on the question."

Capt. James Gillam, another 231st staff member, said that he

[Continued On Page 69, Column 3]

...ically the Governor had said he felt the National Guard is a purely voluntary organization and that he did not want to disturb it.

He also said, the captain continued, "that we should be patient, that segregation was on its way out."

"All we ask," Captain Gillam said, "is that we be allowed to enlist into the 231st Battalion whoever we wanted. We feel that there are many people other than Negroes who would be more useful in the Truck Transportation Battalion than elsewhere in the Guard."

Replying to the accusations, General Reckord said: "Maryland has no responsibility to men who served in Federal forces after they return from active duty. There are plenty of Reserve Units which they can join.

"We have decided the efficiency of the National Guard will be maintained on a higher standard by continuing as we are and not permitting integration."

Newspaper article on Korean War veterans from the Maryland National Guard fighting being returned to their old segregated 231st Transportation Truck Battalion after the Korean War. Article provided by MSG (Ret) Nathaniel Pope.

Appendix N

BIGGEST BECAUSE IT'S THE

Newspaper article about Governor Theodore McKeldin's position on the petition by the officers of the 231st Transportation TRuck Battalion's not to be returned to its former segregated unit. Article provided by MSG (Ret)Nathaniel Pope

# Governor hasn't referred Guard petition to General Reckord or Atty.-Gen. Sybert

Fifteen Maryland National Guard officers who petitioned Gov. Theodore R. McKeldin last July 7 to end racial segregation in the Maryland National Guard have not received a reply.

The matter was brought to light last week when local NAACP attorneys met with Jack Greenberg of the New York national staff.

Mr. Greenberg, Robert Watts, and W. Emerson Brown Jr., attorneys for the 15 officers, conference with the governor last July 7.

They were advised that the governor would talk the matter over with Maj. Gen. Milton Reckord, his Adjutant General, and reply to the petition promptly.

GENERAL RECKORD said last week that he had not received a copy of the officers' petition from the governor.

A spokesman in Attorney General Sybert's office said that he had not been asked to give a ruling whether the state is required under recent Supreme Court decisions to integrate the guard.

When attorneys brought the matter to the attention of the NAACP Legal Redress Committee of the Baltimore Branch, it was agreed that the NAACP should file suit against the state of Maryland and General Reckord to determine whether the state can lawfully operate a segregated guard.

THE PETITION points out that "state imposed racial segregation is unconstitutional" and "without any reasonable justification."

"Congress has declared the National Guard," the petition said, "an integral part of the first line defenses of this nation, Maryland law calls for conforming the State National Guard to the pattern of the regular army which is integrated.

"In time of national emergency, the Maryland National Guard would have to be integrated into the fighting forces of the United States as a whole.

"Segregation in the Maryland National Guard weakens its military efficacy and impairs its fighting effectiveness as a constituent part of the armed forces of the United States.

"Facilities offered colored

erans in the Maryland National Guard are clearly inferior to those available to whites.

"The single unit for colored veterans in Maryland is in Baltimore.

"But white persons throughout the State may participate in National Guard activities in 38 armories in other sections of the state.

"COLORED PERSONS may join only a Transportation Battalion.

White persons may join the Infantry, Artillery, Engineers, a Fighter Squadron, a Medical Unit and an Armored Tank Company.

"It is clear that white persons may avail themselves of the National Guard to obtain training which may be of use to them in civilian life or in further military training. Colored persons do not have the same opportunity.

"It cannot be said that colored members of the Maryland National Guard who served with distinction in the Korean conflict —indeed they were the only units of the Maryland National Guard which served there and suffered Maryland's only casualties in that war—are unfit to associate with their white comrades in arms.

"In Korea, in battle, members of Maryland's colored units served with or commanded mixed units."

THE 1955 budget of the Military Department of Maryland is $623,000 of which $86,000 comes from the Federal Government.

In addition, the Military Department will spend $190,000 this year and $300,000 next year for new buildings.

It has 96 employees, nearly all of whom are white.

THE MILITARY Department operates 38 armories and one rifle range. There are five in Baltimore, three in Baltimore County, and the others in the various ether counties in the state. The complete list is as follows: Salisbury, Centreville, Leonardtown, 5th Regiment, Greenbelt, Cumberland, Westminster, Crisfield, Annapolis, Easton, Laurel, Pocomoke, Silver Spring, Kensington, Chestertown, Denton, Towson, Oakland, Frostburg, Frederick, Hagerstown, Cambridge, Bel Air;

Elkton, Hyattsville, Ellicott City, Prince Frederick, La Plata, Glenburnie, Howard St., 104th Medical, Broadway Market, Army Aviation, Administration Building (Harbor Field), 729 Ordnance Co. (Havre de Grace), Edmondson Avenue, Highfield, Catonsville and Gunpowder Rifle Range.

Only Edmondson Avenue Armory is colored and no colored person can join the guard in any of the other 37 armories in Baltimore City or in the state.

## Nat'l Guard units, too

The Supreme Court decision in the case of recreational facilities brings us to the question of the Maryland National Guard.

The situation in brief is that Maryland expends $651,000 of state taxpayers' money plus $86,000 from the Federal Treasury to operate 38 units in the same number of armories in Baltimore City and every county.

Marylanders, who chance to be born colored, are barred from enjoying or benefiting from all of these units, but one.

And that one is the least desirable.

A total of 130 of them are segregated into a tight little jim crow truck unit in Baltimore City.

Neither Governor McKeldin, who is commander in chief of the Maryland National Guard nor the Guard commander, General Milton Reckord, can justify state action by which white persons may avail themselves of the National Guard to obtain training

in infantry, artillery, engineers, aviation, electronics and medicine which may be of use to them in civilian life or in further military training while colored men are denied these same opportunities.

The governor and General Reckord have handled this National Guard issue in an astounding manner.

Since the petition of colored National Guardsmen for integration was placed [...]ck last July 7, Governor McKeldin, so far as we [...]e been able to learn, ha[...] referred the petition to Ge[...]al Reckord, nor has he ask[...] the attorney general to rule [...]its legality.

We say i[...] clear now that the governor [...]ishes to be compelled by a [...]ourt decision to integrate the [...]aryland National Guard.

The NAACP [...]nder these circumstances, h[...] no other alternative than [...]o seek relief through the [...]ederal courts.

Weather Forecast

THE  SUN FINAL

Vol. 238—No. 4—F | BALTIMORE, MONDAY, NOVEMBER 21, 1955 | 32 Pages | 5 Cents

# McKeldin Abolishes Segregation In National Guard

Sun Newspaper article of November 21, 1955 announcing the end of segregation in the Maryland National Guard. Article provided by MSG (Ret) Nathaniel Pope.

'...ation' Policy

## GENERAL RECKORD SAYS HE WILL COMPLY WITH ORDER 'IMMEDIATELY'

Governor's Action Makes Maryland First Southern State To Drop Racial Barriers In Its Military Service, Guard Officials Note

MILITARY DEPARTMENT
STATE OF MARYLAND
OFFICE OF THE ADJUTANT GENERAL
FIFTH REGIMENT ARMORY
BALTIMORE

General Orders                                        21 November 1955
Number 49

Effective 1 December 1955 any applicant for appointment or
enlistment in the Maryland National Guard (Army or Air) who is
morally, mentally and physically qualified and who meets the other
requirements of appropriate National Guard Regulations pertaining
to appointment or enlistment, will be accepted as a member of the
Maryland National Guard, (Army or Air) regardless of race, creed,
or color provided an appropriate Table of Organization vacancy exists
for such applicant.

BY ORDER OF THE GOVERNOR:

MILTON A. RECKORD
Major General
The Adjutant General

OFFICIAL:

Appendix Q

168

# UNIT COMMANDERS

Captain Thomas H. Lewis
Independent Military Company
Monumental City Guards
1879-1882

Captain Thomas H. Lewis was the founder and organizer of the Monumental City Guard in Baltimore, Maryland. The company was organized February 20th, 1879 originally made up of Negro Personnel by the late CPT. Thomas H. Lewis as an independent Military Company with the hopes of becoming a part of the Maryland National Guard. After many trials and disappointments the dream was realized on February 20th, 1882 the Monumental City Guard Co. was formally recognized as the first separate company in the Maryland National Guard.

CPT. William K Spencer
Monumental City Guards
1st Separate Company Infantry
1882-1917

MAJ William Creigler
Co I ,372nd Infantry
Co A 140th Auxiliary Engineer Battalion
1st Separate Company, 372nd Infantry
1921-1941

LTC William M Brady
Service Company, 372nd Infantry
HHD, 231ST Trans Corps Truck Battalion
1946-1948

LTC Vernon F. Green
HHD, 231ST Trans corps Truck Battalion
HHC, 231st Trans Truck Battalion
1949-1952

CPT Jessie P. Peaker
HHC, 231ST Trans Battalion (Truck)
1953-1955

LTC Vernon F. Green
231st Trans Battalion (Truck)
1955-1960

LTC Melvin H. CADE
229TH transportation Battalion
229th Supply & Transport Battalion
1960-1964

LTC Lester C. Hudgins
229th Supply & Transport Battalion
1964-1966

LTC George M. Brooks
229th Supply & Transport Battalion
1966-1968

MAJ Wayne Thompson
MAJ Ronald Evans
Company C , 103RD engineer Battalion
1968-1975

LT Alex Bishop
CPT Rudolph Walters
Company C, 728th Maintenance Battalion
1968-1975

LT Herbert Parker
2nd Platoon, Company B , 728th Supply & Transport Battalion
FASCOM, company A, 728th Supply & Transport Battalion
1968-1975

CPT Rudolph Walters
734th Maintenance Company
1975-1976

CPT Joseph Mills
MAJ Joseph Langely
MAJ Bruce Blanchard
MAJ Dee Humprhey
MAJ Albert Schwiezer
243rd Engineer Company
1975-1985

CPT Charles Sigmund
CPT Edward Ballard
CPT Walter Hurt
Company C, 58$^{th}$ Support Battalion
1975-1985

LTC Michael N. Schleupner, JR.
229$^{th}$ Supply & Transport Battalion
1985-1988

LTC Michael P. Tangzyn
229$^{th}$ Supply & Transport Battalion
1988-1990

LTC Edward H. Ballard
229$^{th}$ Supply & Transport Battalion
1990-1993

LTC Donald M. Choate
229$^{th}$ Main Support Battalion
1993-1996

LTC Joseph Blume Jr.
229$^{th}$ Main Support Battalion
1996-2000

LTC Donald Krebs
229$^{th}$ Main Support Battalion
2000-2002

LTC Wayne Johnson Sr.
229$^{th}$ Support Battalion
2002-

Program on 100 years celebration of the First Separate Company - from 1879 to 1979 when the unit was called Company C, 243rd Engineers. Program provided by MSG (Ret) Nathaniel Pope.

## HONORS, AWARDS, AND DECO

### **THE BATTLE STREAME

**WORLD WAR I**
Lorraine 1918
Muese-Argonne
Alsace 1918

**WORLD WAR II**
Asiatic-Pacific Theater

**KOREAN WAR**
CCF Intervention
CCF Spring Offensive
Korean Summer-Fall 1952
Korean Summer 1953

First UN Counteroffensive
Second Korean Winter
Third Korean Winter

#### **** DECORATIONS ****
Meritorious Unit Commendation
Meritorious Unit Commendation
Croix De Guerre with Palm
Republic of Korea Presidential Unit Commendation

### PAST COMMANDERS
CPT William Spencer
MAJ William Creigler
LTC William Brady
LTC Vernon Green
CPT Jesse Peaker
LTC Vernon Green
LTC Melvin H. Cade
LTC Lesier Hudgins
LTC George Brooks

### CURRENT COMMANDERS

| | | |
|---|---|---|
| MAJ Wayne Thompson | 103rd Engineers | 1968-1972 |
| MAJ Rodney Evans | 243rd Engineers | 1972-1976 |
| MAJ Joseph Langley | 243rd Engineers | 1976-1978 |
| CPT Rudolph Walters | 728th/734th Mait CO | 1972-1976 |

243rd Engineers — Company C, 58th SPT BN
MAJ Bruce Blanchard — CPT Charles R Singman

## 100 Years

First Seperate Company - Company I, 372nd Int Company A, 140 Auxiliary Eng Bn- First Seperate Company, Int.. Service Company, 372nd Int Reg HHD, 231st Transportation Bn- HHC, 231st Transportation Bn HHC, 229th Transportation Bn- 229th S & T Bn- Company C 103rd Eng Co & Company C 728th Maintenance Bn 243rd Eng Co & 734th Maintenance Co.

1879          COMPANY "C"          1979
             243rd ENGINEERS

## Anniversary Ball

### Melvin H. Cade Armory

### April 7, 1979

# UNIT HISTORY

On 21 February 1879, the First Seperate Company, Monumental City Guard was formed. Two years later it was made part of the Maryland Militia.

Although the Unit saw a brief period of service in the Spanish American War, its real contribution began in World War II where it distinguished itself in the campaigns of the Argonne Forest, Verdun, Sector Five, and Alsace-Lorraine.

The Unit underwent several re-organizations between World War I and 1941. On March 1941, the Unit was inducted into Federal Service.

World War II saw the Unit sent to the Pacific, where it received credit for participation in the Asiatic-Pacific Campaigns.

In the late 1940's, the Unit was upgraded to Battalion Strength, and on 19 August 1950, it was ordered again into Federal Service. The Battalion's service was divided between the United States, Europe, and Korea. It was in Korea that this Unit (The only Maryland Guard Unit activated) distinguished itself further by winning two Meritorious Unit Citations, the Korean Presidential Unit Citations and Eight Battle Streamers! (A complete list of Honors, Awards, and Decorations can be found on the back page of this program.)

After Korea, the Unit's services were called on by both the State and Federal Governments in such diversified areas as Civil Disturbance Control, Flood relief, Emergency Fuel Delivery etc.

On 21 February 1979, the 243rd Engineers and Company C, 58th Support Battalion, the Units which now carry on this proud heritage were called to State Duty to aid in the relief for the Blizzard of 79, thus carrying on the tradition of service on the very day of their 100th Anniversary!

# PROGRAM

8:00 - 9:00 p.m. .......... Cocktails

9:00 - 10:30 p.m. .......... Dinner & Program

10:30 - 1:30 a.m. .......... Dancing & Open Bar

# *** HONORED GUESTS ***

LTG Jeffery Smith .......... Commanding General, First Army

MG Charles Ott .......... Director Nat'l Guard Bureau

MG Edwin Warfield .......... The Adjutant General

Hon. Harry Hughes .......... Governor of Maryland

Hon. Charles Mathias .......... U.S. Senator

Hon. Paul Sarbanes .......... U.S. Senator

Hon. Parren Mitchell .......... Congressman, 7th District

Hon. William D. Schaefer .......... Mayor, City of Baltimore

BG Benjamin Dean .......... Ass't Adjutant General MDANG

BG Raymond Atkins .......... Commander, 58th INF BDF (SEP)

COL George Wallace .......... Chief, Readiness Group Meade

COL Standish Brooks .......... Brigade Senior Advisor

LTC Dennis Bermingham .......... Readiness Group Meade

MAJ John Long .......... Assistor, Readiness Group Meade

The following living Past Commanders of the

Units Celebrating This

100th Anniversary

COLONELS

GREEN, BROOKS, BRADY

HUDGINS

# Brooks named National Guard Brig. General

George M. Brooks has an impressive resume — listing educational, employment, community involvement and military accomplishments.

He also has compiled a list of "firsts" — first black colonel of the Maryland National Guard, first black state director of the Civil Defense and Disaster Preparedness Agency and, most recently, Brooks was promoted to the rank of brigadier general in the Maryland National Guard.

He began his military career in 1943 and served in Europe and the South Pacific in World War II. His unit, the 23rd Transportation Truck Battalion was the only National Guard group from Maryland to be activated to serve in the Korean conflict. Brooks was promoted to captain during that tour of duty.

Before his retirement from the Guard in 1977, Brooks commanded half of the Maryland troops as commander of the 29th Support Center or rear area operations. He was responsible for behind-the-lines security and damage control and supervised operations for civil disturbances and natural disasters.

Brooks's military education includes the Army Command and General Staff College, Industrial College of Armed Forces and specialty courses.

He has received more than 20 military and community awards, including the Legion of Merit Medal, the State of Maryland's Distinguished Service Cross and is a member of the AFRO-AMERICAN Newspapers Honor Roll.

In civilian life, Brooks is currently director of the Maryland Civil Defense, which coordinates emergency services in event of a nuclear attack or natural disaster.

He retired from the Social Security Administration as deputy director of the division of property management. Brooks served more than 30 years as a federal employee.

He accepted the position as Civil Defense director because he said he was so used to being active before he retired.

Brooks holds memberships in several community organizations and has served on two mayor's advisory commissions.

He lives with his wife on North Longwood Street. They have two daughters and one son.

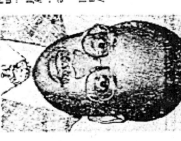

Brig. Gen. George M. Brooks
AFRO Photo by Mark Gail

# Brig. Gen. George Morris Brooks, 77, Md. National Guard's first black colonel

By FREDERICK N. RASMUSSEN
UN STAFF

Brig. Gen. George Morris Brooks, the first African-American colonel in the history of the Maryland National Guard, who also served in World War II and Korea, died Tuesday of cancer at Maryland General Hospital. He was 77 and lived in West Baltimore.

General Brooks enlisted as a private in the Army in 1943, and served with the Infantry in Europe and the Pacific.

In 1946, he was commissioned a second lieutenant in the Maryland National Guard's 231st Transportation Truck Battalion. The battalion traces its history to the First Separate Company (Monumental City Guards), an all-volunteer black unit established in 1879.

"When the Korean War broke out, the unit was federalized and the only Maryland National Guard unit called to active duty," said Lester C. Huggins of Northwest Baltimore, a longtime friend who was discharged from the Maryland National Guard in 1966 with the rank of lieutenant colonel.

The unit, which was integrated while overseas, spent about 15 months in Korea and reached the 38th Parallel. It earned eight Korean War campaign and two meritorious Unit Commendation streamers. "General Brooks was the unit's supply officer, which hauled ammo, rations and dead soldiers," Mr. Huggins said.

Despite President Harry S. Truman's order in 1948 that ended segregation in the military, after the

**George M. Brooks**
supported integration of the Maryland National Guard.

231st returned to Maryland, Maj. Gen. Milton A. Reckord opposed integrating the unit into the regular Maryland National Guard.

"After Korea, we saw no reason not to be integrated. We said there would be no unit unless it was desegregated, and General Brooks was one of the officers who got involved," Mr. Huggins said.

After seeking support from the National Association for the Advancement of Colored People and the Afro-American newspapers, and threatened with the loss of federal funds, Gov. Theodore R. McKeldin signed an executive order in 1955 making Maryland National Guard units open to all.

Philip Sherman, a Baltimore attorney and retired Maryland National Guard brigadier general, said, "He was a dynamic leader and eloquent spokesman for the integration of the Guard. He was well-spoken, a true gentleman and a good comrade in arms."

At the time of his retirement in 1977 with the rank of colonel, he was commander of the 29th Support Center for rear-area operations. In 1979, Gov. Harry R. Hughes promoted him to brigadier general, retired.

During the 1950s, General Brooks worked in Morgan State University's placement office and the personnel office at Aberdeen Proving Ground. From 1966 until retiring in 1978, he was deputy director of the Social Security Administration's division of property management in Woodlawn.

In 1980, Governor Hughes appointed him director of the Maryland Civil Defense and Disaster Preparedness Agency, responsible for coordinating local, state and federal emergency services in the event of a natural disaster or nuclear attack.

General Brooks served on many boards and commissions, including the Baltimore Red Cross, Church Hospital, Maryland World War II Memorial Commission, State Board of Trustees of the State Universities and Colleges, and Mount Ararat Baptist Church, where he was a member.

Born and raised near Harlem Avenue, General Brooks was a 1941 graduate of Douglass High School. He earned a bachelor's degree in mathematics from Morgan State University in 1950.

The Rev. Marion Bascom, director of Morgan's University Christian Center and a longtime friend, said, "He was a man of unbound enthusiasm in the things he believed in, such as his love for Morgan. He always wanted to keep the story straight and alive."

Services will be held at 11 a.m. Wednesday at Union Baptist Church, 1217 Druid Hill Ave., and burial with full military honors at 2 p.m. at Baltimore National Cemetery.

He is survived by his wife of 58 years, the former Amelia J. Soden; a son, Dudley Morris Brooks of Bowie; two daughters, Muriel E. Brooks of Atlanta and Angela A. Brooks of Columbia; a sister, Evelyn E. Brooks of Baltimore; and three grandchildren.

# Army National Guard unit to celebrate 100th birthday

A Maryland Army National Guard unit established for black soliders in 1879 will celebrate its 100th Anniversary April 7 at Cade Armory.

Originally designated the First Separate Company, Monumental City Guard - Maryland State Militia, it was formed Feb. 21, 1879 and located at a former armory known as Richmond Market. The armory site itself was known as one of the first "terminals" for the Underground Railroad in Baltimore.

During its 100-year old history, the unit has been reorganized and was last split into two outfits currently known as Company C, 58th Support Battalion and the 243rd Engineer Company, both of which are headquartered at Cade Armory.

For 100 years members of the nearly all-black unit has served in every war from the Spanish-American to service in the Korean War. Also, it is the only Maryland National Guard unit to be activated for service in Korea.

Among the unit's many commendations and honors is a monument in Manthois, France, dedicated to black soldiers for contributions made by unit members during World War I.

Capt. Charles R. Singman, commanding officer of C Company, 58th Support Battalion said, "This unit has remained a real pillar of strength and inspiration in this community.

"For example, at Christmas this unit helps the Baltimore AFRO-AMERICAN Newspaper's

Mrs. Santa Claus food drive. Unit members donate their time and the unit donates vehicles to distribute food to needy families in the black community," Singman said.

In addition, the unit has sponsored Boy Scout Troop No. 220 for more than 20 years and recently, began to back a Cub Scout Pack.

Among notable unit officers are Colonels George Brooks and William A. "Box" Harris. Col Brooks formerly commanded the Rear Area Operations (RAO) Support Center, one of the two largest military commands in the Maryland Army Guard.

Appendix V

176

Certificate of Appreciation awarded to the 231st Transportation Truck Battalion by the Department of Defense Commemoration Committee for their outstanding support during the 50th Anniveraary of the Korean War, September 15, 2000.

Department of Defense Commemoration Committee

# CERTIFICATE OF APPRECIATION

is Awarded to

*231st Transportation Truck Battalion (MoNG)*

for outstanding support to the
Department of Defense Commemoration for
the 50th Anniversary of the Korean War
*"Freedom Is Not Free"*

SEPT 15, 2000

Secretary of Defense

# The State of Maryland

*Governor of the State of Maryland, to*

231ST TRANSPORTATION CORPS, TRUCK BATTALION **, Greetings:**

*Be it Known: That on behalf of the citizens of this State,*

*in recognition of the courageous service your members provided for the defense of our nation... in honor of the distinguished record that our African-American veterans have compiled throughout the years and the contributions they have made to help ensure equal rights and opportunities for all members of the armed forces; and as an expression of our high regard and sincere gratitude as we join in celebrating African-American Patriots Day in Maryland,*

*we are pleased to confer upon you this*

## Governor's Citation

Given Under My Hand and the Great Seal of the State of Maryland,
the 24th day of February
Two Thousand and one

*Parris N. Glendening*
Governor

*John T. Willis*
Secretary of State

Appendix X

178

LTG(MD) James F. Fretterd
The Adjutant General of Maryland

Presents the

**Dedication Ceremony**
for the

**231ˢᵗ Transportation Truck Battalion**

December 14th, 2002
*LTC Melvin H. Cade Armory*
*Baltimore, Maryland*

*Maryland Army*
*National Guard*

*Soldiers First!*

## Acknowledgements

LTG (MD) James F. Fretterd—Dedication of Plaque
COL (MD) Friedrich L. Martin—Equipment Support
LTC James E. Vandegriff—Editorial Support
LTC Wayne Johnson Sr.—Project Coordinator
Chaplain(LTC) William S. Lee—Historical Narrative
MAJ Andrew Yaukey—Master of Ceremony & Asst. Project Manager
MAJ Drew Stilins—Historical Narrative
MAJ Michael Kohler—Newspaper & Press Release
MAJ Jeff Knopsnider—Equipment Support
CPT Leslie T. Hill—Project Manager
CPT Sandra R. Johnson—231st Coordination & Support Personnel
Chaplain(CPT) Tyson Wood—Spiritual Guidance
CW5 (Ret) James A Bonner—Equipment Support
CSM William Jackson Jr.—Color Guard
CW2 Eric V. Gren—Equipment Set-Up
CSM(Ret) Charlie Frick—Equipment Support
MSG Rudi Thomas—Andor/Virtual Coordinator & Equipment Support
SFC Kevin Russell—Artwork for Program & Invitations
SSG Tracey Driver—Program Support
SSG Derrick Scott—Equipment Support
SSG Eugene Link—NCOIC of MDNG State Colorguard
SGT Maurice White—Equipment Support & Set-Up
SPC Theresa Goldsmith—Caterer of Reception & Administrative Support
SPC Eugenia Lyon—Administrative Support
SPC Krista C. Davey—Administrative Support
Mr. Jennifer Taylor—Equipment Support
1SG (Ret) Lloyd R. Scott—Spokesman for 231st Veterans
MSG (Ret) Nathaniel Pope—231st Historical Research
SFC (Ret) Elgia Butler—231st Coordination
231st Veteran Members—Program Support
State Color Guard Personnel—Posting of the Colors
Co B 229th Soldiers—Overall Support of Ceremony
Mr. Jeff Pitt—Musical Support

## Program

| | |
|---|---|
| 1400 | Arrival of Official Party |
| 1405 | Commander's Welcome—Captain Sandra Johnson |
| 1410 | Introduction of Official Party—Major Andrew Yaukey |
| 1415 | Posting of the Colors & The National Anthem—Command Sergeant Major William Jackson Sr. |
| 1420 | Invocation—Chaplain (Captain) Tyson Wood |
| 1425 | Welcome to Veterans 231st Transportation Truck Battalion—Major Andrew Yaukey |
| 1430 | History of the 231st Transportation Truck Battalion—Major Andrew Yaukey |
| 1435 | The Adjutant General's Remarks—Lieutenant General (MD) James F. Fretterd |
| 1450 | A Soldier's Story—First Sergeant (Ret) Lloyd Scott, Sr. |
| 1455 | Veterans of the 231st Transportation Truck Battalion—Sergeant First Class (Ret) Elgia L. Butler |
| 1500 | Movement to the Plaque Dedication Site |
| 1510 | Dedication of the 231st Transportation Truck Battalion Plaque—Lieutenant General (MD) James F. Fretterd |
| 1520 | Museum Tour |
| 1530 | Reception |

## History of the 231st Transportation Truck Battalion

The roots of the 231st Transportation Truck Battalion go back to 20 February 1879, when a patriotic group of African-Americans from Baltimore organized themselves into an independent military company. Their professionalism, discipline and dedication to duty resulted in their acceptance into the Maryland National Guard on 20 February 1882 as the "Monumental City Guards", a designation that remains a title of honor and pride for all who have served in its ranks since.

In 1896, the unit was re-designated as the 1st Separate Company, Infantry, and found itself activated for federal service during the Spanish-American War. The unit remained bivouacked at Pimlico, Maryland throughout the period of activation. Commanding the 1st Separate Company during this period was Captain William K. Spencer.

On 5 August 1917, the company was federalized for service during World War One and re-designated on 1 January 1918 as Company I, 372nd Infantry. After receiving training at Fort McClellan, Alabama, the unit embarked for France 4 April 1918. Serving with the French Army's IX Corps, the 372nd Infantry entered combat almost immediately. They fought with fierce determination and exceptional gallantry in the 1918 campaigns of Lorraine, Alsace and Meuse-Argonne. The heroic actions of the Company were recognized with the award of the French Croix de Guerre with Palm.

When all of the unit's officers were wounded in the Meuse-Argonne offensive, Sergeant William Creigler of Baltimore took command of Company I and successfully led it to accomplish all of its assigned objectives. For his heroic action and quick thinking, the French Army awarded him, its highest honor—the Croix de Guerre. Sergeant Creigler also received the American Expeditionary Forces Citation Star for Gallantry, which today is called the Silver Star. In a single heroic action, another Baltimorean, Sergeant Rufus Pinckney, saved the life of a French officer and captured 15 German prisoners. For his heroism, he was also individually awarded the French Croix de Guerre for valor.

Following demobilization after World War Two, the unit was activated again into federal service for World War Two on 10 March 1941, as Service Company, 372nd Infantry.

---

immediately integrate the Guard. The petitioning officers quit when the Adjutant General, Maj. Gen. Milton Reckord, directed that a separate unit of the 231st be formed for African-American troops with their own Commander, CPT Jesse Peaker, and Lieutenants appointed from their ranks. The unit was housed in the Edmondson Avenue Armory. Their petition and walk-out was eventually successful, however, as Maryland Governor Theodore McKeldin soon ordered that the Guard be integrated. When issued the orders from Annapolis, General Reckord immediately complied and the Maryland National Guard became the first of the Southern States to integrate. Today, the Maryland National Guard is one of the most progressive and forward thinking organizations in the United States Armed Forces on diversity issues. The legacy of the veterans of the 231st plays a large and important part in that distinction, as they were the pioneers who demonstrated the personal courage to lead the way.

On 1 March 1959, the unit was again reorganized and re-designated as Headquarters & Headquarters Company, 229th Transportation Truck Battalion and assigned to the 29th Infantry Division. That year the unit also moved with great pride into the new Winchester Armory, now known as the LTC Melvin H. Cade Armory. It was and continues to be seen as a "community armory" with resources and space for military and community use. Through two World Wars and the Korean conflict, the lineage of this unit is as proud as any in the National Guard and the United States Army.

In 1985, the unit would become the 229th Supply and Transportation Battalion with the newly re-activated 29th Infantry Division (Light). In August 1990, during Annual Training at Fort Bragg, North Carolina, the unit provided crucial support in loading troops and material for deployment as part of Operation Desert Shield/Desert Storm and the liberation of Kuwait. In 1993, the 229th became the 229th Main Support Battalion as part of reorganization to reflect Active Army force structure. Today the pride, history, and heritage of the 231st Transportation Truck Battalion lives on here at the LTC Melvin H. Cade Armory. Though the 231st remains no more, it's spirit, and the same pride and professionalism are part of every citizen-soldier in the Maryland Army National Guard.

The unit served stateside until being deployed to the Pacific Theater of operations in later stages of the War. For its faithful service, Service Company, 372nd Infantry received credit for participation in the Asiatic-Pacific Theater Campaign.

On 25 April 1947 at Baltimore, Maryland, the unit was again reorganized as Headquarters & Headquarters Detachment, 231st Transportation Truck Battalion. On 1 April 1950, it became the Headquarters & Headquarters Company, 231st Transportation Truck Battalion. The 726th, 147th and 165th Transportation Truck Companies, Maryland Army National Guard were assigned to the 231st Transportation Truck Battalion along with the Headquarters Company. On 19 August 1950, the 231st was mobilized for service in the Korean War. It was the only Maryland National Guard unit to be federalized during that conflict. As a veteran of the 726th would remember: "the Platoon Sergeant marched his soldiers from the Richmond Market Armory at Linden and Howard Streets down to Mount Royal Avenue and the train station. We were excited to do something for Baltimore, for where we came from! It was a great send-off when we left on the train to Camp Edwards, MA for training". The 165th Transportation Truck Company remained stateside during this time period. From Camp Edwards, Massachusetts, Headquarters & Headquarters Company, 231st Transportation Truck Battalion and the 726th Transportation Truck Company departed to Seattle, Washington. From there they were sent to Korea, arriving by ship at Pusan on 31 December 1950, the first Army National Guard units to set foot in Korea.

Meanwhile, following training at Camp Edwards, the battalion's 147th Transportation Truck Company was sent to Germany in the spring of 1951 to support U.S. Army forces in Europe. Although Europe's was not a "hot" war like Korea, the continent was still rebuilding from the Second World War and a stressful and difficult Cold War with the Soviet Union was emerging on the line dividing Eastern and Western Europe. Most of the soldiers in the 231st's Headquarters Company and 726th Transportation Truck Company were young men, inexperienced at war, and not ready for the harsh realities of combat in far away Korea. It was personal character, patriotism, pride and dedication to duty that resulted in the battalion being awarded two U.S. Army Meritorious Unit Citations and the

Republic of Korea Presidential Unit Citation by war's end. Leadership from men like 1st Lt. George M. Brooks and SFC Lloyd Scott mentored the young soldiers of the 231st, enabling them to perform well enough in combat to earn those honors.

The battle lines were so fluid in the Korean War that the truck drivers of the 231st would often transport supplies, ammunition and troops right to the front lines. They would remain in harm's way until their trucks were full of troops to transport, or dead and wounded to be evacuated to the rear. A young 18-year-old, Private Louis Diggs, would remember that "we treated our trucks like they were our right arm". Often, drivers would hang out of the door of their truck with a hand and arm wrapped in a restraining strap and the other hand on the wheel, so they could see the road through the dust or snow kicked up by the vehicle in front of them. Accomplishing their mission was very important to these soldiers. Their proficiency resulted in the 231st eventually having command and control of an additional nine attached truck companies. Though separated while in Korea, the elements of the 231st and 726th were united by an esprit de corps born of a shared home in the Maryland National Guard, shared heritage as African-Americans, and shared pride as American patriots fighting for freedom and democracy in Korea. Their campaign credits for the Korean War are the eight blue and white battle streamers that line the walls of the Cade Armory drill floor. The campaign credits include: Chinese Communist Forces Intervention; First United Nations Counteroffensive; Chinese Communist Forces Spring Offensive; United Nations Summer-Fall Offensive; Second Korean Winter; Korea, Summer-Fall 1952; Third Korean Winter; and Korea, Summer 1953.

On mobilization in 1950, the 231st joined a federal Army that had been desegregated three years earlier by President Truman's executive order. They looked forward to returning to a desegregated National Guard back home. The 231st was released from active service on 21 February 1955. As with all units, individual soldiers from the 231st had been returning from Korea prior to the deactivation. Returning to Maryland from Korea, the veterans of the 231st discovered that despite their hopes for equality, the National Guard in many states, to include Maryland, remained segregated.

Several courageous officers, determined to make a change for the better, petitioned the Adjutant General and the Governor to

# Index

Johnson, W. 101
Johnson, Wayne, Jr.,
    Lt. Colonel 6
Johnson, Wayne, Sr.
    129
Johnson, Wayne,Jr.
    141
Jones, A. 101
Jones, Arthur 96
Jones, C. 71, 101
Jones, Callisah 74
Jones, Charles H. 19
Jones, D. 101
Jones, Davy 19
Jones, E. 71
Jones, Eldridge 139
Jones, H. 71
Jones, J. 71, 101
Jones, Lorenzo S. 19
Jones, Natalie 57
Jones, R. 71
Jones, Robert L. 116
Jones, William H. 19
Jordan, W. 101

## K

Kearsey, E. 71
Keaton, J. 101
Kellum, Vincent T.
    116
Kelly, Alfred 19
Kennard, R. 101
Keyes, F. 101
Keyes, Gladys 57
King, C. 48
King, Evelyn 94
King, Joe 125
King, Joseph
    120, 136, 137, 139
King, L. 101
King, Martin Luther, Dr.
    121
Kinnard, Roy 104
Kirton, E. 101
Koger, A. Briscoe 145
Krebs, Donald 129

## L

La Prade, James 19
Lambert, Cpl 74
Lambson, Percy 71
Lane, B. 102
Langley, Janice
    Celestia Diggs 64
Lapaley, J. 101
Lee, Carol 115

Lee, J. 71
Lee, L. 71
Lee, Rosalind 115
Lewis, Norma 107
Lewis, Thomas H.,
    Captain
    16, 17, 18
Lewis, William 117
Littlejohn, W. 71
Livers, E. 101
Livers, Ernest 105
Livingston, J. 48
Locklear, Joe 35, 138
Locklear, Joseph 48
Locklear, Joseph B.
    38, 39, 40
Locklear, Margaret V.
    39
Locklear, Margaret V.
    Lindsay 39
Lofton, T. 102
Long, Nathaniel 117
Lopes, J. 48

## M

Mackey, Alfred 19
Malone, Alexander 15
Mapp, Hezekiah 19
Marshall, V. 71
Marshall, Vernon 53
Martin, C. 101
Martin, Clarence 135
Mason, Frank 19
Mason, SGT 138
Mason, Warren
    79, 116
Massey, J. 101
Matthews, Grace
    Adams 112
Matthews, H. 71
Matthews, Irdell Jr.
    118
Matthews, Mr. 107
Mayfield, J. 102
McClain, Marvin 138
McDonald, J. 101
McEachin, James 4
McEachin, Mr. 4
McFadden, Calvin 116
McKeldin, Governor
    129, 130
McLugan, W. 101
McMilliam, O. 71
McNamara, Robert S.,
    Secretary of
    Defense 4

Milburn, Paul 53, 71
Miles, Ethel 80
Miller, W. 71
Mills, Joe 80
Mills, Joseph 128
Mills, Joseph H. 116
Mitchell, John 18
Mobray, C. 101
Mondie, George H.
    117
Mondowney, Shirley
    124
Montague, Alice Brown
    86
Montague, Angela 86
Montague, Daryl 86
Montague, Dorothy
    Yates 86
Montague, Douglass
    84
Montague, Douglass,
    Jr. 86
Montague, Ellestine
    86
Montague, Maureen
    86
Monteque, D. 101
Moore, James H. 18
Morse, L. 71
Morton, C. 101
Morton, Matthew W.
    18
Mosby, Charles 19
Mosley, G. 102
Moulton, Herbert 22
Murdock, R. 48
Murrill, Charles L. 116
Murry, Marie 115
Myers, A. 101

## N

Nell, William C 2
Nero, C. 48
Nero. Captain 47
Nevitt. Nathaniel 19
Newby, J. 71
Newby, James 53, 75
Nichols, Clinton
    24, 115
Nichols, Sergeant 115
Nichols, SGM 135
Nichols. Clinton, Sr.
    116
Nickings, N. 71
Nison, Miles C. 116
Noel, Raynette 92

## O

Owens, C. 101
Owens, Lieutenant 99
Owens, T. 101
Owens, Thomas 38
Owens, Washington
    19

## P

Palmer, C. 71
Palmer, Frank
    57, 60, 71, 139
Parago, Edward 116
Parker, C. 48
Parker, Charles 132
Parker, Donald 35, 36
Parker, Donald C. 129
Parker, Herbert 128
Parker, John 117
Parker, L. 71
Parker, R. 71
Parker, Vernell 35
Parren, Elizabeth 57
Parsons, B. 71
Patterson, Claude H.,
    Jr. 41
Patterson, Claude
    Henry, Sr. 41
Patterson, Charles 41
Patterson, Claude
    45, 48, 80, 96,
    135, 138, 144
Patterson, Patsy 41
Patterson, Ruth Harris
    41
Paul, James P. 19
Paxton, R. 101
Paylor, J. 101
Payne, Calvin M. 117
Peacock, James
    135, 137, 138, 139
Peacock, Sergeant
    120
Peaker, Captain 100
Peaker, Jesse
    44, 48, 61, 79, 80,
    110, 119, 120, 124,
    128, 131
Peaker, Warrant
    Officer 132
Peaker. Jesse 11
Pearson, W. 102
Perry, Orville
    86, 92, 101
Phillips, L. 101

Pike, Nicholas A. 19
Pinckney, Rufus 15
Pitts, Gertrude 115
Plato, Robert 136
Pleasant, Henry 116
Plowden, G. 71
Pope, Dawn 124
Pope, Fannie 123
Pope, Hattie 123
Pope, James 123
Pope, Johnny 123
Pope, Nathaniel
    6 18, 20, 23, 24, 30,
    73, 123, 132, 134,
    135, 136, 137, 138,
    139, 140, 142, 143
Pope, Rosalee Sum-
    mers 123
Pope, Sergeant 120
Pope, Shirley
    139, 140
Pope, William 123
Porter, Kevin 34
Porter, Marcia 34
Porter, S. 48
Porter, Samuel A. 34
Porter, Simon 37
Porter, Vanessa
    Antonette 34
Potter, W. 48
Powell, Alfred John 93
Powell, Charles H. 117
Powell, I. 71
Powell, Kedrick
    140, 142, 144
Powell, Kedrick, Mrs.
    140
Powell, Kedrick William
    93
Powell, Lydia Rozell
    94
Powell, Veronica
    Deborah 94
Powell, William Kedrick
    94
Powell. K. 101
Preston, A. 101
Purahan, Stith 18
Purdy, John L. 117

Q

Quarles, P. H. 19
Queen, J. 71

R

Ragin, E. 101

Rainey, J. 101
Ramsey, H. 71
Randall, T. 48
Randolph, A. Philip 3
Rawls, H. 48
Rawson, William 19
Ray, J. 71
Ray, John 18
Reaves, J. 48
Reaves, L. 71
Reckord, General
    11, 43, 44, 119,
    128, 130, 132
Reckord, Milton
    129, 131
Redd, Albert 118
Reddick, Laura 115
Reddick, Walter
    115, 116
Reid, A. 71
Reid, J. 102
Rekord, General 36
Reynolds, Charles 118
Reynolds, Grant 3
Rhee, Sygman,
    President 5
Rhodes, M. 101
Rice, C. 71
Rice, Elmer C. 116
Rice, Mr. 107
Rice, Theodore 135
Richardson, W. 101
Riley, Arno Quincy
    119
Riley, Camelia Ellen
    Ann 119
Riley, Cheryl Juanita
    121
Riley, Doris
    Cunningham 121
Riley, Gary Guy 119
Riley, Jeryl Renita 121
Riley, Patricia Eleanore
    119
Riley, Renee Claudine
    119
Riley, Sarah Flemings
    119
Riley, Sarah Zerita
    121
Riley, Sergeant 96
Riley, Thomas Kenneth
    121
Riley, Timothy
    122, 138, 140, 142
Riley, Timothy Lee
    119

Riley, Tony Keith 121
Riley, William Robert
    119
Riley, William Robert
    Jr., III 119
Robeson, Paul 3
Robin, Willie B. 118
Robinson, L. 71
Robinson, Lillie
    Montague 84
Robinson, William 19
Robinson, Yolanda
    112
Roe, Maxie P. 116
Rogers, Etta 115
Rogers, J. 101
Rogers, Josephine
    115
Rogers, Mr. 107
Rogers, Roland
    115, 116
Ross. Thomas F. 116
Royster, James D.
    117
Ruhl, Harry C. 132
Russel, Vanessa 34
Russell, F. 48
Ryan, Henry 22
Ryan, Henry Jr. 20

S

Salsbury, A. 48
Sanders, Clarence 117
Saunders, W. 71
Savage, H. 71
Savoy, John S. 19
Scheupner, Michael N.,
    Jr. 128
Schwietezer, Albert
    128
Scott, Lloyd R., Sr.
    5, 6, 53, 54, 71, 74
Scott, 1SG and Mrs.
    Lloyd R. Sr. 139
Scott, Anthony 57
Scott, Diane 57
Scott, Edith R. Clary
    93
Scott, Effie Williams
    57
Scott, First Sergeant
    86
Scott, George W. 18
Scott, Geraldine 57
Scott, James 57
Scott, Lloyd 67

Scott, Lloyd, Jr. 57
Scott, Lloyd R.
    120, 142
Scott, Lloyd R., Sr. 6,
    7, 8, 28, 57. 72,
    73, 76, 122, 135,
    137, 138, 139,
    140, 143
Scott, Lt. 100
Scott, Melvin 57
Scott, Michael 57
Scott, Patricia 57
Scott, Richard 57
Scott, Robert Lloyd
    57
Scott, Rochelle 57
Scott, Ronald 57
Scott, Sandra 57
Scott, Saundra 57
Scott, Theodore 131
Scott, Valerie 57
Seaberry, William J.
    118
Seawell, Raymond 92
Sharpe, R. 101
Sheaf, Joseph 19
Shervington, E. Walter
    22
Shields, B. 71
Sigmund, Charles 128
Simmons, W. 71
Simms, Franklin T.
    116
Simpson, Melvin 117
Sivel, A. 101
Smith, Albert J. 29
Smith, C. 102
Smith, Donald 139
Smith, E. 71
Smith, Herman 93
Smith, Irvin 135
Smith, J. 48, 101
Smith, James 117
Smith, James H. 30
Smith, John N. 19
Smith, L. 101
Smith, Lieutenant 82
Smith, Rudolph 118
Smith, W. 71
Snowden. Ida 77
Soden, Ernest
    104, 105
Soden, Ernest, Jr. 101
Sommerville, Albert
    92
Sommerville, J. 101
Sommerville, James

188